The Seed of Abraham

The Seed of Abraham

Intersections of Jewish and Christian Thought

Edited by
MICHAEL M. C. REARDON
& PESACH WOLICKI

Foreword by Gerald R. McDermott

☙PICKWICK *Publications* · Eugene, Oregon

THE SEED OF ABRAHAM
Intersections of Jewish and Christian Thought

Copyright © 2025 Wipf and Stock Publishers. All rights reserved. Except for brief quotations in critical publications or reviews, no part of this book may be reproduced in any manner without prior written permission from the publisher. Write: Permissions, Wipf and Stock Publishers, 199 W. 8th Ave., Suite 3, Eugene, OR 97401.

Pickwick Publications
An Imprint of Wipf and Stock Publishers
199 W. 8th Ave., Suite 3
Eugene, OR 97401

www.wipfandstock.com

PAPERBACK ISBN: 978-1-6667-8252-3
HARDCOVER ISBN: 978-1-6667-8253-0
EBOOK ISBN: 978-1-6667-8254-7

Cataloguing-in-Publication data:

Names: Reardon, Michael M. C. [editor]. | Wolicki, Pesach [editor]. | McDermott, Gerald [foreword writer].

Title: The seed of Abraham : intersections of Jewish and Christian thought / edited by Michael M. C. Reardon and Pesach Wolicki with a foreword by Gerald McDermott.

Description: Eugene, OR: Pickwick Publications, 2025 | Includes bibliographical references and index.

Identifiers: ISBN 978-1-6667-8252-3 (paperback) | ISBN 978-1-6667-8253-0 (hardcover) | ISBN 978-1-6667-8254-7 (ebook)

Subjects: LCSH: Judaism—Relations—Christianity. | Christianity and other religions—Judaism. | Judaism—Doctrines. | Theology, Doctrinal.

Classification: BM535 R43 2025 (paperback) | BM535 (ebook)

VERSION NUMBER 062425

Contents

Permissions | vii
Foreword by Gerald McDermott | ix
Contributors | xiii
Abbreviations | xvi

Introduction | 1
—Michael M. C. Reardon and Pesach Wolicki

PART I: FOUNDATIONAL MATTERS

Chapter 1
The Cost of High-Mindedness: Jews, Gentiles, and Romans 11:2–21 | 21
—Ephraim Radner

Chapter 2
What Else Can We Learn from Each Other? Engaging David Novak on a Jewish Christian Discussion of Faith | 33
—Jonathan Milevsky

PART II: INTERSECTIONS OF JEWISH AND CHRISTIAN THOUGHT

Chapter 3
The Canon as Theological Problem: The Shema as Theological Vision | 47
—Ian Kissell

Chapter 4
Early High Christology in Second Temple Jewish Literature | 63
—J. Luis Dizon

Chapter 5
"You Are Gods": Deification in Christianity and Judaism | 78
—Michael M. C. Reardon

Chapter 6
Holiness That Does Not Separate: Bridging the Gap Between Christian Models of Sanctification and Jewish Approaches to Holiness | 95
—Rafael Bello

Chapter 7
Toward a Holy Disillusion in Qohelet: How the Uniqueness of Israel's God Positions Jews and Christians for Authentic Living Before Him | 107
—Jordan W. Jones

Chapter 8
Jewish and Christian Perspectives on the Problem of Suffering: Discerning the Ways of God in a Fallen World | 121
—Timothy S. Yoder

Chapter 9
The Gift of the Human Body: The Physical Basis of Sexual Ethics in Judeo-Christian Thought | 135
—Jeff Yaneff

PART III: JEWISH-CHRISTIAN RAPPROCHEMENT, RECONCILIATION, AND UNITY

Chapter 10
Οἱ Ἰουδαῖοι and the Gospel of John: Grappling with Anti-Judaism in the New Testament | 153
—Brian K. Gamel

Chapter 11
Lindbeck and Kinzer on the Church: Israel and Gentiles "Mutually Dwelling" in Christ as One People of God? | 174
—Axel Kazadi

Chapter 12
Jewish-Christian Reconciliation Is Inseparable from Christian Leadership: 1 Timothy 3:2 Interpreted in Light of Zizioulas | 186
—Calvin Pais

Epilogue
The Unprecedented Unique Bond Between Christians and Jews | 203
—Charles McVety

Ancient Sources Index | 215
Subject and Name Index | 227

Permissions

Unless otherwise stated, Scripture translations are the authors' own.

Scripture quotations marked BLB are from the Berean Literal Bible.

Scripture quotations marked ESV are from the ESV® Bible (The Holy Bible, English Standard Version®), © 2001 by Crossway, a publishing ministry of Good News Publishers. Used by permission. All rights reserved.

Scripture quotations marked HHB are from the Newer Testament Hebrew Heritage Bible, trans. Brad H. Young, © by Hebrew Heritage Bible Society. Used by permission. All rights reserved.

Scripture quotations marked KJV or AV are from the King James or Authorized Version.

Scripture quotations marked NIV are taken from the Holy Bible, New International Version®, NIV®. Copyright © 2011 by Biblica, Inc.® Used by permission of Zondervan. All rights reserved worldwide.

Scripture quotations marked NKJV are from the New King James Version, copyright © 1982 by Thomas Nelson, Inc. Used by permission. All rights reserved.

Scripture quotations marked NRSV are from the New Revised Standard Version, copyright © 1989, Division of Christian Education of the National Council of the Churches of Christ in the United States of America. Used by permission. All rights reserved.

Foreword

This Kairos Moment

Gerald R. McDermott

THIS BOOK IS A fitting tribute to the kairos moment in which we find ourselves as Christians and Jews. *Kairos* is the Greek word in the New Testament for a time of "crisis" in God's history of redemption—a time that shows God's judgment (the literal meaning of *krisis*) at moments of messianic significance.[1]

Of course, Jews and Christians disagree on the identity of the Messiah and when the messianic age begins. But we agree that this is a kairos moment, if for slightly different reasons.

Jewish-Christian theologian Ephraim Radner in these pages offers the remarkable judgment that according to the apostle Paul's reflection on Jewish and Christian relations, God has broken off the gentile church from the olive tree of Israel. Because of her "ecclesial high-mindedness—pride, disdain, ambition, greed, envy, cruelty, and violence" toward Jews over the last two millennia, God has "not spared" the churches but has "broken [them] off" from the root of the tree.[2]

Radner refers to the following passage in Rom 11:

> You [gentiles] must become exceedingly cautious not to become arrogant over the natural branches. But if you do become proud, remember that it is not you who give life to the root, but rather it is the root that nourishes you.... So do not let yourself feel superior, but rather stand in fear. After all, if God did not spare

---

1. BDAG, "καιρό."
2. This vol., 23–24.

the natural branches, neither will he spare you. . . . You too may be broken off. (Rom 11:18, 20, 22 HHB [adapted])

Radner cautions that he makes no claim to accuracy and that he could in fact be wrong. Nevertheless, his suggestion could indeed be prophetic. It makes plausible the Christian churches' decline over the last centuries marked by divisions, heresy, immorality, and hypocrisy—not to mention massive diminution in numbers and influence.

Most Christians would agree about aspects of this objective decline, but few would see its etiology explained, at least in part, as a prophetic fulfillment of Paul the Jew's admonition to the mostly gentile Roman church two thousand years ago.

This is a Jeremiah-like warning to Christians. It can be helpful and even redemptive if we learn from it.

Our Jewish friend Pesach Wolicki seems to agree that this is a singular moment in the history of redemption, but for three different and intriguing reasons. Rabbi Wolicki first points to the curses in Deut 28 that culminate in the desolation of the land, continuing until "the last generation or era." Almost all Christian English translations translate *ha'acharon* as "later" rather than "last," which is the way it is used in Neh 8:18; 2 Sam 19:12; 23:1; Isa 44:6. In other words, Wolicki suggests, the land of Israel is prophesied by Scripture to continue desolate until a last era.[3]

Second, this last era coincides with what the Bible predicts will be "an awakening that sweeps the world coinciding with the restoration of Israel to the land promised to Abraham, Isaac, and Jacob. Numerous passages from Scripture speak of multitudes among the nations of the world visiting the land and that time, praising God for the ingathering of Israel, which in turn, leads to shared worship of the Lord in Jerusalem."[4] The massive ingathering of Jews back to the land has been occurring since the eighteenth century. And multitudes of Christians have been visiting the land in the last half-century to discover the roots of their faith in the root of Israel.

Third, Wolicki observes that the great Maimonides prophesied that one day Christians would begin to alter their views of Torah and move closer to Jewish positions.[5] Unlike Muslims who reject Torah, Christians would begin to study Scripture with Jews and start to see that the only true God is the God of Israel.

All three of these phenomena are converging at this kairos moment. Israel has flourished since her return to the land. Despite its decline and

3. This vol., 5.
4. This vol., 11.
5. This vol., 10.

division, Christianity is undergoing revival, not only in the Global South but also in the Global North, where—bizarrely—prominent intellectuals are returning to Christian faith. And more and more Christians, often due to their learning from Jews and the land, are repenting of their supersessionism and/or replacement theologies.

Part of this is happening because of growing recognition that Jesus and Paul were far more Jewish than previously imagined. Maimonides might have been right that the Jesus of medieval Christianity led Jews away from Torah, as Rabbi Wolicki reports,[6] but the New Testament Jesus actually holds a supreme reverence for Torah. He insists, "Do not even begin to think that I came to destroy the Torah or the Prophets. I did not come with the purpose to cancel them but rather to interpret them properly. In solemn truth I tell you, until heaven and earth pass away, not even the smallest iota or dot from a letter shall pass away from the Torah until all is accomplished. Whoever then annuls one of the least of Torah's commandments, and teaches others to do the same, will be called least in the kingdom of heaven. However, anyone who practices and teaches them shall be called great in the kingdom of heaven" (Matt 5:17–19 HHB [adapted]).

Paul taught the same reverence for Torah. In his letter to the Roman church he asked, "Do we then overthrow Torah by this faith [in Jesus]? Heaven forbid! On the contrary, we interpret the Torah properly by placing it on a firmer footing. . . . The Torah is holy, and each commandment is sacred and righteous and good" (Rom 3:31; 7:12 HHB).

Paul and Jesus may differ from Jews today on questions pertaining to the Messiah and the messianic age. But they revered Torah, as more and more Christians do today. And this shared reverence for Torah as God's word unites our two faith communities. We Christians are seeing more and more that we have much to learn from our Jewish "older brothers" (as Pope John Paul II used to say).

This volume contains several investigations in line with this sentiment. Ian Kissell, for example, argues that we can derive a greater meaning of the Christian biblical canon from the Shema. J. Luis Dizon demonstrates that Second Temple Jewish texts helpfully illuminate early Christian understandings of the prophesied messiah's identity. Rafael Bello uses Maimonides to inform Christian understandings of holiness, and Michael M. C. Reardon finds surprising intersections with Jewish thought when exploring what is usually thought of as the Christian-exclusive doctrine of deification. Jordan Jones plumbs the depths of Qohelet to unearth "holy disillusion" that can assist Christian spiritual theology. Timothy Yoder discovers a lifeline out of

---

6. This vol., 8.

suffering's abyss in Jewish reflection on free will and God's hiddenness. And Jeff Yaneff uses Jewish conceptions of the material reality of both the human body and cosmos more generally to buttress Christian sexual ethics.

This book also shows how the Jewish vision can help Christians navigate their own ecclesial dilemmas. Alex Kazadi argues that recognizing the "Israelhood" of the church can help prevent her devolving into further supersessionism. Calvin Pais contends that we must see that Christ's hypostasis "of Israel" informs Christian conceptions of leadership. Brian Gamel warns us that faulty interpretations of John's *oi 'ioudaioi* can perpetuate historic supersessionism. And finally, Charles McVety concludes the volume by demonstrating how Gen 12 and its theological implications have blessed the Christian worlds.

In sum, this book shows not only how we Christians can learn from Jews but also how we have neglected to our detriment the 77 percent of the Protestant Bible (and 80 percent of the Anglican and Catholic Bible) that are the Hebrew Scriptures. Let this shared kairos moment be the impetus for us to heed their exhortation: "Let us go up to the Mount of the LORD, to the House of the God of Jacob; That He may instruct us in His ways, and that we may walk in His paths. For instruction shall come forth from Zion, the word of the LORD from Jerusalem" (Isa 2:3).

Contributors

Rafael Bello (PhD, Southern Baptist Theological Seminary) is the recipient of several international grants and awards, including the John Stott Award for Pastoral Engagement, New Visions for Theological Anthropology (NViTA) Award, and the BluePrint 1543 Award for Engagement in Science and Religion (2020). His first book, *Sinless Flesh*, is featured in the Studies in Historical and Systematic Theology Series. He is currently under contract for a monograph on the doctrine of sanctification. In addition to his academic roles, Bello is a research fellow at the Ethics & Religious Liberty Commission (ERLC) and has been involved in ministry in both the United States and Brazil. He is married to Josie, and they have three children.

J. Luis Dizon is a PhD candidate at the University of Toronto in the Department of Near and Middle Eastern Civilizations, specializing in comparative Abrahamic religions. His doctoral research focuses on the polemical and intertextual use of the Bible by Muslim authors. He also researches other topics pertaining to biblical studies and ancient Near Eastern languages. He is a regular guest on the *Reason and Theology* show, speaking on topics relating to Christian apologetics, biblical studies, and comparative religions. He also works as a lay pastoral associate for a Catholic parish in the archdiocese of Toronto, where he teaches sacramental prep classes for children for first communion and confirmation.

Brian K. Gamel is a postdoctoral research fellow at Baylor University's George W. Truett Theological Seminary. He has a PhD in New Testament and theology and has written extensively about the death of Jesus in the Gospel of Mark, including his first book, *Mark 15:39 as a Markan Theology of Revelation: The Centurion's Confession as Apocalyptic Unveiling*. He is currently working on a second book examining the use of athletic imagery in the New Testament.

Jordan W. Jones (PhD, Hebrew Union College) is assistant professor of biblical studies at Regent University School of Divinity in Virginia Beach, Virginia. He writes primarily on the traditional texts of wisdom in the Hebrew Scriptures. He is author of *She Opens Her Hand to the Poor: Gestures and Social Values in Proverbs* (2019) and *Ecclesiastes and Song of Songs* (2024).

Axel Kazadi is an ordained minister in the Wesleyan Church of Canada. He is an assistant professor of theology at Kingswood University in Sussex, NB, and a PhD candidate at Wycliffe College, University of Toronto. His fields of interest include Reformation theology, Jewish-Christian relations, Wesleyan theology, and sacramental theology.

Ian Kissell (PhD, Wycliffe College, University of Toronto) has lived in the United States, Canada, Greece, Tajikistan, South Africa, and Israel, and currently works in theological education in Africa and the Middle East, in both teaching and program development. His interests lie in resourcing both patristic and Eastern Christian thought to help Protestant theology face the challenges of the postmodern era. Ian worships in the Anglican tradition.

Gerald McDermott teaches at Jerusalem Seminary and Reformed Episcopal Seminary. He has written and edited books on Jonathan Edwards, theology of religions, and theology of Israel. His newest book is *A New History of Redemption: The Work of Jesus the Messiah Through the Millennia*. He and his wife live in Charlottesville, Virginia, with their three sons and daughters-in-law and twelve grandchildren.

Charles McVety has served both as the president of Canada Christian College and the national chairman of Christians United for Israel (Canadian chapter) for over three decades. He is also the president of the Evangelical Association and was previously the host of the national weekly television program *Canadian Times*.

Jonathan L. Milevsky (PhD) is the co-head of the Department of Jewish History at TanenbaumCHAT in Toronto, where he lectures on Jewish history and ethics. He is also a distinguished fellow at the Broughton Park Dialogue Group in the UK.

Calvin Pais works adjunctively as the professor of Israelology at Canada Christian College, teaching history and theological approaches for reconciliation between Jews and Christians. He works at an investment bank in Toronto and in his spare time can be found fishing.

Ephraim Radner is professor emeritus of historical theology, Wycliffe College, at the University of Toronto. He is an ordained Anglican priest and author of several books on ecclesiology, pneumatology, and biblical interpretation.

Michael M. C. Reardon (PhD, University of Toronto) is academic dean and professor of New Testament and historical theology at Canada Christian College in Whitby, Ontario. He is also the director of the Eckstein Institute for Jewish-Christian Relations and a Senior Religious Policy Analyst with ARC (Asia Research Center). Michael is co-editor of *Transformed into the Same Image: Constructive Investigations into the Doctrine of Deification* and the author of several articles. He is married to Joyce, and they have three children.

Pesach Wolicki is the executive director of Israel365 Action and author of both *Verses for Zion* and *Cup of Salvation: A Powerful Journey through King David's Psalms of Praise*. He is the host of Eyes on Israel on the Real America Network, cohost of the Shoulder to Shoulder podcast, and a regular contributor to the *Jerusalem Post* and Israel365news.com.

Jeff Yaneff is a PhD candidate at Wycliffe College of the University of Toronto. He has been the professor of biblical theology and philosophy at Canada Christian College for over a decade, where he previously earned a ThD. He has taught at Tyndale University and in addition to his biblical research interests in the subjects of human mortality and immortality, he regularly presents lectures on the intersection of theology with a host of interdisciplinary areas such as energy security, climate change, population science, and other contemporary ethical issues.

Timothy S. Yoder is professor of theological studies at Dallas Theological Seminary, where he is the coordinator for the apologetics program. His book *40 Questions about Apologetics* is forthcoming. He loves teaching and thinking about issues and topics (like the problem of evil) that involve both philosophy and theology. He is married to Lisa, and they live in Mesquite, Texas. Together, they lead the young adult ministry at their church.

Abbreviations

AB	Anchor Bible
Ab.	*De Abrahamo (On the Life of Abraham)*
ANE	Ancient Near Eastern
APOT	*The Apocrypha and Pseudepigrapha of the Old Testament.* Edited by Robert H. Charles. 2 vols. Oxford: Clarendon, 1913
AT	Author's translation
BCOTWP	Baker Commentary on the Old Testament Wisdom and Psalms
BDAG	Danker, Frederick W., Walter Bauer, William F. Arndt, and F. Wilbur Gingrich. *Greek-English Lexicon of the New Testament and Other Early Christian Literature.* 3rd ed. Chicago: University of Chicago Press, 2000 (Danker-Bauer-Arndt-Gingrich)
BHS	*Biblia Hebraica Stuttgartensia.* Edited by Karl Elliger and Wilhelm Rudolph. Stuttgart: Deutsche Bibelgesellschaft, 1983
BibInt	*Biblical Interpretation*
BRev	*Bible Review*
BSac	*Bibliotheca Sacra*
BZNW	Beihefte zur Zeitschrift für die neutestamentliche Wissenschaft
C. Ap.	*Contra Apionem (Against Apion)*
CBQ	*Catholic Biblical Quarterly*
CC	Continental Commentaries
Civ.	*De civitate Dei*
CUFI	Christians United for Israel
CurBR	*Currents in Biblical Research*

Doctr. chr.	*De doctrina christiana (Christian Instruction)*
ETL	*Ephemerides Theologicae Lovanienses*
HCOT	Historical Commentary on the Old Testament
Hor	*Horizons*
HTR	*Harvard Theological Review*
HvTSt	*Hervormde teologiese studies*
IBC	Interpretation: A Bible Commentary for Teaching and Preaching
JBL	*Journal of Biblical Literature*
JES	*Journal of Ecumenical Studies*
JETS	*Journal of the Evangelical Theological Society*
JPS	Jewish Publication Society
JSJ	*Journal for the Study of Judaism in the Persian, Hellenistic, and Roman Periods*
JSNT	*Journal for the Study of the New Testament*
JSNTSup	Journal for the Study of the New Testament Supplement Series
JSOTSup	Journal for the Study of the Old Testament Supplement Series
JTS	*Journal of Theological Studies*
L&N	Louw, Johannes P., and Eugene A. Nida, eds. *Greek-English Lexicon of the New Testament: Based on Semantic Domains.* 2nd ed. New York: United Bible Societies, 1989
LCL	Loeb Classical Library
LEC	Library of Early Christianity
LHBOTS	The Library of Hebrew Bible/Old Testament Studies
LNTS	The Library of New Testament Studies
LSJ	Liddell, Henry George, Robert Scott, Henry Stuart Jones. *A Greek-English Lexicon.* 9th ed. with revised supplement. Oxford: Clarendon, 1996
LSAWS	*Linguistic Studies*
NAC	New American Commentary
NICOT	New International Commentary on the Old Testament
NIGTC	New International Greek Testament Commentary

NovT	Novum Testamentum	
NovTSup	Supplements to Novum Testamentum	
NPNF1	*The Nicene and Post-Nicene Fathers.* 1st ser. Edited by Philip Schaff. 14 vols. Repr., Peabody, MA: Hendrickson, 1994	
NPNF2	*The Nicene and Post-Nicene Fathers.* 2nd ser. Edited by Philip Schaff and Henry Wace. 14 vols. Repr., Peabody, MA: Hendrickson, 1979	
NTL	New Testament Library	
NTS	*New Testament Studies*	
OECS	Oxford Early Christian Studies	
OTL	Old Testament Library	
OTP	*Old Testament Pseudepigrapha.* Edited by James H. Charlesworth. 2 vols. New York: Doubleday, 1983, 1985	
PoE	Problem of evil	
RBS	Resources for Biblical Study	
SemeiaSt	Semeia Studies	
SJLA	Studies in Judaism in Late Antiquity	
SNTSMS	Society for New Testament Studies Monograph Series	
STRev	*Sewanee Theological Review*	
SubBi	Subsidia Biblica	
SupJSJ	Supplements to the Journal for the Study of Judaism	
TBN	Themes in Biblical Narrative	
TDNT	Kittel, Gerhard, and Gerhard Friedrich, eds. *Theological Dictionary of the New Testament.* Translated by Geoffrey W. Bromiley. 10 vols. Grand Rapids: Eerdmans, 1964–76	
TOTC	Tyndale Old Testament Commentaries	
TynBul	*Tyndale Bulletin*	
WBC	Word Biblical Commentary	
WTJ	*Westminster Theological Journal*	
WUNT	Wissenschaftliche Untersuchungen zum Neuen Testament	
ZAC	*Zeitschrift für Antikes Christentum/Journal of Ancient Christianity*	

Introduction

Michael M. C. Reardon and Pesach Wolicki

THE INSPIRATION FOR THIS volume emerged from years of friendship, dialogue, and collaboration between a Jewish rabbi and Christian professor. Leading up to this publication, we created and co-taught multiple seminary courses including the Jewish Roots of Christianity, Comparative Jewish and Christian Hermeneutics, and the History of Israel. We also organized several academic symposia across North America investigating thematic commonalities between Judaism and Christianity. Rabbi Pesach in particular gathered groups of North American Christian professors to visit and experience the land of Israel alongside Jewish scholars and colleagues. And perhaps the most important initiative borne out of these years was the formation of the Eckstein Institute for Jewish-Christian Relations, a grant-funded research initiative that houses many of the aforementioned efforts.

Though this volume was a goal of ours for some time, the unimaginable atrocities inflicted against the Jewish people by Hamas on October 7, 2023, alongside the global explosion of anti-Semitism in the months thereafter created a renewed sense of urgency to complete the project in a timely manner. In a time when Jews are being demonized by the media, openly harassed in public venues, and victimized by government policies, it is imperative that those who identify as Christians, comprising approximately 2.4 billion people worldwide, lend their voice and support to their Jewish brethren. With this in mind, we resumed work on the volume you have in your hands with increased vigor and pray that it engenders a concrete conviction that Christians and Jews need not and should not view each other as "the other," but instead know one another according to their shared conviction: that they worship the God of Israel and identify themselves as the seed of Abraham, whether by blood or through faith.

Now, this certainly does not mean that there are no differences between Christianity and Judaism. The aim of this volume is not to minimize distinctives of the two faiths; nor is it an exercise designed to convert Jews to Christians or Christians to Jews. Jews have a bevy of historical reasons to distrust Christians—ranging from the Crusades to the pogroms—and Christians have theological reasons—whether the identity of the Messiah or the unique path of salvation—to respond likewise. The goal of this book, rather, is to set aside these differences, if even just for a moment, and explore the significant and expansive shared heritage of Jews and Christians. Beyond sharing a set of Scriptures, practitioners of both faiths uphold the absolute supremacy of the God of Abraham, Isaac, and Jacob, possess shared convictions concerning humankind being created in the *imago Dei* (image of God), organize their lives in alignment with common ethical values, and recognize that the world we inhabit today is not the world that will exist in eternity future. While differences exist, this shared understanding of reality binds Jews and Christians together as brethren—ones who can and should feel free to discuss, debate, and dialogue, but nevertheless, as kinfolk who must love, respect, and support one another.

Hence, after much consideration, the majority of the ensuing pages of this introduction are drawn from Rabbi Wolicki's decades-long efforts within the sphere of Jewish-Christian dialogue. Written from a Jewish perspective, and in lieu of him writing an individual chapter for the volume, we felt that an adaptation of his keynote address at the inaugural Eckstein Institute Symposium held at Canada Christian College in 2021 captures the spirit of both of this project and our aforementioned initiatives. The section thereafter previews each of the book's chapters.

TOWARD A NEW THEOLOGY OF THE JEWISH AND CHRISTIAN RELATIONSHIP

> Let them go to the Land and to Jerusalem, build the Temple, raise up the priesthood, principality and Moses with his Law so that they again become Jews and possess the Land. If that happened they should soon see us on their heels and also become Jews.[1]

This passage from Martin Luther is significant for three reasons. First, it provides a context for sharing the Jewish sources below which relate to

---

1. Martin Luther, quoted in Oberman, *Wurzeln des Antisemitismus*, 82–83n137. I am grateful to Johannes Gerloff for translating this passage in an email (Dec. 4, 2017).

Christianity. Some of what these Jewish commentators say will, at the least, not be especially complimentary. But they are important Jewish voices that help us to understand both the traditional and contemporary landscape of Jewish attitudes Christianity. Indeed, playing a so-called "tit-for-tat" exchange in which we examine ancient Jewish and Christian writings in order to see which side is more insulting to the other's religion, we would find no end to such outlooks.

Second, this line from Luther provides an entry point into the Jewish mindset regarding Christianity. Significantly, Jews are far more aware of Christian anti-Jewish sentiment than the majority of Christians are, and this awareness greatly informs how modern-day Jews feel about Christianity to this day. This is a significant disconnect between the two faiths—while most Christians are unaware of this history, the Jewish self-understanding views the atrocities committed against them in the name of Christianity over the past two thousand years as ever present.

Last, this quote is significant it that it raises both a challenge and question to modern day people of faith. Indeed, it is a challenge that we must face if we are honest and genuine seekers of truth. The challenge is related to our inherited theological outlooks. On the one hand, we should be and often are obedient adherents to our faith systems. This includes theological axioms and interpretations from great thinkers in our respective traditions that we utilize as frameworks to guide our own thinking. Our current systematic theologies are built upon the groundwork laid by those who came before us, and thus, we revere and cherish the thinkers of past centuries. For many Christians and Jews, we are wary of departing from their pronouncements.

Yet, we cannot lose sight of a simple reality: all theological assertions are contextual. For example, even setting aside the sarcastic tone of Luther's remark, how would his theology pertaining to the Jews have differed if the modern state of Israel existed during his lifetime? Or reaching further back in the annals of history, how would Augustine's understanding of the Jews have shifted if Israel's borders, including Jerusalem, had already been restored? While it's surely doubtful that Luther would have made good on his promise to convert to Judaism, it is readily apparent that he could have never made the quoted statement above. The reality of an independent and prosperous Jewish state in the land of Israel would surely have forced him to arrive at a very different conclusion.

Augustine famously defined theology as an exercise of "faith seeking understanding." That is an especially insightful definition. It is the *seeking* that we must embrace. All too often, we make the mistake of thinking that theology is "faith *achieving* understanding," and in doing so, purport that the endgame of theological inquiry is absolute certainty. But to state what should be obvious to most readers, God is not a theologian. Neither in Scripture nor in his governance of the cosmos, God never speaks in the language of systematic theology, nor does he articulate a clear set of axioms wherein everything logically fits together. In fact, God speaks through the prophet Isaiah to convey a diametrically opposed notion: "My thoughts are not your thoughts, my ways are not your ways" (Isa 55:8). This verse does not speak about whether God knows things that he hasn't told us yet or that he's smarter than us (though of course, both of these statements are true). Rather, this verse is point to a different reality: God's thoughts and ways are not merely unknown to us—they are ultimately unknowable at all.

To state this differently, if as limited human creatures we believe that our systematic theological conclusions are satisfying and logical, and that due to this we have arrived at a comprehensive understanding of God, we can be certain that we are mistaken. How and why we are mistaken may never be revealed to us—or if God mercifully intends it to be so, it may be revealed only to future generations. Regardless of either possibility, the first axiom of theology that we must accept as genuine seekers of truth is that all theology is ultimately a speculative human endeavor which desires to attain to the unattainable. It is faith *seeking* understanding; not achieving it.

Theologians, as a portion of our readership likely aspire to be, are charged with the task of interpreting and explaining God—hence, the term *theo*logy, the study of God. In a Bible-based belief system this means studying both the tapestry of Scripture and the world we inhabit—that is, the world in which God acts. Great theologians draw from both of these sources—human history up until their lifetime and the text of the Bible—to draw conclusions about who God is and what he is doing in relation to humanity, time, and space.

This is true of all theological positions. For example, the well-trod question of theodicy: how to understand divine justice in a divinely created world that nevertheless contains evil. In examining this issue, theologians must determine what Scripture reveals about the character of God—that is, what the Bible says about God's mercy and justice as well as what it says about the God who punishes the wicked and rewards the righteous. They then must take these insights and place them in dialogue with how the material cosmos actually operates. With these combined inputs, the reality of the earth today and what the Bible reveals regarding God, theologians can begin to promulgate their positions.

The same is true when grappling with questions related to biblical prophecies and material human history. We now live in a period of human history in which the nation of Israel has returned to their land after two thousand years of exile. This should be a significant event for any theologian, and specifically, Christian theologians.

After the curses listed in Deut 28 culminate in the exile of Israel thereafter, Deut 29:22 speaks of the desolation of the land continuing to *hador ha'acharon*—"the last generation" or "era"—in other words, a very long time. It should be noted that almost all Christian English translations of this verse render *ha'acharon* as "later" rather than "last." I believe that this translation is inaccurate as *acharon* literally means "latest" or "last" (see how the same word is translated in Neh 8:18; 2 Sam 19:12; 23:1; Isa 44:6). When taken as true, Deut 30 then describes how the nation of Israel will return from being scattered to the ends of the heavens to the land of Israel, take possession of this land, and become "more numerous and more prosperous than their ancestors" (Deut 30:5). These events are no longer future-tense prophecies. Everything in this verse has occurred in the past several decades. Any theological position related to Israel and prophecies related to Israel must take these monumental changes into account—even if this entails a questioning or reconsideration of long-held theological positions inherited from theologians before us.

There exists a dilemma on both the Jewish and Christian sides of the theological aisle. There is both a distaste and fear of reexamining or renouncing on traditional ways of thinking. We revere the thinkers who came before us and operate within traditions in which they play a formative and authoritative role. Most, though not all, are extremely cautious about becoming too radical in our theologies or worldviews. Yet, at the same time, we live in a very different world, especially in relation to Israel, and this necessitates new ways of thinking. Simply stated, God has acted in history in a momentous manner and we incorporate this change into our theological frameworks; we must continue to seek understanding of God.

I would like to suggest a way forward in respect to this conundrum. A few years ago, the great historian Barbara Tuchman published *Bible and Sword*. The volume surveys the history of the relationship between British Christianity, the land of Israel, and the prophecies related to Israel from the origins of the Christian church up until the twentieth century. Tuchman clearly details how, for centuries, the role of the land of Israel, though of central importance to some Christians, was at best a marginal concern to most the Christian world. Yet in more recent centuries, especially due to the rise and influence of the Puritans, Israel was assigned greater theological import. And thus, today the land of Israel is increasingly important and formative within the faith of hundreds of millions of Christians worldwide.

My point in including this historical survey is that we don't necessarily need to "turn our backs" on the entirety of our faith tradition to embrace

God's move in human history. Sometimes, our tradition includes options and flexibility which, whether dormant or marginal in past centuries, are proven to be right, even to the point of being of vital importance, in later eras.

We now turn to Jewish understandings of Christianity, for which I want to draw from a few passages from Maimonides—the single most influential Jewish theologian of the past two thousand years. Maimonides was a medieval legal scholar and philosopher who lived from 1140 to 1205, and is universally recognized as the foremost Jewish thinker of the entire post-talmudic era. While this does not mean that every consensus of modern Jewish thought aligns with every position he held, every discussion of Jewish thought must deal with his outlooks.

Though he lived in the twelfth century, a time of Christian persecution against Jews throughout Europe, what he wrote about Christianity serves as a useful window into difficult issues that the Jewish side of Jewish-Christian dialogue presently encounters. To be sure, in his legal writings, Maimonides wrote harshly about Christianity. He championed the position that Christianity is a form of idolatry.[2] For Maimonides, the combination of physical icons in worship and the Trinitarian compromise on the oneness of God were enough to definitively make such a ruling. It's worth mentioning that not all Jewish legal authorities—even in Maimonides's own time—concurred with his assessment. Today, with countless developments in Christian theology and the rise of divergent denominations and practices, the question of Christianity's status according to Jewish law remains a hotly debated issue.

Yet, we set this aside for the time being, because the following two passages from Maimonides are especially fascinating in light of his position that Christianity is idolatrous. In Maimonides's *Responsa*, a question was posed to him regarding the permissibility of teaching Torah to non-Jews. This is important, because the Talmud forbids teaching Torah to non-Jews, which in talmudic times generally referred to pagans. The questioner asked if this ruling still applies "today" (i.e., the twelfth century). Maimonides replied as follows:

> It is permissible to teach the commandments and commentaries to Christians and to draw them closer to our faith. This is not permissible to Ishmaelites [i.e., Muslims]; as you know that it is their belief that the Torah is not from heaven. Therefore, when you teach them something of what is written, and they find it contradicting that which they have invented according to the corruption of the stories mixing up of subject matter in

---

2. Maimonides, *Commentary on Mishnah Aboda Zara* 1:3.

> their tradition, it will prove nothing to them because of their errors and they will explain it according to their mistaken assumptions. They will respond to us with their claims and will be stumbling block to Jews who are forbidden among them. But Christians believe that the text of the Torah has not changed. They merely offer explanations that are mistaken that are known to them. And if they are told the correct explanation it is possible that they will return to the correct way. And even if they do not return to the correct way when we want them to it will not produce any stumbling block for us as there is no difference in their scriptures from ours.[3]

In other words, Maimonides saw value in teaching and discussing Scripture with Christians because of their shared faith in the divine authority of Scripture. He saw value in drawing Christians closer to the Jewish faith. We need to be clear here: Judaism has not and does not seek converts. Maimonides is not talking here about drawing Christians to convert to Judaism. Rather, he is referring to the value in drawing Christians, and more broadly Christianity, closer to Judaism on the basis of shared faith related to the divine authority of Scripture.

To fully understand why Maimonides saw this as a valuable endeavor we need to examine a second text. The *Mishneh Torah*, Maimonides's monumental legal code, remains the most important and comprehensive treatment of rabbinic law to this day. Though modern Jewish practice does not follow Maimonides's rulings completely, all rabbinic Jewish law since Maimonides is based upon his system. In the final pages of his encyclopedic work, Maimonides deals with issues relating to the concept of "Messiah." He lays out what the Jewish definition of Messiah is and what the qualifications are for someone to earn the title. Within that context, he devotes several lines to discussing Christianity. After explaining, from his standpoint, why Jesus does not qualify as Messiah—including the disastrous results for the Jewish community that have resulted from Christian anti-Semitism during events such the Crusades—he makes a fascinating theological statement:

> Jesus the Nazarene, as well, who imagined that he was the messiah and was killed by the court, Daniel had prophesied regarding him as it states "Those rebellious among your own people will rise up in fulfillment of the vision, but will fail." And is there a greater failure than this? That all of the prophets spoke of the Messiah redeeming Israel, saving them, gathering in their dispersed and strengthening their observance of the

---

3. *Responsa of Maimonides*, no. 149.

commandments; and this one caused their loss by the sword, the exile of their remnant, their suppression, replacing their law, and leading most of the world astray to serve a god other than Hashem.

However, the thoughts of the creator of the world—man is not capable of conceiving of them—for His ways are not our ways and our thoughts are not His thoughts. And all of these matters of Jesus the Nazarene—and of the Ishmaelite who arose after him—were solely in order to pave the path for the king Messiah and to repair the entire world to serve Hashem together as it states, "Then I will purify the lips of the peoples, that all of them may call on the name of the Lord and serve him shoulder to shoulder."

How so? The entire world has now been filled with the concept of the Messiah, the concepts of the Torah, and the concepts of the commandments. These matters have spread to the most distant lands and to many primitive nations [lit. nations of uncircumcised hearts]. They discuss these matters. Regarding the commandments of the Torah—some say these commandments were true but have since been negated in our days and were not to be practiced for the future. Others say that hidden matters are meant by them and that they are not meant to be understood according to their simple meaning, but that the Messiah has already come and revealed their secrets.

And when the true king Messiah will arise and will succeed and be exalted—as a direct result they all will retract and know that their ancestors bequeathed falsehood to them and that their prophets led them astray.[4]

Maimonides is known for the great precision of his writing. His choice of words was extremely careful; this is especially true of his legal code. It is well known in the world of Jewish scholarship that Maimonides's exact words, order of ideas, and choices of cited verses are deliberate and worthy of study. With this in mind, let us carefully analyze this passage so that we fully appreciate the points that he just made.

As mentioned, the context of the statement is the discussion of the concept of the Messiah from a Jewish legal perspective. Maimonides lays out the definition of the term and the qualifications of a would-be claimant to the title. In this context, he makes the following four points:

---

4. Maimonides, *Mishneh Torah, Kings and Wars* 11.1 AT.

1. Jesus was not the Messiah because he had the opposite effect of expectations surrounding the Jewish Messiah (e.g., he led the Jews away from Torah, into greater suffering and a deepened exile).
2. Nevertheless, Jesus was the catalyst of God's plan "to pave the path for the king Messiah and to repair the entire world to serve Hashem together."
3. This "paving" and "repairing" come about through the spreading of the core ideas and ideals of the Torah to the entire world.
4. When the real Messiah will arrive Christianity will be proven false and will be rejected by its adherents in favor of an entirely Jewish form of faith.

For the purposes of our discussion, it is critical to take note of two divisions within what Maimonides wrote about Christianity.

First, on one hand, he describes the negative effect of Christianity on the Jewish people, which Maimonides describes as an unmitigated disaster—the polar opposite of the Jewish definition of Messiah. Yet, he also details the positive effect of Christianity on the nations of the world. He describes Christianity a powerful move of God designed, in his words, "to pave the path for the coming of the Messiah"—the catalyst for the shared faith in and worship of the God of Israel by all humanity.

The second distinction, related to the first and perhaps even a restatement of the first, is between what Christianity has been in the *past* (i.e., a cause of oppression, deepened exile for Israel, and the world being led astray) and what it contributes to the *future* (i.e., bringing knowledge of the concepts of the biblical faith to the entire world and paving the way for universal redemption).

To fully appreciate what Maimonides is saying we first must understand how Judaism defines itself. From Abraham being charged with teaching justice and morality to all the peoples of the earth, through the Lord calling on Israel to be a "kingdom of priests" (Exod 19) to the prophecies of Isaiah and Zechariah laying out the vision of all of humanity believing in and serving the one God together—Judaism has a universal mission. The goal and mission of Israel is to bring all of humanity to know God. The temple in Jerusalem of the future is called "a house of prayer for all nations" by Isaiah. While the Jewish eschaton does not see everyone as Jewish, it does see everyone as serving the same God, the God of Israel.

To paraphrase Maimonides, the groundwork for all humanity serving the God of the Bible is for the knowledge of the Bible to be spread throughout the world. Why would the nations stream to Jerusalem at the time of the ingathering of Israel to seek the Lord as Zechariah prophesied (e.g., Zech 8) unless they know who this God is? As Maimonides points out, the reason that so much of the world today knows the God of the Bible is due to Christianity. The same Christians who were persecuting Jews for centuries simultaneously spread knowledge of the Bible to all of humanity. This familiarity with the Bible paves the way for the ultimate shared worship to come in the future.

The "endgame" of Judaism is that all humanity has faith in the God of the Bible. Christianity moves the world in that direction. The partnership is natural. At the same time, there is trauma in the relationship. Christian anti-Semitism and forced conversions of Jews to Christianity have resulted in strong visceral discomfort related to Jewish-Christian dialogue for most Jews.

Maimonides looks past that negative history—a history that was still going strong during his lifetime with the Crusades, claims of blood libel, and expulsions from European countries—to argue for a longer-term eschatological vision in which Christianity and Judaism are partners all along, whether they know it or not.

This brings us back to the first passage I cited, the *responsum* regarding teaching Torah to Christians. While it may appear strange that Maimonides permits teaching Torah to Christians even though he argued that Christianity was a form of idolatry, the second passage in *Mishneh Torah* explains this ruling. Maimonides's determination that Christianity was idolatrous was due to the technical nature of the Trinity and the use of icons in worship—both *anathema* to the principles of Jewish faith and practice. This ruling has no bearing on the ultimate purpose and trajectory of the Christian faith as it relates to the historical development of universal faith in the God of the Bible.

We should note Maimonides's precise words towards the end of the *responsum*, "And even if they do not return to the correct way *when we want them to*."[5] It is inescapable that Maimonides posited that there is a historical process underway and that there will come a time in the future when Christians will begin to alter their understanding of the Bible such that their beliefs will draw closer to the positions of Judaism. Maimonides saw the study of Scripture with Christians as a positive endeavor to advance this process.

Much has changed since Maimonides wrote these words in the twelfth century. Most notably, the Reformation, with all that flowed from that monumental change, and the success of the modern state of Israel, inclusive of changing Christian attitudes toward the Jewish people. When I speak

---

5. *Responsa of Maimonides*, no. 149; emphasis added.

to Jewish audiences, I regularly cite Maimonides and ask them, "If Maimonides, living at the time of the crusades, when medieval Christianity was openly hostile to Judaism, was able to see past that reality to a larger vision of cooperation and shared faith, how about us who live when we do?"

Scripture speaks of an awakening that sweeps the world coinciding with the restoration of Israel to the land promised to Abraham, Isaac, and Jacob. Numerous passages from Scripture speak of multitudes among the nations of the world visiting the land and that time, praising God for the ingathering of Israel, which in turn, leads to shared worship of the Lord in Jerusalem.

In talks and articles to the Jewish community, I often rhetorically ask, "Do you believe that the biblically foretold ingathering of Deuteronomy 30 is underway? Well, that ingathering is meant to be accompanied by multitudes among the nations who are a part of that as well." The shifting attitudes in the Christian world, from the Vatican's radical redefinition of its doctrines regarding the Jews and Israel to the rise of Christian political support for the Jewish state to the fact that millions of Christian tourists visit Israel every year, a simple fact is clear: there exists a special relationship between our faiths that is being further developed.

It's true that we cannot ignore the harsh realities of the past. But we are not bound by them as we shape the future. Maimonides points the way. It is true that the past was disastrous for the Jewish people. At the same time, looking forward to the fulfillment of the biblical vision of a universal faith in the Lord, Christianity and Judaism are partners in paving the path to that reality.

We must be humble, yet bold. Humble enough to recognize that no matter how rational and elegant our systematic theology, we must never be too sure of ourselves. And we must be bold enough to embrace and respond to changing realities. This endeavor can be challenging. For Jews, we are challenged by our long memories. Paradigms are not easy to break. But things are changing, and sometimes, human political realities can help clarify what these changes might be.

The fact is that Christians are facing the same adversaries as Jews—both culturally in the West and militarily in Africa and the Middle East where Christians are persecuted daily. This should play a role in waking people up to the reality of our changing relationship. Christians who are attacked all over the Middle East simply for being Christians are attacked by the exact same people who hate Jews. Indeed, if I, a Jewish rabbi, had been standing beside the French priest who was publicly murdered in his church a few years ago, the murderer would have gladly murdered me as well.

It is not a nod to so-called intersectionality to say that if someone is murdered for a reason that applies to me equally, that an attack on that person for that reason is an attack on me as well. As strange as it sounds, in our current reality, when Christians in Nigeria are murdered by radical Muslims for being Christian, I, as a Jew, am under attack as well. All people of the God of the Bible are under attack. One need look no further than the attacks on Christmas and Easter celebrations in the name of hatred for the state of Israel that we have seen in recent months.

This is perhaps a negative spin on our current relationship—shared victimhood. But this commonality speaks to a much deeper and positive connection. As Maimonides wrote, we have a natural affinity of ideas based on our shared reverence for Scripture which transcends other differences. This commonality points the way to an exchange of ideas that results in a real partnership.

Much of the Jewish community resists looking at these issues in a new way. Old paradigms are stubborn things. Many in our intellectual and theological community resist reexamining theological positions of old for fear of breaking down boundaries set by great minds of the past. But increasingly, more and more eyes, minds, and hearts are being illuminated.

To be clear, differences between Christians and Jews remain and will continue to remain. We do not seek for the two faiths to be theologically harmonized on every point. There are different paths to the one God, the God of Abraham, Isaac, and Jacob. But in the Jewish community, as well as in the world of Christianity, we must be willing to see that things have changed and continue to change. We must be bold enough to embrace these changes and allow ourselves to be challenged theologically. As noted at the outset, theology is contextual, and today's context is not what it was in the past. Just as the theologians of the past took bold steps in staking out positions based on what they saw before them, we are in the same position today.

We are not blind to the significant points of departure between our faiths; yet, at the same time, we must seek a stronger bond of partnership and a relationship built on an appreciation for the vast amount that we share. The prophet Zephaniah spoke of a time when all peoples would serve the God of Israel *shechem echad*—"as one shoulder" (Zeph 3:9). That time is coming closer every day.

WHAT LIES AHEAD

The volume in your hands is divided into three parts, the first of which is entitled "Foundational Matters." Ephraim Radner's "The Cost of

High-Mindedness: Jews, Gentiles, and Romans 11:20–21" opens the section by valorizing the virtue of uncertainty related to who—whether Jew or gentile—will be "in" or "out" of "the Great Assize of creation's transfiguration." As a Jewish convert and Anglican priest, Radner calls the gentile church both to humility and to repentance in relation to her historic posture toward the Jewish people. According to Radner, gentiles, for far too long, have exhibited antipathy toward Jews; as a result, he argues that "the gentile church, because of her high-mindedness, has been 'spared not' by God," and in fact, has been "broken off" of the olive tree spoken of in Rom 11.[6] Taking this claim as a starting point, he goes on to discuss the implications of this ecclesial reality: first, as it relates to Christian evangelization of Jews; next as it relates to the character of the gentile church; and finally in respect to the revelation of Christ's form, character, and cosmic significance.

The second chapter, Jonathan Milevsky's "What Else Can We Learn from Each Other? Engaging David Novak on a Jewish Christian Discussion of Faith" examines the intellectual topography of eminent Jewish philosopher and theologian David Novak. Milevsky detects difficulties related to locating content in Novak's Jewish-Christian dialogue, and furthermore, argues that inconsistencies of such dialogue are best understood with Novak's developing natural law theory. Hence, with reference to the talmudic concept of *qitrug*, Milevsky suggests an alternative approach that allows Jews and Christians to engage each other's faiths, while simultaneously resolving some of the difficulties he contends are inherent to Novak's approach.

The second and longest section of this volume contains six impressive investigations that illuminate various intersections of Jewish and Christian thought. Ian Kissell's "The Canon as Theological Problem: The Shema as Theological Vision" argues that a distinctive feature of the Judeo-Christian tradition (as well as Islam) is that it is "text centered" to a degree that other religious traditions are not. While this has long been recognized by scholars, how this text-centrality has been imagined has shifted significantly in the modern era; in Western Christian theology, discussions of canon came to emphasize questions of authority and monovocality. Kissell argues, however, that this modern understanding of canon ought to be reconsidered. A close reading of Irenaeus's *Against Heresies* demonstrates a different understanding of canon, one which pictures not a single, authoritative voice, but a harmonious chorus emerging from distinct voices. According to Kissell, this canonical vision is deeply rooted in the Hebrew Scriptures, especially the Shema, and paying attention to this fact brings into focus the distinct

6. This vol., 23.

features of the Judeo-Christian tradition, as well as how these two traditions have their own emphases.

The next essay, J. Luis Dizon's "Early High Christology in Second Temple Jewish Literature," rejects the commonly held notion that the Christian doctrine of a divine-human Messiah is a departure from prevailing beliefs in Second Temple Judaism about the Messiah, which past scholars have argued would have imagined the Messiah as no more than a human being. In support of this claim, Dizon carefully examines Jewish texts such as the Dead Sea Scrolls, 4 Ezra, and the book of Enoch show how a portion of Jewish thinkers conceived of a Messiah who was more than human—even possessing divine attributes, titles, and prerogatives. Dizon goes on to conduct a comparative study of the Christology of these texts and the Christology of the Gospel of Mark (often considered to be the earliest of the four gospels) to demonstrate that these texts share common motifs, which ultimately, point toward a divine-human Messiah. While not as well developed as the Christology of Mark, he concludes that the aforementioned Second Temple texts create a trajectory of thought that the later Christian affirmation of a divine-human Messiah extends from.

Michael M. C. Reardon's "'You Are Gods': Deification in Christianity and Judaism" traces a similar trajectory as the previous chapter, but does so not merely in relation to the Messiah, but to all human beings. Reardon begins by outlining what deification does and does not entail within orthodox Christian thought and suggests that this framework is equally applicable to other monotheistic traditions, including Judaism. After introducing a spectrum of philosophical frameworks informing portrayals of Christian deification, Reardon turns to outline the scriptural bases for Christian deification. In the next section, he analyzes several Second Temple Jewish scriptural commentaries which hold both similar and dissimilar concepts related to the deification of human beings. He concludes with a brief comparison of how deification is conceived of in both faiths and provides a way forward for future dialogue between the two faith traditions in relation to deification.

In "Holiness That Does Not Separate: Bridging the Gap Between Christian Models of Sanctification and Jewish Approaches to Holiness," Rafael Bello retrieves insights from the Jewish tradition related to holiness in order to bridge the gap between divergent Christian models of sanctification: specifically, those found in the Wesleyan, Keswick, and Reformed traditions. Despite some variation in Orthodox Judaism, Bello contends that the concept of holiness and/or sanctification boasts common loci and explanations across traditions, broadly construed. He goes on to analyze Maimonides's conception of holiness as virtue and moderation within Jewish thought and concludes that relating virtue and the Mosaic law is, in fact, a profitable way forward to bridge between differing Christian models of sanctification, as well as bring these competing models into dialogue with Jewish conceptions of holiness.

Jordan W. Jones's essay, "Toward a Holy Disillusion in Qohelet: How the Uniqueness of Israel's God Positions Jews and Christians for Authentic Living Before Him," engages with the radical assertions of Qohelet, popularly known as the "preacher" or "teacher" of Ecclesiastes. Qohelet's world featured systems of belief that contradicted the way of God taught in the Hebrew Scriptures—on the one hand, the religious ideologies of the ancient Near East had worshippers futilely attempting to control life's outcomes through manipulation of the gods; on the other hand, certain Hebrews, like the interlocutors of Job, held to the similarly false belief that the outcomes of life could be accurately predicted through ritual obedience to and right living before YHWH. According to Jones, Qohelet rejects these false systems by presenting the God of Israel as wholly other and "in every good way infinite"; hence God-fearers are called to embrace a "holy disillusion," that is, the scriptural teaching of an infinite God and the opportunity provided by that God to live joyful, simple (that is to say, "authentic") lives in reverential obedience before him.

In "Jewish and Christian Perspectives on the Problem of Suffering: Discerning the Ways of God in a Fallen World," Timothy Yoder examines both the commonalities and the distinctives of Jewish and Christian approaches to the presence of suffering in our world. From the book of Job to the present day, followers of Yahweh have labored to discern the ways of a good God in a fallen and suffering world. Accordingly, Yoder examines the reflection of medieval thinkers like Saadiah Gaon, Maimonides, and Augustine, as well as contemporary scholars like Abraham Herschel and Eliezer Berkovits, Marilyn McCord Adams and Alvin Plantinga. In a post-Shoah world still filled with horrendous evils, Yoder rightly contends that Jews and Christian still find it necessary to think deeply about human free will and the hiddenness of God, the role of sin and punishment in our relationship to God and what it means to follow God in a world of persecution and darkness.

Jeff Yaneff's "The Gift of the Human Body: The Physical Basis of Sexual Ethics in Judeo-Christian Thought" explores the highly contentious issue of same-sex unions and transgenderism in relation to the historic Judeo-Christian tradition. For Yaneff, there is an unexpected shared presupposition in Jewish and Christian thinking, who have jointly disavowed such practices within their ethical frameworks. He contends that the Judeo-Christian sexual ethic locates ultimate authority in relation to gender and sexuality within the material world. This shared commitment, he suggests, is rooted in the presumption that the entire cosmos is a divinely given (and good) gift to be received with thanksgiving by its beneficiaries. The alternative LGBTQ affirming ethic, he contends, does not locate its ultimate authority for sexual ethics within the visible cosmos, but in invisible structures such as passions, emotions, personalities, and the alike. Yaneff goes on to demonstrate through analysis of Jewish and Christian texts that the prioritization of unseen impulse and desires above material concerns is deemed problematic within the Judeo-Christian sexual ethic based upon the notion that same-sex pairing "tells a lie" about the identity of those involved—that is, identical, noncomplementary, visible, material bodies are presented as something they are not, that is, the opposite, complementary gender.

The final section of the volume, entitled "Jewish-Christian Rapprochement, Reconciliation, and Unity," is comprised of four essays—three written within the context of academic exegesis and theology, and thereafter, an epilogue which aptly "bookends" the volume by offering a Christian pastoral and historical perspective in favor of Jewish-Christian dialogue.

The first, Brian Gamel's "Οἱ Ἰουδαῖοι and the Gospel of John: Grappling with Anti-Judaism in the New Testament," argues that John's use of the phrase οἱ Ἰουδαῖοι—which is often translated "the Jews"—is a theological problem disguised as a linguistic one. While interpreters have frequently tried to offer more precision to the referent behind that phrase—through innovative translations, historical context, and appeals to its symbolic meaning—Gamel contends that the problematic nature of this English translation is often unacknowledged. A failure to recognize and own this dangerous and hurtful language in the Fourth Gospel, he suggests, is an impediment to contemporary Jewish-Christian dialogue and an evasion of Christian responsibility to name and confess sin in the interest of apologetics. In light of this contention, Gamel discusses a possible solution which both acknowledge this problem within John while still regarding the text as authoritative Scripture through the method of content criticism (i.e., *Sachkritik*).

In "Lindbeck and Kinzer on the Church: Israel and Gentiles 'Mutually Dwelling' in Christ as One People of God?," Axel Kazadi demonstrates that George Lindbeck's Israel-like concept of the church may assist Christians in recognizing that the gentile and Jewish fragments of the Church are fundamentally connected as a single, inseparable people—which nevertheless does not obliterate their particularities. Dividing these two fragments, Kazadi suggests, has irreversible supersessionist consequences and breeds violence against the vulnerable fragment. It has historically been the Jews who have suffered at the hands of Christians in the medieval, Reformation, and modern periods, due to their tendency to self-define themselves as being apart from and severed from Israel's actual life. Kazadi goes on to argue that

Israel and the church were one people during the patristic era because there was no theologically presumed break in continuity between them. While he also discusses Mark Kinzer's concerns related to bilateral ecclesiology, Kazadi ultimately contends that Lindbeck's Israel-like concept of the church satisfactorily affirms the single peoplehood of Jewish and gentile believers.

In "Jewish Christian Reconciliation Is Inseparable from Christian Leadership: 1 Timothy 3:1–2 Interpreted in Light of Zizioulas," Calvin Pais draws from the work of one of the most influential Eastern Orthodox theologians and bishops of recent memory—John Zizioulas—to provide a theological interpretation of 1 Tim 3:1–2 in the service of Jewish-Christian unity. Pais begins his essay with a novel but altogether appropriate translation of the verse referenced in the essay's title, which he renders "faithful is God." As an Evangelical, Pais contends that God's faithfulness is axiomatic and synonymous with an enduring loyalty, which he further contends is the interpretive logic for everything within the created cosmos. This logic is seen especially in God's marriage to Israel. God's own marital faithfulness to Israel—through great pains—is not only the very salvific basis for Christians, but is also constitutive of Christian leadership and their congregations, which in turn, relates to their ministries within God's own marital life and reconciliation.

The volume's epilogue, Charles McVety's "The Unprecedented Unique Bond Between Christians and Jews," is an especially important piece for lay Christians who are otherwise not regularly engaged with theological scholarship. McVety has served both the president of the Canadian chapter of Christians United for Israel (CUFI) and the president of Canada Christian College and School of Graduate Theological Studies for multiple decades. In the latter role, he provided partial funding, as well as the venue, for the first academic symposium of the Eckstein Institute for Jewish-Christian Relations—several of the essays in this volume were originally presented at that event. His essay traces the relationship between the rise of Evangelicalism, Pentecostalism, and Christian Zionism and interprets this history theologically through the lens of the promise in Gen 12 that those who bless Israel will also be blessed. McVety begins by introducing William Blackstone, a Christian Zionist who organized a conference of hundreds of Christian leaders in support of Israeli statehood several years before the beginning of the Jewish Zionist movement. Thereafter, he details the important work that has been done in the past decades to strengthen both political and familial bonds between Jews and Christians. Ultimately, McVety suggests that Jews and Christians have a unique, unbreakable bond both in the face of common enemies and in light of their joint worship of the God of Israel, and that from a Christian perspective, the rise of Christian Zionism aligned with the great blessing of both Evangelicalism and Pentecostalism achieving exponential growth in the past century.

While the essays of this volume collectively cover extensive ground, we trust that readers come away from it with a fresh realization of a simple reality: though Christians and Jews have numerous particularities distinguishing themselves from one another, they perhaps share much more that binds them together as kinfolk. Whether it be shared understandings of God's justice, a common notion of both the creation and telos of humanity, tethered political and social realities, or fidelity to the same set of Scriptures and same Creator of the cosmos, we pray and hope that Christians and Jews will be emboldened to cease looking at one another as the "other," but rather, as brethren who both identify as the seed of Abraham—whether by blood or through faith—and praise, worship, honor, and glorify the God of Israel.

BIBLIOGRAPHY

Maimonides. *Commentary on Mishnah Aboda Zara.* [In Hebrew.] Wikisource. https://he.m.wikisource.org/wiki/במר%22ם_לע_הדובע_הרז_א.

———. *Mishneh Torah, Kings and Wars.* Sefaria, n.d. From *Mishneh Torah*, translated by Eliyahu Touger (Jerusalem: Moznaim, 1986–2007). https://www.sefaria.org/Mishneh_Torah%2C_Kings_and_Wars.11.1?lang=bi&with=About&lang2=en.

———. *Responsa of Maimonides.* Vol. 1. Edited by Joshua Blau et al. Jerusalem: Machon Yerushalayim, 2016.

Oberman, Heiko Augustinus. *Wurzeln des Antisemitismus: Christenangst und Judenplage im Zeitalter von Humanismus und Reformation.* 2nd ed. Berlin: Severin und Siedler, 1981.

Tuchman, Barbara W. *Bible and Sword; England and Palestine from the Bronze Age to Balfour.* New York: New York University Press, 1956.

PART I

Foundational Matters

Chapter 1

The Cost of High-Mindedness
Jews, Gentiles, and Romans 11:2–21

Ephraim Radner

THIS ESSAY IS A reflection on what it might mean if we take Scripture seriously with respect to the experienced *history* of Jews and gentiles. History is a key category here. One of the places where the Scripture reveals the meaning of history is in prophecy, so I will be focusing on that. My perspective is deeply Christian, and thus I am not trying to say what a Jew should or shouldn't think about God and history. I am addressing gentiles in particular.

Let me begin with comments by the prominent Jewish philosopher and theologian David Novak. In a recent popular, but quite complex, article, Novak has argued that some form of "supersessionism" lies at the "core" of the Christian gospel; supersessionism also lies, he would add, at the core of Jewish self-identity.[1] *Supersessionism* is the modern term given to the view that, in its Christian application, the Christian gospel (and thus, church) "supersedes" and supplants or replaces Judaism, or otherwise takes Judaism's place as the religious location of salvation. Claims like the following are therefore "supersessionist": the new covenant replaces the old covenant; Jesus replaces temple; the cross replaces temple sacrifice; the gospel replaces the law; and so on.

---

1. Novak, "Supersessionism Hard and Soft."

Supersessionism, in this general meaning, has been under some attack over the past decades in theological circles, as the idea that Christianity replaces Judaism as the site of God's salvation has been judged to lie behind the horrors of Christian anti-Semitism and its murderous consequences. But, as Novak argues, it is hard to get away from, given the logic of either Christianity or Judaism, according to which each religion sees itself as the ultimate truth, and thus sees the other as a degradation, obfuscation, or rejection of that truth. Both religions are supersessionist, simply because each is defined by a truth that sees itself as supreme, and thus exclusive. While Novak argues that there is a huge moral and ultimately appropriately theological difference between what he calls a "hard" supersessionism—which is bad—and a "soft" supersessionism—which is good—supersessionism itself, he says, is nonetheless inevitable if you are a genuine Christian or Jew. I agree with Novak. While I am less certain of his distinction between hard and soft supersessionism (which I won't try to explain in this abbreviated forum), I also agree with Novak's final suggestion in his article: he concludes that, in the end, it is *God* who is the great and original supersessionist, for it is God who will completely upend our human expectations (however theologically astute they may be) about who is "in" or "out," Jew or Christian, at the Great Assize of creation's transfiguration. God's truth will supersede our own limited articulations and orderings of the truth as we have apprehended it.

My reflections here are aimed at this particular possibility of "God the Supersessionist." They are based on a rather simple claim: viz, that history, and in particular our history of Jews and the Christian church, demonstrates this divine supersessionism in the form of prophetic warning and its fulfillment. The particular prophetic warning I have in mind, which follows a well-known form used by Paul (1 Cor 10:11) is both obvious and ignored, and is found in Rom 11:2–21: "Well: because of unbelief they were broken off, and thou standest by faith. Be not high-minded but fear: For if God spared not the natural branches, take heed lest he also spare thee not" (AT). The "natural branches" in this case are the Jews of Israel who did believe in Jesus as the Christ/Messiah; and the "you" here are the "wild olive branches" who are the gentile believers in Jesus, "grafted in" to Israel. To the gentile believers, Paul says, "take heed that God destroy you not because of your high-mindedness"—the word translated here as "high-mindedness" is used in 1 Tim 6:17 to describe the proud rich of the world; and related words are used by Jesus to describe self-justifiers whom God will literally bring "down" (Luke 16:15). The sense is clear enough.

The notion that prophetic warnings are issued and then only retrospectively seen to have been fulfilled is well founded in Scripture, and the books of Kings trade on this reality over and over. Take, for example, the astonishing account of King Josiah's cleansing of Israel's irreligion, where the warning of an anonymous "man of God" to Jeroboam centuries earlier (1 Kgs 13:1–10) is unveiled as now fulfilled in Josiah's shockingly violent reformation of the nation's religious life (2 Kgs 23:16–18): it was all happening "according to the word of the Lord which the man of God proclaimed" so long before. So too with others, like King Ahab and David himself. Retrospectively, then, I suggest that Rom 11:20–21 has now found its fulfillment: what we see today is "according to the word of the Lord that Paul proclaimed." That is my foundational assertion: the gentile church, because of her high-mindedness, has been "spared not" by God.

I am not going to argue for this retrospectively apprehended fulfillment. Rather, I want to reflect on what such a fulfillment might mean. It is up to all of us to discern the workings of God's will, and I make no claims to accuracy on this score. But I think that this retrospective judgment is at least plausible; and further, even if it is not, considering its plausibility at least shows us how fragile our pragmatic energies with respect to the church may actually be in the face of God's own determinative strength.

As to the plausibility of Rom 11:20–21's fulfillment, I will mention three things that are historically demonstrable. First, with respect to the church that we are talking about: when we say "church" we mean specifically the gentile church. This may have been less the case when Paul was speaking to the Romans, although this is debated. In any case, most historians are in agreement that by AD 100, more or less, the Christian church was almost wholly gentile in membership, as it has remained until quite recently.[2] The rise of Messianic Judaism, itself a complex phenomenon ethnically, has done little to change this fact at least with regard to what we call "the church." To be sure, Jews *did* enter this gentile church from time to time—including in my family—but in miniscule numbers, and through strange and often contorted mechanisms of social and psychological pressure. To say "Christian church" in history—Western, Eastern, global—is to say "gentile." I take this as axiomatic. I do not mean to dismiss a profoundly divine significance and vocation granted to Jews who *did* so enter the gentile church, but that is another topic.

Second, the "high-mindedness" of the gentile church, not only but in particular towards the Jews, is horribly undeniable, and I will not linger on this fact. No historico-logical gymnastics can obscure the depths and lengths to which ecclesial high-mindedness—pride, disdain, ambition,

---

2. Sim, "How Many Jews Became Christians."

greed, envy, cruelty, and violence—drove gentile Christians in their relations to Jews. I take this as a given.

Finally, has God in fact "not spared" this high-minded gentile church? Look only at Europe, increasingly North America, and the moral shape of the gentile church elsewhere: the so-called "triumph of the church" at the least requires rather subtle arguments to establish in our day, unless one's main criterion is money. We will each have to judge for ourselves on this matter; though God will provide the final sentence.

So let us assume (though this may be wrong) that Paul's warning has been fulfilled at least in some major respects: the gentile church, perverted by "high-mindedness," in particular towards the Jews, has not been spared by God, but instead "broken off" in their turn. What might be the implications? I will group these implications into three categories. First, there are the secondary implications, as they touch upon the Christian evangelization of Jews. Second, there are more immediate implications as they touch upon the character of the gentile church. Finally, there are the deep implications that touch upon the very revelation of Christ—his form, character, and cosmic significance. Let me examine each in turn.

EVANGELIZATION

If the gentile church has not been "spared" by God; and if this means, in Paul's language, somehow being "cut off" from the root of Israel in a fashion that is both real if often opaque, at the least we must say that what witness the church gives to Jews will be of a "negative" nature. The posture of a negative witness is well and repeatedly described in Scripture with respect to Israel herself in her visible condition before the nations. A classic, though hardly unique, expression of this is Ezek 5:14–15:

> Moreover I will make thee [Israel] waste, and a reproach among the nations that [are] round about thee, in the sight of all that pass by. So shall be a reproach and a taunt, an instruction and an astonishment unto the nations that [are] round about thee, when I shall execute judgments in thee in anger and in fury and in furious rebukes. I the LORD have spoken [it]. (AT)

The notion that the Jews as Israel were to remain in such a posture before the church—"astonishing" the church by her (Israel's) fall from grace—was (in)famously articulated by Augustine, and it became in fact one of the bases upon which Jews were, ironically, seen as demanding protection, though not blessing, by the Church of the West throughout the Middle Ages. As long as there were Jews—though Jews living within the limits of strict control and liabilities—the church would be properly reminded of her own call to faithfulness, of the dangers of unbelief, and of what God might do to those who rebelled against the Christ and the Christian truth.[3] So may it be, then, for the gentile church now, in a reversal that, after all, is quite evangelical in its dynamics, according to the One who has "brought down the mighty from their seats, and exalted them of low degree" (Luke 1:52).

But although we might rightly call the church's own fall from grace a divine "witness" it is not exactly what we have in mind when we use the term "evangelization." In light of the fulfillment of Paul's warning, therefore, perhaps we should say that only Jews can evangelize Jews. This is a possibility that has motivated Messianic Jewish proselytization, at least in theory (practice, however, being quite another thing). As a member of the gentile church, who has even recently been increasingly involved with other Jewish members of the gentile church, for me this possibility is challenging.[4] And note well: the challenge is not just strategic, pursued according to missiological claims about "who is the best evangelizer of a given people." The challenge is utterly moral and further, one that touches the very purposes of God's judgment and providence: the only way gentiles can witness to Jews, in this light, is through their own specifically gentile ecclesial failures.

Indeed, one might wonder about the status of "gentilized Jews," like my father, and like many other quite prominent Christian Jews: with whom ought they to tie their wagon, and more than that, to suffer God's judgments, as it were? The Jewish theologian Michael Wyschogrod (and to a lesser extent, the Messianic Jewish theologian Mark Kinzer) have suggested that Jewish believers in Yeshua as Messiah are in fact called to keep the Mosaic law in many, if not most, respects, if they are indeed to claim their blessing of affiliation, even now, to the "root" of Israel (in Paul's terms).[5]

These are deep matters of formal and existential ordering, for individuals and groups. I hope we can see that how we discern the ways of God and his warnings will determine the very course of our lives and ministries. Many practical matters tied up with the ministerial relations of Christians and Jews get complicated if Rom 11:20–21 is viewed as somehow "fulfilled."

---

3. A subtle—perhaps overly subtle—discussion here is Fredriksen, *Augustine and the Jews*; other perspectives on the historical trajectory of Augustine's views can be found in Cohen, *From Witness to Witchcraft*.

4. I am an Anglican priest who has worked around the Anglican Communion (e.g., Africa, Asia) among the "gentile" members of the communion's churches. But, spurred in part by one side of my family's Jewish identity, I have become interested in Jewish-Christian relations, as well as in Jewish Christianity (see yachad-beyeshua.org).

5. Wyschogrod, "Letter to a Friend"; Kinzer, *Post-Missionary Messianic Judaism*.

THE CHARACTER OF THE GENTILE CHURCH

Yet, for all that, these are but secondary implications of the fulfillment of Rom 11:20–21. Let us move on to some larger corporate consequences, and ask about the character of the gentile church herself, if Paul's words turn out to be prophetic in their demand.

I have already mentioned how scripturally concrete are Paul's words here: God will be "unsparing" towards the gentile church, they will be "broken off" just as were the many branches of unbelieving Israel. The seriousness invoked here touches upon the core of our beings as gentile Christians and gentile churches: we are "perishing," to use the frequently translated English word for the Hebrew *abad* and Greek *apollumi* (Num 17:12; Deut 30:18; Matt 8:25; John 3:15). In the gospels, it is also translated as "lostness"—as the father exclaims who embraces his "prodigal" son: "He was lost, and is found" (Luke 15:24 AV). Obviously, to be lost does not mean "never to be found," and it is for the perishing and lost that the Lord God of the universe humbled himself that he might take them up (Matt 18:11). But it is the condition of perishing and lostness, nonetheless, to which Paul would point in his warning.

Hence, the specifically gentile church, if Paul is right, has been set in a place where its own character as a subsisting and enduring body can only be characterized by seeking, penitence, and crying out to God. I suppose that this too is a form of witness, just as the Publican in some strange way speaks to the Pharisee before God (Luke 18). It must said, however, that a posture of beseeching penitence is almost by definition invisible to others, and has no value in its visibility (Matt 6): pray in your closet, not before others on this matter (6:6). In any case, *survivability* is to be given in penitence, nothing less—without penitence, we die—and the One who comes to the perishing renders such cries into years.

I might add as well that just such penitence, that might characterize the church, ought also to reshape the framework of Christian theology itself, which has always been, by definition, gentile theology. After all, can the blind lead the blind (Luke 6:39)? Can lost gentiles lead gentiles, let alone Jews? On what basis can a theology shaped by a church cascading into the waves of unsparing lostness provide guidance for a future of penance? In my own experience, I have found less and less to hang on to in the great canon of classical gentile theology, and more and more to hold on to within the corners and crevices of otherwise ignored believers, gentile to be sure, but even more among Jewish writers. It is a pointer I first heard from my mentor George Lindbeck, who (without explaining with much detail) was among the first quite Christian theologians to urge a reappraisal of the value of specifically *rabbinic* Jewish theology for the church;[6] and this in the face not only of centuries of disdain for rabbinic theology, but even contemporary ecumenical judgments (including Novak's) that rabbinic theology, coming after the so-called "parting of the ways" between Judaism and the gentile church, is a kind of intra-Jewish affair that should be of no interest and pertinence to Christians. Yet, perhaps rabbinic theology is now more pertinent to the gentile church than ever before.

I certainly would not say that classical gentile theology is useless—whether from masters like Augustine or Aquinas, Luther or Calvin, let alone contemporary gentiles from Karl Barth to James Cone and Sarah Coakley. But I would suggest that Rom 11:20–21 demands a novel and acutely aimed critical spirit directed at these sources. It is not the case that one can simply purge the anti-Semitism or anti-Judaism of the past from an otherwise pure material; after all, a "little leaven leavens the whole lump" (Gal 5:9), to borrow another Pauline warning with something else in mind, and we have been eating from a progressively rotting bread for a long time.

In any case, if Paul's words are now finding their fulfillment, then humility must shape the core identity of the gentile church. Of course, this was always the church's calling, as something like Phil 2 makes so pressingly clear. Just this fact has deep providential and christological implications, as I shall note in a moment: God fulfills his plan "one way or the other," for the plan—that the humble, and only the humble, shall be exalted—must order all things and all peoples, Jew and gentile together; and the divine plan is itself the figure of salvation. Still, the call into this plan is one aimed at willingness, and the gentile church is perhaps today being called to a *willing* humiliation, now that its unwillingness has been so starkly exposed. Dare I say that COVID-19 was part of this exposure (along with any number of other burdens, including division, sexual abuse, complicity in war, and so on)? But what deep challenges then have come upon us from the Lord, who has graciously, but now firmly, made clear that the church's press for regaining cultural power, for instance—political or otherwise—is profoundly mistaken! Unravel this press, and so much of what have been doing, and what we continue to do as Christians, in our congregations, our denominations, our organizations, and our schools, must dissolve in some other pool

---

6. "One final example of what Christians can gain from understanding the church as Israel in nonsupersessionist terms is that it frees them to hear God speak not only through Old Testament Israelites, but also through postbiblical Jews; this freedom follows from the belief that the covenant with Israel has not been revoked. The Jews remain God's chosen people and are thus a primary source for Christian understandings of God's intentions" (Lindbeck, "What of the Future," 386–87).

of tears. This too comes as both warning and calling, in regard to current conflicts in our midst, as ecclesial and civil societies both.

How one discerns Paul's words has enormous consequences. Only recently have theologians begun to unravel some of these fateful and even dreadful possibilities.[7]

THE REVELATION OF CHRIST

Let me now turn to the deepest implication of these words of Rom 11:20–21, as I have suggested their fulfillment. This implication touches upon the very revelation of the Christ's own character: the deepest, hardest, least "practical" implications, but most important for reconsidering Jewish-gentile (Christian) relations. Furthermore, it is precisely because this deep implication is not unique to this text, but reflects many other texts in Scripture, that the earlier implications I have sketched seem to be to have a presumptive plausibility.

I begin with premise: It seems to me that Scripture teaches us that the Jewish-gentile nexus is fundamental to human creaturely life: there are only two "kinds" of human beings, as Moses says:

> Remember the days of old, consider the years of many generations: ask thy father, and he will shew thee; thy elders, and they will tell thee. When the most High divided to the nations their inheritance, when he separated the sons of Adam, he set the bounds of the people according to the number of the children of Israel. (Deut 32:7–8 AV)

The rendering of this last verse in the Septuagint is more metaphysically allusive: the sons of Adam are separated according to the number of the "angels of God," the Greek says, as if the peoples are given over to angels. In any case, there are, on the one hand, the Nations, divided up according to a given divine calculus. Now Moses goes on, in Deut 32:9, and says: But, on the other hand, "the Lord's portion [is] his people; Jacob [is] the lot of his inheritance." Thus, there is Israel, and there are the Nations—that is all. And however various and culturally distinct in permanent ways these last may be, as both Gen 11 and Rev 7 make it clear, the deepest distinction, bound to God's own personal claim, is between Jew and gentile (that is, a member of the nations).

---

7. See the recent work of the Catholic theologian Paul J. Griffiths, *Israel: A Christian Grammar*.

It is true that, as Paul says in Acts 17, God "hath made of one blood all nations of men for to dwell on all the face of the earth, and hath determined the times before appointed, and the bounds of their habitation" (v. 26). Yet these two human kinds of Jew and gentile, even though of "one blood," exist in a mysterious relationship of *struggle*, that is figured from the beginning (as both Jewish and Christian commentators recognized, if attributing reversed referents to each) in the narratives of Cain and Abel, and then Jacob and Esau, and in their historical out-workings. The distinction becomes a dichotomy, and the dichotomy becomes a chasm. It is a chasm that only God himself, in the "unsearchable" mystery of his purposes as Paul writes at the end of Rom 11 (32–36), can bridge. Thus, in the incomprehensible act of his incarnation and coming as Messiah, Jesus the Christ is given over to Jew and gentile both, and becomes their "peace." Their peace, "our peace" (Eph 2:14). In him alone can they embrace.

Yet this peace is incomprehensible. It is beyond understanding (Phil 4:7), because, as Paul notes, it is given on a cross (Eph 2:16), by the shedding of the Messiah's, God's incarnate self "in the flesh," (v. 15) "blood" (v. 13): "For he is our peace, who hath made both one, and hath broken down the middle wall of partition [between us]; having abolished in his flesh the enmity . . . for to make in himself of twain one new man, [so] making peace; And that he might reconcile both unto God in one body by the cross, having slain the enmity thereby" (AT).

Our theological focus over the centuries on the *mechanism* of Christ's atonement and reconciliation—here, indeed, is a gentile distortion, brought by narrowness of vision—has turned into a platitude; and the platitude has obscured the reality here of the bloodied rejectedness that is at the center of God's act: the Messiah/Son of God/God himself is to be "rejected." That is who the saving God *is*. Obviously, this is a gospel claim, and one tied, as we know to Isaiah's divine words (Isa 53:3). The problem is that the gentile church saw this as a past event whose mechanized accomplishments— "overcoming" division and "the law"—constituted a present resolution. Perhaps that seemed plausible at the time, and it is certainly possible to read Hebrews and parts of Paul in just this way, such that a central supersessionist vision did not seem to demand intrinsically Christian "high-mindedness." But that is not what this "history" (or prophecy) of Rom 11 implies. Rather, what is implied is that "peace on the *cross*," the peace of blood, the peace of rejectedness, is the very nature of the Christ; and that God is thus a rejected God at the heart of his being, at least vis à vis human creation: for "there is none righteous, no not one" (Rom 3:10 AV), and "all have sinned and come short of the glory of God" (Rom 3:23 AV) and God has "concluded them all in unbelief" (even now and into the future [Rom 11:32 AV]). God, for human beings, comes to us first as rejected. Reconciliation, in the great divide of Israel and the nations, of people with people—reconciliation with God and with one another—comes through adherence to and being grasped by this God-who-is-being-rejected, even by me, by Jew and by every gentile people of the world. This marks a key aspect of God's comprehensive grasp of human beings.

I do not claim to understand this mystery. It is one that the early church fathers continually attempted to articulate, Irenaeus, and of course Athanasius, and then Leo the Great most insistently, pressed this central aspect of the gospel that we might simply call "divine reversal" or "interchange": the rich become poor, so that the poor might become rich (2 Cor 8:9); the divinity became creature that creature might become divine (2 Pet 1:4; 1 John 3:1–3); righteousness becomes sin, so that sinner might become righteous—perhaps the most astonishing way of putting it (by Paul, no less [Rom 5:19; 2 Cor 5:21]), the first shall be last, (so that) the last shall be first—perhaps, in practice, and even more astonishing claim, because it comes from the lips of Jesus himself (Matt 20:16; Phil 2:6–8), who, though himself "the first and the last" (Rev 2:8), chooses to be *only* the last (Mark 10:42–45). To be caught up by God as Jew and gentile is to be ever caught up in this reversal, whose historical forms, of course, will shift over time—as the powerful become weak, and the weak powerful. If Christian supersessionism is built into the Christian gospel—as David Novak rightly, in my mind, believes—it is into *this* reality right here: a divine reversal that is utterly complete.

Of course, the Rejected God is the Redeeming God, as Barth emphatically elaborated. But this is so not in some serial or chronologically-effected sequence, where one simply moves from rejectedness to redemption, as from a stepping stone to a summit. Somehow, stone and crest are one. Furthermore, such a divine reality provides, as I have insisted, a paradoxical consequence evangelically: this means that the gentile Christian is never in a position to determine the place and trajectory of God's grasp of the Jew; and we should say, with Novak, vice versa: I can never assert categorically in this conversation between Jews and gentiles that "you do not know God," or "the God you know is a mistaken God." Rather, the God you know will change our places, will bring good from evil, will make the lowly sit in the place of princes. We, Jew and gentile both, have yet even to begin to plumb the depths of this truth, which must ever bring us to tears of fear, as Paul says in Rom 11:20; but also of awe and joy. "O the depth of the riches both of the wisdom and knowledge of God! How unsearchable [are] his judgments, and his ways past finding out!" (Rom 11:33 AV).

In conclusion, let me return to the more abstract description I gave at the very beginning of what I have tried to do, that is, understand what

Scripture says about *history*. The question of "history's pressure"[8] on scriptural sense-making (or sense-providing) is important to me. Since I think that what we call temporal history is actually *internal* to the scriptural reality (understood somehow metaphysically), it is not really a matter of external human experience somehow shaping scriptural meaning—it is not the case that things that happen *change* the meaning of Scripture—so much as it is the case of our experience, over time, coming into view as something bound to Scripture.

To take a major example in the context of Jewish-Christian relations and self-identities, the Holocaust: Does the Holocaust having happened historically somehow alter how we should read the scriptural claims about Israel and the church, or about Jews and gentiles? In a way, it does: the (gentile) church is shown, through this unspeakably tragic historical event and many events leading to it, to be horrendously unfaithful in her relation to "Israel." This judgment is generally accepted in our day. But what does one make of this? For many—not just Jews, of course, but Christians especially—the Holocaust as historical reality has somehow delegitimated Christian evangelism vis à vis Jews altogether. This reasoning could be applied to others as well (e.g., colonized indigenous peoples: the sins of the colonial missionizers of the past subverts Christian mission to these people today). And if that is the case, then many things that are said in Scripture about the church's mission and vocation are also somehow rendered inapplicable or (as many would claim) even false. I can perhaps be read as implying this.

But if so, this is an erroneous conclusion, and stems from a misapprehension of what "historical experience" is. In the example above, I would say that the Holocaust is itself scripturally located, given, and explained. It is "already there" in Scripture, lurking about and waiting to be noticed and taken seriously. How this may be so is not obvious, and requires trembling scrutiny. But, for instance, Rom 11 (not to mention Rom 2–3, and the vast scriptural network within which these texts emerge) has much to say about this particular and horrendous set of events, both in terms of the actual and the conditional: "all have fallen short," and "take heed lest he spare not ye" and "fear." Historical experience, in this case, drives us to the creative texts that are at work in the shape of our lives; but that is because our lives are already given within these texts, as it were. Given what Scripture says about who we are, we should not be *surprised*—only rendered profoundly sorrowful—by what awful things we have done, even we, the followers of Jesus.

To be sure, I may be mistaken in my reading of the "fulfillment" of Rom 11:20–21. But I know that I am *not* wrong in believing that this text—among

---

8. Rowe, "Biblical Pressure and Trinitarian Hermeneutics."

others—is one that we cannot skim over or brush aside. One of the permanent features of created existence, including our "histories," in relation to Scripture, is that we are ever pressed back to the text, particular texts, hard texts, by the hardest aspect of our historical existence, in order to discover *within* the text who we are, just where our histories are most burdensome. This is true for any text of Scripture. It is true for Rom 11:20–21. All I am pleading for is that we do not shrink back from such a self-discovery, no matter what it amounts to. For it is in just such shrinking back, as Hebrews says (10:39), that we are "destroyed"; and it is in going forward, with the One whose very life is found within the Scriptures, that we too find our lives.

BIBLIOGRAPHY

Cohen, Jeremy, ed. *From Witness to Witchcraft: Jews and Judaism in Medieval Christian Thought*. Wolfenbuttler Mittelalter-Studien 11. Wiesbaden: Harrassowitz, 1996.

Fredriksen, Paula. *Augustine and the Jews: A Christian Defense of Jews and Judaism*. New York: Doubleday, 2008.

Griffiths, Paul J. *Israel: A Christian Grammar*. Minneapolis: Fortress, 2023.

Kinzer, Mark S. *Post-Missionary Messianic Judaism: Redefining Christian Engagement with the Jewish People*. Grand Rapids: Brazos, 2005.

Lindbeck, George. "What of the Future? A Christian Response." In *Christianity in Jewish Terms*, edited by Tikva Frymer-Kensky et al., 378–87. Radical Traditions. Boulder, CO: Westview, 2000.

Novak, David. "Supersessionism Hard and Soft." *First Things*, Feb. 1, 2019. https://www.firstthings.com/article/2019/02/supersessionism-hard-and-soft.

Rowe, C. Kavin. "Biblical Pressure and Trinitarian Hermeneutics" *Pro Ecclesia* 11 (2002) 295–312.

Sim, David C. "How Many Jews Became Christians in the First Century? The failure of the Christian Mission to the Jews. *HvTSt* 61 (2005) 417–40.

Wyschogrod, Michael. "Letter to a Friend." *Modern Theology* 11 (1995) 165–71.

Chapter 2

What Else Can We Learn from Each Other?

Jonathan Milevsky

INTRODUCTION

IN AN ARTICLE IN *First Things*, theologian David Novak writes that Jewish dialogue with Christians runs along parallel rather than perpendicular lines. As he puts it, the content of the discussion is merely an affirmation of "our common beginnings."[1] In his *Jewish-Christian Dialogue*, as well as his *Talking with Christians*, it is clear that the dialogue he proposes is based on natural law, to the extent that moral norms—which Novak associates with the Noahide code, the rabbinic universal legal framework which prohibits idolatry, adultery, theft, and the like—can be located within both traditions. Elsewhere, Novak defines this common ground as a border concept, in the Kantian sense of *Grentzbegriff*, inasmuch as moral imperatives form a perimeter shared by both faiths. If this ethical common ground shared between Jews and Christians is not simply an expression of a Rawlsian overlapping consensus but a common vision of human nature, however, which he indeed goes on to suggest,[2] it would seem to be more than a mere border

---

1. Novak, "Jews, Christians, and Civil Society," 32.
2. Novak, "Is Natural Law a Border Concept," 249.

concept, particularly because the natural law is later grounded by Novak in the *imago Dei*, which has profound legal and theological implications for both faiths. Further, in the same article in *First Things*, Novak writes in more detail about the commonalities between Jews and Christians:

> So our greatest commonality, our most lasting intersection in this world, takes place when we understand each other to be waiting for the Kingdom of God—the coming world—and refuse to settle for anything in this world as a substitute.[3]

Based on this description of the commonality between Jews and Christians, it stands to reason that the discussion takes place beyond the aforementioned border. Indeed, Novak states that the conversation can be about faith.[4] In this paper, I explore the content of such a Jewish-Christian discussion of faith, and I introduce two problems this creates for Novak's thought. The problems include the fact that it is incompatible with Novak's later, as opposed to earlier, accounts of natural law theory, and that the discussion he proposes ultimately has no content. In the final part of this chapter, I attempt to identify the parameters of such a discussion. Specifically, by reference to the talmudic concept of *qitrug*, I suggest an alternative approach which may help us identify the content of potential Jewish-Christian dialogue but also helps us resolve some of the difficulties we face with Novak's approach.

I note at the outset that I am not discussing pluralism. In his article for *Menorah Review*, Novak states that there are multiple aspects of truth in God's creation,[5] and in his *Jewish-Christian Dialogue*, Novak builds on Aristotle's concept of potentiality to argue that Judaism and Christianity can both be privy to revelation.[6] We will not be pursuing this line of thought, for the obvious reason that neither side of the dialogue can speak with any tradition or authority about the other truth, but also because neither partner in that dialogue would be sharing anything in common. Indeed, Novak himself writes that religion is not subjective, and that we present our faith as the fullest truth of God's relationship with the world.[7] If that is true, then we speak of objective facts when we discuss faith, which would not be the case if we refer to truth that neither dialogue partner can access. Along these lines, I will not touch on Yiftach Fehige's work about the use of God's voice,

---

3. Novak, "Jews, Christians, and Civil Society," 33.
4. Novak, *Talking with Christians*, 44–45.
5. Novak, "Jewish View of Christianity."
6. Novak, *Jewish-Christian Dialogue*, 133–35.
7. Novak, *Talking with Christians*, 162.

as a way of representing a plurality of faith communities,[8] since Fehige's approach runs into similar difficulty.

We begin with Novak's *The Image of the Non-Jew in Judaism*, where Novak writes as follows about the implications of non-Jews conforming to moral norms:

> Clearly the Noahide laws were persistently invoked as a criterion in the Jewish judgment of the moral status of any gentile society. The fact that some societies passed this test and others failed indicates that Noahide law was considered to be still binding and that gentiles were morally capable of living up to it.[9]

That is to say the Noahide code allowed the rabbis to bestow legal status upon non-Jews in the Roman Empire. Although Novak does not yet develop his approach to Jewish-Christian dialogue at that point, it stands to reason that any discussion with non-Jews involving natural law as it is presented there would only take place along legal, comparative lines. Given that non-Jews are only held to these standards because they are reasonable and thus attainable through ratiocination, it is not surprising that Novak adds that the recognition of non-Jews depends on whether rationality is an important factor in Judaism.[10] The implication therefore is that a dialogue with Christians based solely on that criteria would be limited to discovering the shared rational grounds for moral law.

This approach offers some advantages. One of them is that such discussion would avoid the triumphalism of the past, in the sense that both traditions come as partners but also that it would avoid parallelism.[11] On the latter Novak writes,

> In fact, my reservations about current parallelism are over its insufficient research in the sources of one's particular tradition. As such, most parallelism is not particular enough. And, on the other hand, it is too particular in its fixation on the comparative dimension of ethics and not sufficiently cosmic in its thrust so as to be able to deal with the ontological questions our theological and philosophical forebearers loved to tackle and were properly prepared to tackle.[12]

---

8. Fehige, *Offenbarungsparadox*, 22–38.
9. Novak, *Image of the Non-Jew*, 145.
10. Novak, *Image of the Non-Jew*, 147.
11. Novak, "Is Natural Law a Border Concept," 240.
12. Novak, "Is Natural Law a Border Concept," 241.

But is the conversation between Jews and Christians limited to natural law and does it therefore fall into parallelism? Novak seems to suggest otherwise. In *Talking with Christians*, in fact, he states that Jews have learned from Christian piety and that Jews and Christians can learn from each other's beliefs and practices.[13] Elsewhere, Novak even describes this task as a commandment. From Mal 3:16, Novak tells us to unite with other faiths:

> In this vein have those who revere God been talking to one another. God has heard and noted it, and a scroll of remembrance has been written at God's behest concerning those who revere God and esteem the holy name.[14]

Before attempting to sketch out the content of such a discussion, it is important to identify the role that the *imago Dei* would have in this dialogue. To do so, we first need to formulate a viable conception of the term in Novak's thought. While he acknowledges that there are several explanations for the *imago Dei*, he writes in *Talking with Christians* that the one he finds "most attractive here and now" is "the one that sees the image of God (the *tzelem elohim* or *imago Dei*) as human existence being the object of unique divine interest, so much so that God regarded human beings as worthy enough for God to directly speak to them—to us. And that speech is what my late, revered teacher, Abraham Joshua Heschel, called God's anthropology, not man's theology."[15] Read alongside with Novak's inspiration for this idea, namely Heschel's thesis that it is God's concern for humans that allows humans to seek God),[16] we can conclude that moral law, which again is grounded for Novak in the *imago Dei*, cannot be separated from the human search for God. That is to say, separated from the performance of the commandments, the *imago Dei* in Novak's conception is the type that gives humans the capacity to search for God.

In support of the claim that this idea is crucial to Novak's natural law theory, we need to look no further than its three main components. As I demonstrate in an article entitled "Reason with Baggage," for Novak, natural law combines three elements, namely, commandedness, createdness, and response.[17] That is to say the fact that humans are created by God constitutes a state of commandedness, which in turn requires a human response, and that manifests through our minimal and maximal obligations towards other

---

13. Novak, *Talking with Christians*, 44–45.
14. Novak, *Jewish-Christian Dialogue*, 155.
15. Novak, *Talking with Christians*, 201; Heschel, *God in Search of Man*, 412.
16. Heschel, *God in Search of Man*, 413.
17. Milevsky, "Reason with Baggage."

human beings. Seen in this way, the discovery of our human "finitude," to use Martin Kavka and Randi Rashkover formulation,[18] which corresponds to the creativeness-commandedness aspects of Novak's theory, requires a response which we can formulate with others who are similarly obligated to respond.

Further support for the fact that the response is shared comes from the phenomenological turn Novak takes in his writings. First, a little background: Novak originally assumes that the Thomistic view of human flourishing is self-evident. In *Law and Theology in Judaism*, he writes that "recognizing the essentially rational nature of the prohibition of bloodshed is the moral meaning of the general truth that human life is structured towards its own self preservation and enhancement."[19] He later comes to realize that that is not the case. Based on the fact that the world was facing nuclear war in the 1980s, Novak states in his *Halakhah in a Theological Dimension*, that "the absolute sanctity of human life is by no means self-evident."[20] This development marks a change in Novak's thought and drives him to describe only the benefits of moral norms (or what is *ratio ad quod nos*) as commonly recognized. As for the wisdom that underpins the norms, he begins to describe that phenomenologically:

> Indeed, human sociality presupposes a physical order surrounding it, upon which it can depend for its own continuity. But humans discover their own essential order, their own essential law, from their own social experience. Only thereafter do they discover the order of the nonhuman realm by analogy.[21]

As I explain elsewhere, the reason that Novak takes this phenomenological turn is because human beings can no longer be assumed to have access to this deeper ground. Thus, the only way they can access this realm, according to Novak, is through the experience of living within a society. More to the point, it is by being confronted with other human beings, that we discover what Novak calls their own "essential law." Given that the discovery is gained independently of a covenantal community, it is also the case that this confrontation is a common experience of all human beings. It also follows that this experience is something that human beings can put into context together, using common terms.

---

18. Rashkover, "Introduction," xv.
19. Novak, *Law and Theology in Judaism*, 115.
20. Novak, *Halakhah in a Theological Dimension*, 113.
21. Novak, *Natural Law in Judaism*, 38.

As a result, a discussion based on natural law, seeing as it is grounded on the notion of human beings in the image of God, is by definition one that is shared. What then would be the topic of conversation? To answer this question, it is necessary to note that Novak's reference to the "primacy of God's commandments for human action" is synonymous with his treatment of the *ta'amei hamitzvot*. By the former Novak means the reasons why we act morally, while by the latter he means the rational basis for the reasons for the commandments, where he begins to locate natural law in his article "Natural Law, Halakhah, and the Covenant." Since these two concepts can be identified with one another, we can gain more insight into the content of the dialogue by delving into his treatment of *taamei ha-mitzvot* in his *Natural Law in Judaism*.

There, Novak writes that whether one performs commandments because of their purpose or because God commanded it, such performance requires knowledge of who God is, which in turn informs us why he is to be obeyed.[22] It follows that if we are to focus on God's commandment as the driving force for human moral conduct in our dialogue, it is also the case that Jews and Christians will require a common conception of God for that discussion to begin. We thus arrive at two problems for Novak's thought. The first is the lack of content. The second is the incompatibility with his developed natural law theory. We will take these problems up now.

A LACK OF CONTENT

In Novak's 1989 work, *Jewish-Christian Dialogue*, he writes that any Jewish constitution of non-Jews must be based on Noahide law. As he puts it,

> The dialogue, then, is to be constituted on the common anthropological border between Judaism and Christianity. It is to be ever cognizant of what is common and what is uncommon.[23]

According to Novak, the dialogue must be grounded in theonomous ethics, which "emphasizes the primacy of God's commandments for human action." Given that "both Judaism and Christianity affirm creation as the necessary background for their respective revelations," they can discuss God's commandments by reference to this commonality.[24] By affirming God's creation as a necessary background, Novak means here that the basis for moral conduct is received through a covenantal community's tradition. This

---

22. Novak, *Natural Law in Judaism*, 65–66.
23. Novak, *Jewish-Christian Dialogue*, 141.
24. Novak, *Jewish-Christian Dialogue*, 142.

concept is what he elsewhere calls "wisdom," which means the metaphysical truths that underpin moral norms. But even within these communities, such knowledge is not readily available. As he writes earlier,

> The developing insight of the seriously committed and intelligent student of nature and the Torah will enable one, however, to see more and more of the Divine wisdom in the law, as one comes to recognize the aptness of that law to human nature.[25]

Perhaps because of this reason, the discussion itself is inherently limited to the norms themselves. Novak makes this point explicit in his *Jewish-Christian Dialogue*:

> Both Jews and Christians must obey the commandments as God has revealed them to their respective communities. Only fidelity to the commandments enables Jews and Christians to engage in the dialogue with their respective identities intact. They will not then expect from it either too little or too much.[26]

In this sense, I agree with scholar Randi Rashkover's suggestion that dialogue for Novak does not go as far as it should, but not for the reason she offers. For Rashkover, dialogue ought to be based on the "logic of the law," by which she means the dialectical relationship between desire and law, meaning that dialogue should focus on that tension.[27] While this is a promising area of dialogue, it does not appear to be as fundamental to the discussion as a conception of God, without which, any discussion of moral human action loses its justification. Nevertheless, Novak's dialogue is prevented from broaching the subject.

Further, this type of discussion is at odds with the scriptural proof which Novak offers as the basis for the dialogue. Recall that Novak draws on Mal 3:16 as a source for a conversation with other lovers of God. The problem is that the conversation implies that something substantial is discussed. Indeed, the term employed by the verse is not the one used for shared adherence to commandments—the word should have the root *shmar* rather than *dbr*, which means speech. There must therefore be more to the conversation than prohibitions that hold for both communities of faith.

---

25. Novak, "Commandments," 4.
26. Novak, *Jewish-Christian Dialogue*, 92–93.
27. Rashkover, *Freedom and Law*, 170, 178–82, 220.

THE TRAJECTORY OF NOVAK'S THOUGHT

The second difficulty that emerges from Novak's suggested dialogue is that he originally locates natural law in Judaism only within the Noahide code, and not even all of it; he finds it specifically in the prohibition against murder.[28] This account differs substantially from his later, more developed account, which locates natural law in the rabbinic enactments and the reasons for the commandments as well. The essential difference between these accounts is that the earlier account is grounded in reason. Thus, the prohibition against murder is easily identified as the expression of natural law. Along the same lines, when Novak rules on matters concerning abortion, he does so by reference to reason, namely, on the basis that the prohibition of murder is self explanatory.

The change from grounding natural law in reason to basing it on the metaphysics of moral norms only happens after Novak first expands the concept of natural law to include Israel's acceptance of the Mosaic law at Mount Sinai, which includes even the so-called nonrational commandments. Novak's point in doing so is that, although the Israelites could have been aware of the benefits of the commandments at that point, they were willing to accept it on the basis of their existing relationship with God. In other words, they had trust that the commandments would be reasonable because of their source. With the definition thus broadened beyond merely self-explanatory, or what Novak frequently calls *ratio per se*, he is able to expand natural law to other areas within Judaism.[29]

Put differently, natural law ceases to mean rationally attainable laws and begins to refer to the suitability of moral law to human beings. Without such a broadened definition, the three areas in which Novak locates natural law are simply too diverse to fit a narrow definition. The Noahide code are commandments whose benefit can be widely understood, while rabbinic enactments are decrees that the rabbis find to be compelling. And although the reasons for the commandments do resemble the rational basis for the Noahide code, it is clear from all of his writings on the topic that Novak does not mean the reasonableness of the commandments when he speaks about *ta'amei hamitzvot*. What Novak means is the act of ascertaining the purpose of the commandments, that is to say the process of reasoning about the commandments themselves. Given this definition, it is simply not feasible to identify all these areas with natural law because they are reasonable in themselves. Conversely, natural law cannot be confined to legal matters

---

28. Novak, *Law and Theology in Judaism*, 115.
29. Milevsky, *Evolving Meaning of Reason*, 15–71.

either. The concepts that Novak associates with natural law are properly called anthropological. Thus, a broader definition becomes necessary.

It follows from this development that a dialogue with Christians based on natural law must take place on anthropological borders, but it is difficult to see how that can be possible given the limitations we have mentioned. It is as if Novak's dialogue has not caught up with his natural law theory.

Qitrug

In this final section of the paper, I will try to resolve the outstanding difficulties by proposing the content for Jewish-Christian dialogue. Part of the challenge will be that, assuming that faith itself is to be discussed, we ultimately run into differences in the conception of God, particularly with respect to Jewish theology and Christology. I propose that the rabbinic concept of *qitrug* represents a way forward. The idea means modes of conduct or even specific items that put Israel's behavior in a negative spotlight, either because the behavior or item in question is reminiscent of Israel's previous misdeed or because it contrasts with her ongoing conduct and makes Israel look bad by comparison. Crucially, this concept also includes behaviors with which the nations of the world are credited and simultaneously reflect negatively on Jews. An example would be the city of Nineveh, which repented after the warning of only one prophet, while Israel repeatedly ignored the warnings of many of God's messengers. Because of this discrepancy, the rabbis speak favorably of Nineveh in Gen. Rab. 15:4.

אָמַר רַבִּי יוֹסֵי בַּר חֲנִינָא כָּל הַמַּלְכֻיּוֹת נִקְרְאוּ עַל שֵׁם נִינְוֵה, עַל שֵׁם שֶׁהֵם מִתְנָאוֹת מִיִּשְׂרָאֵל

(*Amar Rabi Yosi bar Hanina kol ha-malkhuyot niqre'u al shem nineveh, al shem she-hem mit'na'ot me-yisrael*)

Rabbi Yosi son of Hanina said that all the kingdoms are called by Nineveh's name, because they were more beautiful than Israel.

The implication of this statement is that the behavior of Nineveh forms a stark contrast with that of Israel. And by extension, Israel is expected to live up to the standard set by its adversary. If God judges Israel when they do not live up to those standards, it stands to reason that we are allowed to investigate what those standards are.

Another example appears in Midrash Tehilim. In reference to David's plea that his enemies have come to "eat his flesh" in Ps 27:2, the midrash interprets this verse as referring to the nations of the world.

שֶׁהֵן בָּאִין לְקַטְרֵג אֶת יִשְׂרָאֵל וְאוֹמְרִים לִפְנֵי הַקָּדוֹשׁ בָּרוּךְ הוּא אֵלּוּ עוֹבְדֵי עֲבוֹדָה זָרָה וְאֵלּוּ עוֹבְדֵי עֲבוֹדָה זָרָה

(*Shehen ba'in le-qatreg et yisrael ve-omrim lifnei Ha-Qadosh ba-rukh hu elu ovdei avodah zara ve-elu ovdei avodah zara.*)

That they come and accuse Israel and they say before the Holy One Blessed be He, these are worshippers of idolatry and these are worshippers of idolatry.

In this teaching, the nations of the world themselves come with the claim that the Jews have been sinful and that the latter are no better than the pagans. Here as well, the concept is that the behavior of the nations of the world is a standard which can and should be applied to Israel. If their conduct is honorable, the conduct of Israel should be no different. And if their conduct is deplorable, it is up to Israel to do better.

Although I am unaware of any thinkers who have used this concept in a positive way, it can be argued that if a standard is implied negatively, it can be applied in a positive sense as well. Indeed, the Talmud states that the standard used for reward is exponentially more generous than that used for punishment.[30] By that logic, a standard that is used to criticize Israel must also be available for constructive purposes. In other words, instead of using a given standard as a measure of when Israel falls short, it is equally possible to use that standard to highlight areas in which Israel can improve. That is to say, what if *qitrug* is seen in a positive light?

If that would be the case, however, we would still need to determine what the content of the conversation would be. Since the content of both faiths—Christology on the one hand and the Torah in its entirety—are a chasm which cannot yet be overcome, what standards can then be discussed? I propose that faithfulness itself can be used to measure Israel's faith. Placed in the context of dialogue, the application of this concept would mean the conversation between Jews and Christians can include the conduct of Christian saints, since that behavior can serve as a standard by which to measure Israel's faith.

The benefits of extending this concept to Jewish-Christian dialogue is that it prevents the difficulties we have found in Novak's proposal. To wit, Jewish and Christians can speak about in detail about the intensity of their faith or devotion to God's teachings because neither are unique to either one: both communities are sustained by, and are devoted to, their faith. The conversation does not have to be limited to prohibitions and limitations but can have positive content, i.e., what both communities can and should

---

30. b. Sotah 11a.

actively pursue. And the dialogue does not in any way undermine the wisdom that either Jews or Christians receive from their communities.

Before I conclude, I would like to raise the possibility that *qitrug* can be a fruitful tool for Christians as well. Needless to say, I make this suggestion with the awareness that I am speaking from a Jewish perspective, but a corollary with the Christian gospels might represent a promising area of research. I refer specifically to Jesus's critique of the Pharisees in Matt 23. There, Jesus accuses the Pharisees of acting "to be seen of men," meaning their broad phylacteries and the borders of their garment—by which he means *tzitzit*, the traditional fringes—are not a mark of sincerity but simply a visible sign of their piety. While this is not an unproblematic passage from a Jewish perspective, it nevertheless assumes a common moral standard of measurement, not unlike a *qitrug*. Indeed, much like a *qitrug*, where the conduct of an external yet analogous exemplar is used to illustrate one's shortcoming, an internal shortcoming is illustrated by the gap between visible acts of piety and internal humility, and it represents the standard Jesus sets for his followers. Thus, *qitrug* represents a positive and meaningful standard that can serve as the content of the conversation between Jews and Christians.

CONCLUSION

In this chapter, I have shown that Novak's suggestion that Jews and Christians can engage in a discussion of faith is never fully developed in his thought. Further, such content is ultimately inconsistent not only with his emphasis on natural law as the grounds for discussion but also with his fully developed natural law theory, which puts the wisdom, or metaphysical explanation for moral norms, in a rarefied realm which cannot be shared outside of one's own covenantal community. As a direct result of these factors, the discussion that Novak advocates is ultimately restricted to moral law. In an attempt to avoid these issues, I have picked up where Novak leaves off, so to speak, and suggested that a fruitful and substantial discussion can be based on what the rabbis call *qitrug*, that is, a standard by which Israel falls short. Though this term appears exclusively in a negative sense, the positive counterpart would be to learn and be inspired in areas of faith. It is this type of content that represents a way forward in future dialogue between lovers of God—Jews and Christians.

BIBLIOGRAPHY

Fehige, Yiftach. *Das Offenbarungsparadox: Zur Dialogfähigkeit von Juden und Christen.* Paderborn: Schöningh, 2012.

Heschel, Abraham Joshua. *God in Search of Man: a Philosophy of Judaism.* New York: Farrar, Straus and Cudahy, 1955.

Milevsky, Jonathan L. "Reason with Baggage." *Journal of Religious Ethics* 47 (2019) 696–715.

———. *Understanding the Evolving Meaning of Reason in David Novak's Natural Law Theory.* Philosophy of Religion—World Religions 10. Leiden: Brill, 2022.

Novak, David. "The Commandments: Divine Will or Divine Wisdom." Supplement, *Hawaii Jewish News* (Nov. 4, 1987) 4.

———. *Halakhah in a Theological Dimension: Essays on the Interpenetration of Law & Theology in Judaism.* Brown Judaic Studies. Chico, CA: Scholars, 1985.

———. *The Image of the Non-Jew in Judaism.* 2nd ed. Littman Library of Jewish Civilization. Oxford: Littman Library of Jewish Civilization, 2011.

———. "Is Natural Law a Border Concept Between Judaism and Christianity?" *Journal of Religious Ethics* 32 (2004) 237–54.

———. *Jewish-Christian Dialogue: A Jewish Justification.* New York: Oxford University Press, 1989.

———. "A Jewish View of Christianity: Recognition Without Surrender." *Menorah Review* 32 (1994) 1–2.

———. "Jews, Christians, and Civil Society." *First Things* 120 (2002) 26–43.

———. *Law and Theology in Judaism.* New York: Ktav, 1974.

———. *Law and Theology in Judaism.* 2nd ser. New York: Ktav, 1976.

———. "Natural Law, Halakhah, and the Covenant." *Jewish Law Annual* 7 (1988) 43–67.

———. *Natural Law in Judaism.* Cambridge: Cambridge University Press, 1998.

———. *Talking with Christians: Musings of a Jewish Theologian.* Radical Traditions. Grand Rapids: Eerdmans, 2005.

Rashkover, Randi. *Freedom and Law: A Jewish-Christian Apologetics.* New York: Fordham University Press, 2011.

———. "Introduction." In *Tradition in the Public Square: A David Novak Reader*, by David Novak, edited by Randi L. Rashkover and Martin Kavka, xi–xxxiv. Radical Traditions. Grand Rapids: Eerdmans, 2008.

PART II

Intersections of Jewish and Christian Thought

Chapter 3

The Canon as Theological Problem
The Shema as Theological Vision

Ian Kissell

IT IS A CURIOSITY of history that, in a relatively brief period of five centuries, three text-centered religions emerged in the Near East. "Many religions have sacred books associated with their traditions or their worship," writes F. F. Bruce, "but Jews, Christians and Muslims have come to be known as 'people of the book' in a special sense.... Among 'people of the book' the 'book' has a regulative function: conformity to what the book prescribes is a major test of loyalty to their religious faith and practice."[1] Text-centered religions seem perfectly natural—even inevitable—in a world accustomed to literacy, but given the religious milieu of the ancient Near East, it is actually quite remarkable.

By the twelfth century, Europe had achieved widespread literacy, with texts occupying a remarkably central position. Brian Stock concludes from his study of the period that, in no small part because of the influence of Judaism and Christianity,[2] Europe had been transformed into "textual communities," which refers to a "community whose life, thought, sense of identity and relations with outsiders are organized around an authoritative text,"

---

1. Bruce, *Canon of Scripture*, 18–19.

2. An interesting testament to the emergence of literacy from the Jewish and Christian religions is Abelard, *Dialogue*, written in the early twelfth century. The three interlocuters note from the start that while all three follow "religions," the Philosopher "is satisfied with the natural law. But the other two have Scriptures" (19).

and where the authority of an interpreter is derived from their mastery of an authoritative text.[3] Noted Egyptologist Jan Assmann has sought to ground these "transformations" far earlier in "the rise of monotheism" which led to "the development of writing and literacy" which began with the advent of Hebrew monotheism.[4]

Since, as Assmann notes, "there is not a single monotheistic religion that is not based on a canon of holy writ,"[5] he concludes that monotheism requires canonization, which he defines as the codification of official cultural memory, or in other words, a singular, official interpretation of the past:

> Faith . . . is just another word for "memory," for it is all about not forgetting what was said to the ancestors and about trusting the authenticity of their experience and testimony. The absence of exterior evidence is compensated for by an interior or spiritual representation, that is, memory and its codification in Scripture. . . . The appeal to memory is so decisive that right from the start a religion based on revealed truth has had to have recourse to techniques of recording—that is, to writing—in order to fight the ever-present danger of forgetting. Moreover, it had had to invest writing with the highest authority and to develop a new form of tradition, namely, canonization.[6]

This treats "canon" and "authority" as roughly synonymous: religious authority is derived from religious texts and is predicated on skillful interpretation of those texts.[7] While this genealogy is certainly not without historical merit, it betrays fundamentally modern epistemological concerns about the grounds for authoritative interpretation, obscuring the far more radical claims of the Judeo-Christian tradition. In this essay, my goal is not to disregard these modern concerns, but to de-emphasize them so that a more fundamental one can emerge more clearly.

---

3. Heath, "Textual Communities," 5, referring to Stock, *Implications of Literacy*, 90–91.

4. Assmann, *Of God and Gods*, 90.

5. Assmann, *Of God and Gods*, 91.

6. Assmann, *Of God and Gods*, 91–92.

7. "Very often we use the term 'canon' broadly to refer to Scripture itself or to the function of Scripture as norm in the church, i.e., to the authority of Scripture" (Yoder, "Authority of the Canon," 265).

CANON IN MODERN THEOLOGY

Discussions of canon in the nineteenth and twentieth centuries have focused on historical concerns of authorship and composition, essentially seeking to determine on what basis the texts were considered to be authoritative by their original textual communities.[8] The work of Gerhard von Rad and Brevard Childs on the Hebrew Scriptures disrupted this consensus by calling biblical scholars in the dominant historical-critical tradition to move beyond questions of source and reception, and instead pursue a holistic approach which evaluates the canon qua canon as a literary whole. Rolf Rendtorff summarizes the approach as:

> assum[ing] the canonical basis of the Hebrew Bible but also making the texts themselves, in their present "canonical" shape, the point of departure for the account. This interpretation of the text occurs within a context of historical-critical biblical research. It goes a step beyond methodological approaches in widespread current use by . . . focusing its primary attention on this final form.[9] . . .
>
> The predominant interest in the final shape of the texts is grounded largely in the fact that the texts in this form became the foundations of faith.[10]

This so-called "canonical approach" has lacked enthusiasm among proponents both of traditional historical-critical biblical studies, who dismiss it as a return to precritical naïveté, and evangelical scholars, who condemn it as ahistorical and not providing a sufficient grounds for the authority of the text.

JOHN PIPER'S CRITIQUE OF CANONICAL INTERPRETATION

A helpful illustration of the latter is provided by a 1976 article in the *Journal of the Evangelical Theological Society* by evangelical pastor and theologian John Piper, not because the article received a great deal of engagement, but

---

8. For a taxonomy of views of canon in the modern period, see Yoder, "Authority of the Canon"; for a theological appraisal, Wilson, "Canon and Theology." The magisterial work from Protestant New Testament scholarship is Bruce, *Canon of Scripture*, as well as a more recent contribution by Kruger, *Canon Revisited*.

9. Rendtorff, *Canonical Hebrew Bible*, 1.

10. Rendtorff, *Canonical Hebrew Bible*, 2.

because it clearly displays the points of disagreement. Piper immediately frames the question of canon as one of authority for a textual community. He asks the question "On what *basis* do we claim that the Christian canon is authoritative?"[11] and charges that "the burden of [canon critics] is to set forth and defend the Christian canon as the authority on which a new and fruitful Biblical theology can be based."[12] Notably, Piper's critique is that the canonical approach is unable to defend biblical authority because of a flawed view of inspiration:

> [The "canonical" position] is a significant shift away from the historical particularity of divine revelation. The alternative position is that inspiration is a past, once-for-all event that resulted in concrete historical meanings in written documents that have been faithfully preserved in the Christian canon. All our theological thinking should be oriented to and judged by those meanings as they are contained in the text of Scripture.... The clear implication [of the canonical approach] is that the canonical shape of the Christian Scriptures has a "trans-historical capacity" to confront every generation with the Word of God *apart from* the rigorous historical research of Biblical scholars. While this will have wide appeal to laymen, it is surely not true.[13]

Piper's position grants religious authority to professional interpreters who derive their authority from the canon by means of faithfully translating the voice of the Lord in the past into the present.

Canon as a Priori

The claim of the canon critics is that the authority of the canon is a faith claim of the community. In other words, canon is a theological a priori which is confessed but not confirmed by the community, since the authority of the documents is not objectively demonstrable.[14] Piper objects that the authority of the canon cannot rest on the decision of the community, otherwise it would be self-affirming, and must instead rest on authorship and content.

---

11. Piper, "Authority and Meaning," 88; emphasis in original.
12. Piper, "Authority and Meaning," 87.
13. Piper, "Authority and Meaning," 94–95; emphasis in original.
14. For a concise summary of the approach, see "A Canonical Approach to Old Testament Theology," in Childs, *Old Testament Theology*, 6–13.

Piper calls as his witness John Calvin, who "does not 'presuppose' the authority of the canon"[15] but rather seeks a ground for that authority in the content and origin of the books, not in the "authoritative reception of sacred tradition."[16] However, a close reading of the *Institutes* reveals Calvin's own position—one that does not fit nicely with Piper's argument.[17] He is right to claim that Calvin argues that the church (or any religious community) does not possess authority over their texts, nor could they even claim to be the authoritative interpreters, since the community is founded by the word of God, and thus derives its position from Scripture and not the other way around.[18] In other words, the church (and by extrapolation the synagogue) is a textual community in the sense that it is founded by the command of God as recorded in a text, and is shaped by reading that text across the generations, but not in the sense that it possesses and has ownership of that text.

However, Calvin's own argument demonstrates more depth than this single claim when he turns to the question of those who "both wish and demand rational proof that Moses and the prophets spoke divinely," a question which sounds very much like that of the modern biblical scholars, including Piper.[19] Calvin's answer is succinct—there is none. The authority of Scripture is not established rationally, but is instead a communal religious faith claim. For this reason, confirmation of the value of the text is found in God's presence with the community, not in the text itself:

> Illumined by his power, we believe neither by our own nor by anyone else's judgment that Scripture is from God; but above human judgment we affirm with utter certainty . . . that it has flowed to us from the very mouth of God by the ministry of men. . . . God, therefore, very rightly proclaims through Isaiah that the prophets together with the whole people are witnesses to him; for they, instructed by prophecies, unhesitatingly held that God has spoken without deceit or ambiguity. Such, then, is a conviction that requires no reasons; such, a knowledge with which the best reason agrees—in which the mind truly reposes more securely and constantly than in any reasons; such, finally, a feeling that can be born only of heavenly revelation. I speak of nothing other than what each believer experiences within

---

15. Piper, "Authority and Meaning," 89.
16. Piper, "Authority and Meaning," 90.
17. Calvin, *Institutes*, 1:vii.
18. "If the teaching of the prophets and apostles is the foundation, this must have had authority before the church began to exist" (Calvin, *Institutes*, 1:vii.2).
19. Calvin, *Institutes*, 1:vii.4.

himself—though my words fall far beneath a just explanation of the matter.[20]

In this view, there can be no authoritative interpreters, merely communities more or less faithful to the task of hearing the voice of the Lord emerge polyvocally from the canonical text.

The Canon and the Cosmos

Piper's conclusion is that his own theological tradition precludes Child's approach, since "Calvin, like the early Church before him, sought to ground the authority of the canon not in its affirmation by the believing community but in the qualities of its content and the nature of its origin. I see very little continuity between Calvin's approach to the authority of the canon and the Childs-Sheppard approach."[21] Based on this conclusion, Piper counters that the canon should be considered authoritative now on the same basis as each document was admitted into the canon in the beginning—content and authorship.

Piper here not only misappropriates Calvin but also distorts the tradition on which Calvin is drawing, misshaping it into the modern discussion to which it is ill fit. Calvin, Piper, and certainly even Childs would agree that the authority of the texts are not predicated on the declaration of the community—on this much they all wholeheartedly agree. However, the very terminology of canon was originally leveraged neither for authority, nor even for an official list of texts, but rather as a middle term concerning the relationship of God to the cosmos which proceeds from the fundamental shared claim of the Judeo-Christian tradition, the Shema of Deut 6.

IRENAEUS AND THE CANON OF FAITH

Likely the earliest uses of canonical terminology in Christian literature is the work of Irenaeus of Lyons; the *Refutation and Overthrowal of Knowledge Falsely So-Called*, commonly referred to collectively as *Against Heresies*, was written as five books over a period of two decades in the latter half of the second century.[22] While, as the title suggests, the expressed subject is the nature of religious knowledge, undergirding this is a conflict over the religious interpretation of the cosmos.

20. Calvin, *Institutes*, 1:vii.5.
21. Piper, "Authority and Meaning," 90.
22. Behr, *Irenaeus of Lyon*, 21–22.

Irenaeus's opponents are a number of schismatic groups, likely all operating in Rome, who in his mind mutilate Scripture in the name of justifying a religious vision that is contrary to the witness of Scripture. Each of these opponents proposes a distinct array of aeons who are responsible for the generation and government of the world, and which are alluded to indirectly in Scripture.[23] For instance:

> The Duodecad [group of twelve] of the Aeons is indicated by the fact that the Lord was twelve years of age when He disputed with the teachers of the law, and by the election of the apostles, for of these there were twelve. The other eighteen Aeons are made manifest in that the Lord conversed with His disciples for eighteen months after His resurrection from the dead. They also affirm that these eighteen Aeons are indicated by the first two letters of His name, namely *Iota* and *Eta*. And, in like manner, they assert that the ten Aeons are pointed out by the letter *Iota*, which begins His name; while, for the same reason, they tell us the Savior said, One *Iota*, or one tittle, shall by no means pass away until all be fulfilled.[24]

While Irenaeus considers this method of reading Scripture absurd, his opponents justify it cosmologically. The world, they propose, emerges through a conflict of the aeons, as some penetrate the inner life of the supreme spiritual beings and seek to reveal this to humanity, and others intentionally seek to obscure such knowledge; still others are simply incompetent or unwittingly deceive humanity.[25]

The cosmos, being the production of such a dizzying array of spiritual principles, is in need of a hypothesis (ὑπόθεσις), or a supposition around which the complicated matter might be organized.[26] Naturally, this leads to the question of authority, for the text, like all material things, is a vague shadow of the truth, and ultimately insufficient for deducing such a hypothesis. True religious knowledge is only found when an enlightened interpreter with a clarified spiritual understanding properly synthesizes the competing elements into a religious hypothesis. Of course, each of the religious leaders Irenaeus opposes presents themselves as just such a leader, with the result

---

23. "Aeons" or "eternities" in the gnostic system are "divine partial aspects" that emanate from the singular God (the Absolute "Monad") "who is utterly other-worldly and unknowable," and thus form a celestial hierarchy of partial knowledge which leads from the natural world to the Absolute (Markschies, *Gnosis*, 89–90).

24. Irenaeus, *Haer.* 1.3.2 AT.

25. Irenaeus, *Haer.* 1.1–1.5.

26. Irenaeus, *Haer.* 1.4.4; 8.1; 9.2–9.4; 9.28.

that the schismatic groups had fragmented around their preferred religious authority.

Irenaeus's rebuttal is that the true church confesses a cosmic order that is governed by "one Lord through one Word," a repeated mantra throughout all five books.[27] The result is a unity to the cosmic order: "For the Son, being present with His own handiwork from the beginning, reveals the Father to all; to whom He wills, and when He wills, and as the Father wills. Wherefore, then, in all things, and through all things, there is one God, the Father, and one Word, and one Son, and one Spirit, and one salvation to all who believe in Him."[28]

For Irenaeus, the Christian tradition does not utilize a *hypothesis* but a *canon* (often translated as "rule") of truth, which is demonstrated by how the church utilizes Scripture:

> A sound mind ... which is devoted to piety and the love of truth will eagerly meditate upon those things which God has placed within the power of humanity and has subjected to our knowledge ... rendering the knowledge of them accessible to those who study. These things ... are clearly and unambiguously set forth in Sacred Scriptures.... Therefore the parables ought not to be warped to ambiguous expressions ... [but] receive a single interpretation from all, so that the body of truth remains whole, with a harmonious adaptation of its parts. . . . [Otherwise] no one will possess the "canon" of truth; but for each person who explains the parables there will be found another system of truth in opposition to each other.[29]

What Irenaeus lays out in *Against Heresies* is a canonical vision for the interpretation of Scripture that is defended by a canonical cosmology. He does not, strictly speaking, defend his interpretive method; rather, his defense of religious knowledge follows a priori from an interpretation of the

---

27. The first use of this formula is instructive: "Such is the account which they all give of their Pleroma, and of the formation of the universe, striving, as they do, to adapt the good words of revelation to their own wicked innovations. And it is not only from the writings of the evangelists and the apostles that they endeavor to derive proofs for their opinions by means of deficient interpretations and deceitful explanations: they deal in the same way with the law and the prophets, which contain many parables and allegories that can frequently be interpreted various ways, according to the kind of exegesis to which they are subjected. And others of them, with great craftiness, adapting such parts of Scripture to their own imaginations, lead away captive from the truth those who do not retain a steadfast faith in one God, the Father Almighty, and in one Lord Jesus Christ, the Son of God" (Irenaeus, *Haer.* 1.3.6 AT).

28. Irenaeus, *Haer.* 4.6.7.

29. Irenaeus, *Haer.* 2.27.1 AT.

cosmos based on the religious claims of the Scriptures. What also emerges from Irenaeus's argument is that the canon is community formative: those who read the text in faith as portraying a harmonious (canonical) vision are themselves formed into a unified community.

The Relationship Between Canon and Monotheism

Irenaeus's argument for a canonical rather than a hypothetical conception of the cosmos is, in fact, part of a larger ideological revolution taking place at the time, for which philosophers of history such as Giorgio Agamben credit the Judeo-Christian tradition.[30] However, if Irenaeus's opponents believe that the material world is a deficient guide to religious knowledge, the modern period is characterized by a swing in the other direction, to the complete perspicuity of truth. The prevailing wisdom of the last two hundred years has been that the emergence of text-centered religions is a consequence of the transition from polytheism to monotheism, which itself was an inevitable watershed in the progress of human reason. In polytheism, the forces of nature that subjugated humanity's existence were mythologized and arranged into pantheons, but eventually humanity awoke to the more reasonable conclusion that there could only be one deity, a singular Lord of the cosmos. This evolutionary explanation presumes that monotheism is, by necessity, a more coherent explanation for the world.

This consensus is well summarized by philosopher of history Karl Jaspers, who coined the term "Axial Age" to refer to the period between 800 and 300 BCE in which "rationality and rationally clarified experience launched a struggle against the myth (*logos* against *mythos*); a further struggle developed for the transcendence of the One God against non-existent demons, and finally an ethical rebellion took place against the unreal figures of the gods."[31] The inevitability of monotheism based on the reasonableness of humanity was held not just by the philosophers, but even theologians who on most scores would disagree considerably with Jaspers's conception of the purpose and telos of history. For instance, C. S. Lewis would state with little attempt at argument that

> monotheism should not be regarded as the rival of polytheism, but rather as its maturity. Where you find polytheism, combined with any speculative power and any leisure for speculation, monotheism will sooner or later arise as a natural development.

30. Agamben, *Kingdom and the Glory*.
31. Jaspers, *Origin and Goal of History*, 3.

> The principle, I understand, is well illustrated in the history of Indian religion. Behind the gods arises the One, and the gods as well as the men are only his dreams. That is one way of disposing of the Many. European thought did not follow the same path, but it was faced with the same problem. The best minds embrace monotheism.[32]

What is lost in this simple progression is the fact that every religious system implies a certain ordering of humanity, nature, and God—what I have called a cosmology—and it is far from axiomatic that monotheism's cosmology more easily accounts for lived experience. In fact, it is arguably easier to explain many of the tragic elements of the world within dualistic frameworks where there are a multitude of equally powerful divinities who favor some and not others, and some of whom are intent on destruction and chaos. The world becomes much more difficult to account for if one intends to defend that (1) there is one God who has ultimate agency over all things, and (2) that God is consistent and not capricious. To do this, an underlying harmony must emerge from conflict. The question, then, is how to substantiate this harmony.

Polytheism operated on what I will call a *political cosmology*, terminology derived from pre-Aristotelean Greek philosophy. "Political" here comes from the idea that the city (Gk. *polis*) is the most apt illustration for how the cosmos operates. The life of a city emerges from an equilibrium of a host of distinct and often contradictory forces; this equilibrium is established and maintained by power and may or may not be stable. Political visions are amiable to polytheistic systems, where the various forces at play in the polis are analogous to divine forces, arranged in a hierarchy, which regulate the order of the cosmos.

The breakup of the political vision is described in Pseudo-Aristotle's writings which propose a new, "economic image" for the cosmos, which substitutes the house (Gk. *oikos*) as the primary image. "Economy and politics differ not only in accordance with the house and the city (for these are, in the end, similar), but more so in that politics resides in many hands, but the economy is a monarchy."[33] This economic vision is even more strongly expressed in Pseudo-Aristotle's work *De mundo*, written likely in the second century and roughly contemporaneous to Irenaeus.

> Some people, however, have wondered how the cosmos, if it is composed of the "opposite" principles . . . has not long ago been destroyed and perished; it is as if men should wonder how a

---

32. Lewis, *Allegory of Love*, 57.
33. Pseudo-Aristotle, Οἰκονομικά 1.1343a AT.

city survives, composed as it is of the most opposite classes (I mean poor and rich, young and old, weak and strong, bad and good). They do not recognize that the most wonderful thing of all about the harmonious working of a city-community is this: that out of plurality and diversity it achieves a homogeneous unity capable of admitting every variation of nature and degree. But perhaps nature actually has a liking for opposites; perhaps it is from them that she creates harmony, and not from similar things, in just the same way as she has joined the male to the female, and not each of them to another of the same sex, thus making the first harmonious community not of similar but of opposite things.[34]

The emergence of text-centralized religions are, in all likelihood, part of a larger intellectual revolution, a comprehensive reconception of the world. The self-confidence in progress of modernity obscured both how radical the monotheistic claim was, as well as the stakes of that claim.

WHAT DOES IT MEAN THAT "GOD IS ONE"?

Monotheism supports an "economic cosmology," yet for a century it has been recognized that two variations of the economic images exist—a Monarchic version, where all disparate forces are arranged in submission to a singular principle and a canonical, where each agent is included into a harmonious whole. The Judeo-Christian tradition is the primary source for the canonical vision, as evidenced by the canonical form of the sacred texts of this tradition.

Shahādah and the Oneness of God

While the three Abrahamic religions are all monotheistic and each centralizes a sacred text, there is a significant difference in the cosmology which emerges from them. The central claim of Islam is the *Shahādah*: "There is no God but Allah," and the recitation of this creed is a pillar of the religion. After a long philosophical-theological debate around the turn of the first millennium, the prevailing understanding of this statement of faith is known as *al tawḥīd*, which is the doctrine of how the order of the world is maintained by means of the supreme oneness of God.[35] Preeminent twentieth-century

---

34. Pseudo-Aristotle, Περι Κοσμος 5 AT.

35. A common Surah to quote for this is Al-Anbya (21) 22: "Had there been other gods besides Allah in the heavens or the earth, both realms would have surely been corrupted" (Yusuf Ali).

Islamic scholar Ismail Al-Faruqi claims emphatically that "there can be no doubt that the essence of Islamic civilization is Islam; or that the essence of Islam is *al tawḥīd*, the act of affirming Allah (SWT) to be the One, the absolute, transcendent Creator, the Lord and Matter of all that is. . . . Without *al tawḥīd* there can be no Islam."[36]

Al tawḥīd claims a cosmic order based on the normativity[37] of one God as the lawgiver, and defines worship as the universal call to all to enter into one relationship with the one God by means of submission to the universal law, for "since Allah (SWT) alone is God, it follows that His commandments are valid for all humans."[38] The monotheistic vision *al tawḥīd* could be briefly summarized by the word *singularness*, which supports a monarchic cosmology: there is one God, and thus one norm, and therefore the telos is for all to be one. This cosmology is reflected in the structure of the Qur'an, which is not a canon, but rather an authoritative revelation from a single prophet.

Shema and the Uniqueness of God

Al-Farugi charges Jewish and Christian monotheism with corrupting God's transcendence: the former betraying it by conceiving of a covenantal relationship between God and Israel, and the latter even more by arguing for an incarnation.[39] The basis for this conflict is the difference between the *Shahādah* and the Shema, which "refers to Judaism's fundamental profession of belief in and commitment to the unity and uniqueness of *God," and is an inseparable and repeated confession in the worship of Judaism.[40] The words of the Shema come from Deut 6:5–6: "Hear, O Israel! The Lord is our God, the Lord alone. You shall love the Lord your God with all your heart and with all your soul and with all your might." This confession at the same time establishes the uniqueness of God and entangles the unique, transcendent God with the material cosmos.

This cosmic vision emerges from the Shema because, as Jewish philosopher Hermann Cohen argues, the stress of Judaism's monotheistic claim is not on oneness. Rather, "it is God's uniqueness, rather than his oneness,

---

36. Al-Faruqi, *Al Tawhid*, 17–18.

37. "To be a Muslim is precisely to perceive God alone . . . as normative, His will along as commandment, His pattern alone as constituting the ethical desiderate of creation" (Al-Faruqi, *Al Tawhid*, 15).

38. Al-Faruqi, *Al Tawhid*, 185.

39. Al-Faruqi, *Al Tawhid*, 20–23.

40. "Shema," in Baskin, *Cambridge Dictionary of Judaism*, 547.

that we posit as the essential content of monotheism. Oneness signifies only an opposition to the plurality of gods. It is questionable whether this idea was the primary idea of monotheism, whether it by itself was capable of prevailing against polytheism."[41]

The revolutionary aspect of the Shema is not simply to replace many with one; in a sense, a political cosmology already did this through violence and power as one principle prevailed over the rest. What the Judeo-Christian tradition does is overturn power through harmony, which it does by reconciling the material with the divine:

> If monotheism opposed polytheism, it also had to change God's relation to the universe in accordance with its new idea of God. ... Thus, from the very outset the concept of God's oneness involves a relation to nature. This oneness immediately acquires a significance that takes it beyond the opposition to plurality and elevates it even beyond mere opposition to the notion of composition. The notion of composition contains a relation to nature.[42]

As Assmann notes, "The power structure of a pantheon reflects the power structure of a society";[43] therefore, any reconfiguration of the idea of the relation of the divine to the cosmos will initiate social restructuring, even if society takes some time to catch up with the religious belief. Cohen also observes, "It is already striking that Judaism presents its chief sources in literary documents, whereas polytheism possesses them above all in monuments of plastic art."[44] This, I argue, is because the canon itself was a part of the ideological revolution of the Judeo-Christian tradition.

THE SHEMA AS CANONICAL VISION

If the first half of the Shema entangles the unique God with the cosmos, the second half does the same for the individual human and the worshipping community. Two questions immediately proceed from the brief command to "love the LORD your God with all your heart and with all your soul and with all your might." First, how do you command someone to love something, as love does not operate on command, and second, what is the relationship between love and instruction (Torah)? The answers to these

---

41. Cohen, *Religion of Reason*, 35.
42. Cohen, *Religion of Reason*, 35.
43. Assman, *Of God and Gods*, 59.
44. Cohen, *Religion of Reason*, 37.

questions distill the unique contribution of the Judeo-Christian tradition by means of a *canon* of faith, as well as clarify some ways in which the Jewish and Christian traditions differ.

The call to love God in a holistic fashion—heart, soul, and strength—is, in a way, its own canonical vision, integrating the human subject in a struggle with self that mirrors humanity's struggle with the material world. Significantly, it is not a passive task either, but rather a call to love as active submission. This would indicate that the communion with God that leads to inspiration includes a holistic harmony of the person, which is further reflected in the form of the Scriptures as a holistic harmony of these inspired individuals who deliver the voice of the Lord to the community.

This, I argue, is the true meaning of canon: it is why the Judeo-Christian tradition has pioneered textual communities (and literacy with it), and why canonical reading of the sacred text should be understood as a return to the premodern conception seen in Calvin and Irenaeus. The modern period's disastrous infatuation with harmonization through power betrays an adherence to alternative cosmologies, whether it be the *Reichstheologie*'s Catholic defense of Hitler based on a monarchic cosmology[45] or Marx's return to a political cosmology by cogently stating (in direct contrast to *De mundo*) that all of history was the story of the conflict of irreconcilable forces.[46] Reflection on the Scriptures must face its modern presuppositions, which begins by seeing canon foremost as a faith claim: that the various voices harmonize not by subjugation of some but by allowing each to speak to the community as they read them in faith.

It is not that the texts are authoritative because the community says so, but rather the community exists because they read the texts as speaking singularly though polyvocally. This canonical reading is an affirmation of faith that God delivers the word of the Lord through the voice of human authors, and God does this precisely because the call to holistic love for God is a call to a canonical cosmic vision which includes God's covenantal love for his people. The difference between submission to the instruction of an authoritative text and active engagement with God by means of a community formulated by that text is, in my estimation, the central shared component, even if not always recognized, of the Judeo-Christian religious tradition.

---

45. Schmidt, *Political Theology*. For a Jewish response, Rosenstock, "Monotheism as a Political Problem."

46. "The history of all hitherto existing society is the history of class struggles" (Marx and Engels, *Communist Manifesto*, 19).

BIBLIOGRAPHY

Abelard, Peter. *Dialogue Between a Philosopher, a Jew, and a Christian.* Translated by Pierre Payer. Toronto: Pontifical Institute of Medieval Studies, 1979.

Agamben, Giorgio. *The Kingdom and the Glory.* Edited by Werner Hamacher. Translated by Lorenzo Chiesa. Stanford, CA: Stanford University Press, 2011.

Al-Faruqi, Isma'il Raji. *Al Tawhid: Its Implications for Thought and Life.* Herndon, VA: International Institute of Islamic Thought, 1982.

Aristotle. *Metaphysics, Books 10–14. Oeconomica. Magna Moralia.* Translated by Hugh Tredennick and G. Cyril Armstrong. LCL 287. Cambridge, MA: Harvard University Press, 1935.

———. *On Sophistical Refutations. On Coming-to-Be and Passing Away. On the Cosmos.* Translated by E. S. Forster and D. J. Furley. LCL 400. Cambridge, MA: Harvard University Press, 1955.

Assmann, Jan. *Of God and Gods: Egypt, Israel, and the Rise of Monotheism.* George L. Mosse Series in Modern European Cultural and Intellectual History. Madison: University of Wisconsin Press, 2008.

Baskin, Judith R., ed. *The Cambridge Dictionary of Judaism and Jewish Culture.* Cambridge University Press, 2011.

Behr, John. *Irenaeus of Lyons: Identifying Christianity.* Christian Theology in Context. Oxford: Oxford University Press, 2013.

Bruce, F. F. *The Canon of Scripture.* Downers Grove, IL: InterVarsity, 1988.

Calvin, John. *Institutes of the Christian Religion.* Edited by John T. McNeill. Translated by Ford Lewis Battles. 2 vols. Louisville: Westminster John Knox, 2011.

Childs, Brevard S. *Old Testament Theology in a Canonical Context.* Philadelphia: Fortress, 1985.

Cohen, Hermann. *Religion of Reason: Out of the Sources of Judaism.* Translated by Simon Kaplan. 2nd ed. AAR Religions in Translation. Atlanta: Scholars, 1972.

Heath, Jane. "'Textual Communities': Brian Stock's Concept and Recent Scholarship on Antiquity." In *Scriptural Interpretation at the Interface Between Education and Religion: In Memory of Hans Conzelmann*, edited by Florian Wilk, 5–35. TBN 22. Leiden: Brill, 2018.

Jaspers, Karl. *The Origin and Goal of History.* Translated by Michael Bullock. New Haven, CT: Yale University Press, 1953.

Kruger, Michael J. *Canon Revisited: Establishing the Origins and Authority of the New Testament Books.* Wheaton, IL: Crossway, 2012.

Lewis, C. S. *The Allegory of Love: Study in Medieval Tradition.* London: Oxford University Press, 1936.

Markschies, Christoph. *Gnosis: An Introduction.* Translated by John Bowden. London: T&T Clark, 2003.

Marx, Karl, and Friedrich Engels. *The Communist Manifesto.* Translated by Yanis Varoufakis. London: Vintage, 2010.

McDonald, Lee Martin. *The Biblical Canon: Its Origin, Transmission, and Authority.* Grand Rapids: Baker, 2007.

Piper, John. "The Authority and Meaning of the Christian Canon: A Response to Gerald Sheppard on Canon Criticism." *JETS* 19 (1976) 87–96.

Rendtorff, Rolf. *The Canonical Hebrew Bible: A Theology of the Old Testament.* Tools for Biblical Study. Leiden: Deo, 2005.

Rosenstock, Bruce. "Monotheism as a Political Problem: The Critique of Political Theology out of the Sources of Judaism." In *Judaism, Liberalism, and Political Theology*, edited by Randy Rashkover and Martin Kavka, 321–44. Bloomington: Indiana University Press, 2013.

Schmidt, Carl. *Political Theology: Four Chapters on the Concept of Sovereignty*. Translated by George Schwab. Chicago: University of Chicago Press, 2005.

Stock, Brian. *The Implications of Literacy: Written Language and Models of Interpretation in the Eleventh and Twelfth Centuries*. Princeton, NJ: Princeton University Press, 1987.

Wilson, Jonathan R. "Canon and Theology: What Is at Stake?" In *Exploring the Origins of the Bible Canon Formation in Historical, Literary, and Theological Perspective*, edited by Craig A. Evans and Emmanuel Tov, 241–53. Acadia Studies in Bible and Theology. Grand Rapids: Baker Academic, 2008.

Yoder, John H. "The Authority of the Canon." In *Essays on Biblical Interpretation: Anabaptist-Mennonite Perspectives*, edited by Willard M. Swartley, 265–90. Elkhart, IN: Institute of Mennonite Studies, 1984.

Chapter 4

Early High Christology in Second Temple Jewish Literature

J. Luis Dizon

ONE OF THE MAJOR differences between Christianity and Judaism concerns their belief regarding the nature of God. Christianity has historically confessed belief in God as Trinity. To quote the Articles of Religion of the Anglican Church, "In unity of this Godhead there be three Persons, of one substance, power, and eternity; the Father, the Son, and the Holy Ghost."[1] Moreover, Christianity has confessed that the second person of the Trinity, Jesus Christ, was incarnated as a man, based upon New Testament passages such as John 1:14; Phil 2:6–11; 1 Tim 3:16; and several more. Christian reflection on these passages has further resulted in an understanding of Christ as being divine, and even God incarnate.

By contrast, Judaism has rejected the Christian concept of a triune God. Maimonides, in formulating the thirteen articles of the Jewish faith, stressed the undifferentiated oneness of God and his incorporeality in the first three articles, which to be sure, were written to preclude any notion of Trinitarianism or of a corporeal deity.[2] Furthermore, contemporary Judaism conceives of the Messiah as merely a human figure that is neither heavenly or divine in any way. Although this individual may have great power

---

1. Anglican Church of Canada, "39 Articles of Religion," art. 1.
2. Kohler and Hirsch, "Articles of Faith."

and authority, it is nevertheless the power and authority of an exalted and anointed man, not of God incarnate.

What is true of medieval and modern Judaism, however, is not necessarily informative of Jewish theological positions during the time of Jesus. In fact, as far as Jewish views of the Messiah go, many of the notions that characterize the branch of theology known as "Christology" actually originated during the Second Temple period of Jewish history. While mainstream of Judaism condemns the idea of the Messiah as God incarnate, it would be incorrect to presume that no Jewish scholars recognize elements of multi-personality within God or even incarnational theology within their own tradition. For example, Benjamin Sommer in *The Bodies of God and the World of Ancient Israel* argues that the Hebrew Bible[3] contains the teaching that God is, in fact, corporeal in nature, and more strikingly, that God can be corporeally manifested in more than one place at once.[4]

On the basis of this argument, Sommer contends that modern Jewish reactions to the Christian notion of God being incarnate must be reevaluated, since this idea is not so foreign to ancient Jewish thought:

> Some Jews regard Christianity's claim to be a monotheistic religion with grave suspicion, both because of the doctrine of the trinity (how can three equal one?) and because of Christianity's core belief that God took bodily form. What I have attempted to point out here is that biblical Israel knew very similar doctrines, and these doctrines did not disappear from Judaism after the biblical period. . . . No Jew sensitive to Judaism's own classical sources, however, can fault the theological model Christianity employs when it avows belief in a God who has an earthly body as well as a Holy Spirit and a heavenly manifestation, for that model, we have seen, is a perfectly Jewish one. A religion whose scripture contains the fluidity traditions, whose teachings emphasize the multiplicity of the *shekhinah*, and whose thinkers speak of the *sephirot* does not differ in its theological essentials from a religion that adores the triune God.[5]

Another Jewish scholar who offers similar insights into the relationship between ancient Judaism and Christianity's view of the nature of God is Daniel Boyarin. In several of his works, Boyarin discusses the cross-pollination that has taken place between Jewish and Christian thought, how the two

---

3. The terms "Hebrew Bible" and "Old Testament" are used interchangeably throughout this essay.

4. Sommer, *Bodies of God*, 1.

5. Sommer, *Bodies of God*, 135.

outlooks were originally intertwined with one another, and how a "parting of the ways" towards the end of the first century led to the separation of Judaism and Christianity into separate religions, which in turn led to mutually distinct ideas about God and the Messiah. Concerning this, Boyarin states:

> I'm going to tell a very different historical story, a story of a time when Jews and Christians were much more mixed up with each other than they are now, when there were many Jews who believed in something quite like the Father and the Son and even in something quite like the incarnation of the Son in the Messiah, and when followers of Jesus kept kosher as Jews, and accordingly a time in which the question of the difference between Judaism and Christianity just didn't exist as it does now. Jesus, when he came, came in a form that many, many Jews were expecting: a second divine figure incarnated in a human. The question was not "Is a divine Messiah coming?" but only "Is this carpenter from Nazareth the One we are expecting?" Not surprisingly, some Jews said yes and some said no. Today we call the first group Christians and the second group Jews, but it was not like that then, not at all.[6]

The goal of this essay is to examine the evidence for such claims in extant literature from the Second Temple period to show that reverence for Jesus, including attribution of divine honors and prerogatives, has its roots in late Second Temple Jewish developments in messianic thought. When one considers the Jewish messianism of the Jewish literature in the century or so leading up to the founding of Christianity and writing of the New Testament, there emerges a growing tendency to regard the Messiah (or "Son of Man," as the two figures came to be equated, as will be shown in the later discussions of 1 Enoch and 4 Ezra) in increasingly exalted terms. Thus, when the gospels attribute divine honors and powers to Jesus, they do so in a context where similar thinking is already prevalent.

"TWO POWERS IN HEAVEN" AND PHILO

One of the most interesting phenomena to appear in Second Temple Judaism are various strands of theology that are collectively known as "two powers" beliefs. The most ground-breaking work on this set of beliefs is Alan Segal's *Two Powers in Heaven*. Segal demonstrates that arguments over "two powers" theology, though primarily emerging after Second Temple

---

6. Boyarin, *Jewish Gospels*, 1–2.

Judaism,[7] can nevertheless be traced back to writings during the Second Temple period. Perhaps one of the most explicit examples of this is found in the writings of Philo of Alexandria (20 BCE—50 CE).[8] Writing in the decades prior to the destruction of the Second Temple, Philo observes that in some biblical texts, there appear to be two figures simultaneously referred to by the divine name Yahweh. He exegetes these passages by positing a *Deuteros Theos* (lit. Second God). An example of this interpretation is his discussion of Gen 31:13, a verse which contains an interesting variant. Rather than the Masoretic Text's reading, "I am the God of Beth-El,"[9] the LXX reads, "I am the God who appears to you in the place of God."[10] Philo exegetes this passage in *De somniis* to mean that there are, to use his terms, "two Gods." He writes:

> And do not fail to mark the language used, but carefully inquire whether there are two Gods; for we read "I am the God that appeared to thee," not "in my place" but "in the place of God," as though it were another's. What, then, are we to say? He that is truly God is One, but those that are improperly so called are more than one. Accordingly the holy word in the present instance has indicated Him Who is truly God by means of the articles saying "I am the God," while it omits the article when mentioning him who is improperly so called, saying "Who appeared to thee in the place" not "of the God," but simply "of God."[11]

Regarding this, Segal notes that the expression "two Gods" was considered a synonym for "two powers" in rabbinic thought. He further notes that Philo does not use the phrase in a negative light, as later rabbis would, but uses it as an explanation for the many anthropomorphic depictions of God that appear in the Hebrew Bible.[12]

Further on in the same paragraph, Philo equates the second instance of God that appears in Gen 31:13 with the *logos*:

> Here it gives the title of "God" to His chief Word, not from any superstitious nicety in applying names, but with one aim before him, to use words to express facts. Thus in another place, when he had inquired whether He that IS has any name, he came to

---

7. Boyarin, *Jewish Gospels*, 33–155.
8. Boyarin, *Jewish Gospels*, 159–81.
9. Heb. *Anokhī 'ēl Beth-'ēl*.
10. Gk. *Egō eimi o theos o ophtheis soi en topō theou*.
11. Philo, *Philo*, 5:417–19. See also Segal, *Two Powers in Heaven*, 159.
12. Segal, *Two Powers in Heaven*, 159; see also 162–63.

> know full well that He has no proper name, and that whatever name anyone may use of Him he will use by licence of language; for it is not the nature of Him that IS to be spoken of, but simply to be.[13]

According to Segal, Philo "derives the idea that the *logos* is a separate, second divine hypostasis from the fact that "God" is repeated in "place of God" instead of using the pronoun (i.e., *My* place) as one would normally expect." Furthermore, because of this identification of the second instance of *theos* in the text as the *logos*, "the *logos* is properly a god and may be called by the divine names."[14]

Besides Philo, ideas resembling "two powers" theology can also be found in apocalyptic texts such as the Similitudes of Enoch (which comprise chs. 37–71 of the book of 1 Enoch), 4 Ezra, and some of the Dead Sea Scrolls, in their presentation of the Messiah (or "Son of Man") as an otherworldly heavenly figure, to whom preexistence and divine prerogatives are attributed. The germ for these ideas can be traced even further back, to the book of Daniel and its enigmatic description of "one like a Son of Man" (Dan 7:13).[15] In order to trace the development of this thought, we shall now turn to these texts.

One like the Son of Man

One of the major motifs that plays into "two powers" theological speculation is the idea of the "Son of Man." The earliest uses of this phrase as they are contained in the Psalms and the earlier prophetic books of the Old Testament refer to an ordinary human being. For example, Ps 8:4 states, "What is man, that you think of him, or a son of man, that you care for him?" Similar uses abound in Ezekiel, where God frequently addresses the prophet as a "son of man" when giving him instructions on what to do next.

Over time, however, this phrase began to be used as a title for a superhuman figure whose power and authority far transcend those of ordinary human beings. The most famous example of this is in the book of Daniel. In Dan 7:9–14, thrones are set up and then two figures are presented. First, there is the ancient of days (*attīq yōmīn*), who sits on one of these thrones (vv. 9–10). The second figure is described as "one like a son of man" (*bar enash*, אֱנָשׁ). The description provided of this figure in vv. 13–14 is interesting:

13. Philo, *Philo*, 5:419.

14. Segal, *Two Powers in Heaven*, 162; emphasis added.

15. English translations are my own from the original Hebrew and Aramaic texts as found in the *BHS*.

> I kept looking in the night visions, and behold, with the clouds of heaven, one like a son of man was coming, and to the ancient of days he came, and before him he was presented. And to him was given dominion, and glory, and a kingdom; that peoples, nations, and tongues might serve him. His dominion is an eternal dominion that will not end, and his kingdom is one that will not be destroyed. (Dan 7:13–14)

Regarding the prerogatives attributed to this heavenly Son of Man, Adela Yarbro Collins describes Dan 7:13–14 as speaking of a form of "functional divinity," where a being is described as exercising divine attributes, such as: "ruling over a universal kingdom, sitting on a heavenly throne, judging human beings in the end-time [and] traveling on the clouds, a typically divine mode of transport." She distinguishes this from "ontological divinity," which is when a being is described as being divine in nature, such as how Paul describes Jesus as being "in the form of God" in Phil 2.[16] Based upon these attributes, Boyarin concludes that the Ancient of Days and the one like a Son of Man together constitute the divine nature, arguing that "at least since Daniel and almost surely earlier, there had been a tradition within Israel that saw God as doubled in the form of an old man and a younger human-like figure, sharing the divine throne (or sharing, rather, two equal thrones)."[17]

The figure of the "Son of Man" that appears in Daniel is further developed in later Jewish tradition. Various documents from the first century BCE and early first century BCE latch onto this figure and expand his role, giving more detailed descriptions of his origins, identity and authority. Two such texts are the Similitudes of Enoch and 4 Ezra.

The Son of Man in the Similitudes of Enoch

Of all the later Jewish texts that speak of a divine Son of Man, one of the most noteworthy, and one which has been the subject of much discussion and debate, is a subsection of the book of 1 Enoch known as the Similitudes of Enoch (or Parables of Enoch).[18]

The first mention of the "Son of Man" occurs in the first parable: "And when the Righteous One appears before the faces of the righteous and chosen, whose works depend upon the Lord of Spirits" (1 En. 38:2).[19] Daniel

---

16. A. Collins, "How on Earth."
17. Boyarin, "Enoch, Ezra," 337.
18. Charlesworth, "Date and Provenience." According to Charlesworth, this subsection of Enoch was written during the time of Herod the Great.
19. Olson, *Enoch*. The translations of R. H. Charles and E. Isaac have also been consulted, although I prefer Olson's as it is the most up to date of the three.

C. Olson suggests that a parallel between the use of the title "the Righteous One" here and in Isa 53:11 exists, the latter of which details how the Suffering Servant is referred to by God as "the righteous one" (Heb. *tzaddīq*). Olson thus proposes that the title was originally derived from this biblical passage.[20] George Nickelsburg, commenting on this passage, notes that this character is given the prerogative of judging, which is something normally reserved for God alone. He notes that "instead of the deity in the company of the holy ones, it is the Righteous one who appears in the midst of the congregation of the righteous. He, rather than God, presides over the judgment."[21]

This figure, who is at some points called "the Righteous One" and in others called "the Chosen One," is mentioned in passing a few more times in the next few chapters. The next major description of this figure occurs in the second parable. Here, he is described as such:

> On that Day,
> my chosen One will sit on the throne of glory,
> and he will discern how they have conducted themselves,
> and their places of rest will be numberless.
> Their spirits will be strengthened within them when they see my
>   Chosen One—
> those who have made their appeal to my glorious Name.
> On that Day,
> I will cause my Chosen One to dwell among them,
> I will transform heaven and make it forever a blessing, and light.
>   (1 En. 45:3–4; see also 51:3; 55:4; 61:8; 62:2–5)

The description of this figure continues into the next chapter, where the connection with Dan 7:9–14 is further strengthened when the text begins to refer to God as the "head of days" (1 En. 46:1) and "the Antecedent of Days" (v. 2). It then explicitly calls the messianic figure "the Son of Man" (vv. 3–4). The description that follows reads like an expansion of Dan 7:14. Although many common themes occur in this passage, other details are added which are not present in Daniel, and certain details from Daniel are omitted here.[22] In this chapter, it is said that righteousness belongs to and abides with the Son of Man. He is said to reveal all of the hidden treasures of Heaven, and to triumph over all the kings and nations of the world, hurling them down from their thrones. Further on in ch. 47, there seems to be some hints that the Son of Man would suffer, since the chapter contains two passing references

---

20. Olson, *Enoch*, 74.
21. Nickelsburg and VanderKam, *1 Enoch 2*, 95.
22. Nickelsburg and VanderKam, *1 Enoch 2*, 155.

to "the blood of the Righteous One" (1 En. 47:1, 4). Olson contends that the author of Enoch is presenting this figure as experiencing suffering, pointing to the parallel with Isa 53:11 as evidence. He also sees a possible allusion to this passage in Matt 27:24–25.[23]

And then, in 1 En. 48:2–3, the preexistence of the Son of Man is affirmed. Here, it states:

> At that hour,
> that Son of Man was named
> in the presence of the Lord of Spirits
> and his name
> before the Antecedent of Days.
> Before ever the sun or the heavenly signs were created, before the stars of heaven were made, his name was named before the Lord of Spirits.

Finally, in vv. 5–6, not only preexistence but worship is attributed to the Son of Man:

> All who dwell on the earth will fall down and worship before him and will praise and bless and celebrate with son the Name of the Lord of Spirits. Because of all this, he has been chosen and hidden in his presence before the creation of the world and forever.

Based on all of these descriptions of the son of man in the Similitudes of Enoch, Collins attributes "functional divinity" to the figure.[24] Although he is not described as having "ontological divinity," the fact that he is described as preexistent and receiving worship comes close. Hence, Boyarin can rightly say that the Similitudes "provides us with our most explicit evidence that the Son of Man as a divine-human Redeemer arose by Jesus' time from reading the Book of Daniel."[25] Further on, he says:

> What we learn from this is that there was controversy among Jews about the Son of Man long before the Gospels were written. Some Jews accepted and some rejected the idea of a Divine Messiah. The Similitudes are evidence for the tradition of interpretation of the Son of Man as such a divine person, the tradition that

---

23. Olson, *Enoch*, 90. Hamilton also notes that the theme of innocent blood found in Matt 27:24–25 connects with another part of the book of 1 Enoch, the book of the watchers (chs. 6–11), lending evidence to the idea that Matthew was aware of the Enoch traditions. See Hamilton, *Death of Jesus*, 47–70.

24. A. Collins, "How on Earth," 57.

25. Boyarin, *Jewish Gospels*, 76.

fed into the Jesus movement as well. It is only centuries later, of course, that this difference in belief would become the marker and touchstone of the difference between two religions.[26]

The Son of Man in 4 Ezra

Another important document that is relevant to the question of Second Temple Jewish ideas about the nature of the Messiah is the book of 4 Ezra. Although the text of 4 Ezra was originally composed in Hebrew, it survives only in Latin and Coptic manuscripts.[27] In its final form, the book is believed to have been composed during the first century, shortly after the destruction of the Second Temple.[28] However, sections of it may have been composed earlier. R. H. Charles has noted that the final form of the text of 4 Ezra was likely to have been put together by a redactor from five separate sources which preceded him. Of these five sources, source M (which contains ch. 13, the one which we are examining) is thought to have been written prior to the destruction of the Second Temple.[29]

The first thirteen verses of 4 Ezra 13 present a vision of a heavenly warrior figure who emerges from the sea. The first paragraph describes him as such:

> After seven days I dreamed a dream in the night; and behold, a wind arose from the sea and stirred up all its waves. And I looked, and behold, this wind made something like the figure of a man come up out of the heart of the sea. And I looked, and behold, that man flew with the clouds of heaven; and wherever he turned his face to look, everything under his gaze trembled, and whenever his voice issued from his mouth, all who heard his voice melted as wax melts when it feels the fire. (4 Ezra 13:1-4)

The rest of the chapter talks about how numerous nations are gathered together from the four winds of heaven to make war against the messianic figure, but that by a breath of fire that issues from his mouth, he destroys all of his enemies. After this, a multitude, some of whom were joyful and some sorrowful, came to this figure, some of whom were bringing offerings (4 Ezra 13:5-13). Here, John Collins sees allusions not just to Dan 7, but

26. Boyarin, *Jewish Gospels*, 77.
27. Stone, *Fourth Ezra*, 1.
28. Stone, *Fourth Ezra*, 9-10. See also Nickelsburg, *Jewish Literature Between*, 270, 276-77.
29. *APOT* 5:551.

also to Ps 2, which speaks of God establishing the Messiah on Mt. Zion and causing him to be triumphant over his foes.[30]

What follows this is a request from Ezra for an interpretation of the vision (4 Ezra 13:14–20). This interpretation is given in vv. 21–58. Two excerpts from this interpretation are highly significant, as they shed light on the person and nature of the mysterious figure in Ezra's vision:

> This is the interpretation of the vision: As for your seeing a man come up from the heart of the sea, this is he whom the Most High has been keeping for many ages, who will himself deliver his creation; and he will direct those who are left. (4 Ezra 13:25–26)
>
> And when these things come to pass and the signs occur which I showed you before, then my Son will be revealed, whom you saw as a man coming up from the sea. (4 Ezra 13:32)
>
> And he, my Son, will reprove the assembled nations for their ungodliness (this was symbolized by the storm). (4 Ezra 13:37)
>
> I said, "O Sovereign Lord, explain this to me: Why did I see the man coming up from the heart of the sea?" He said to me, "Just as no one can explore or know what is in the depths of the sea, so no one on earth can see my Son or those who are with him, except in the time of his day." (4 Ezra 13:51–52)

The interpretation of the vision is significant for our understanding of 4 Ezra's conception of the Son of Man figure that he has just described, because he is posited to have preexisted prior to his revelation to the world. For this reason, Collins describes him as "a pre-existent, transcendent figure."[31] Verses 32 onwards then state that this figure will make an appearance at a decisive point in history, when he is said to conquer his enemies and judge the world.

From these descriptions, it is clear that, just like Dan 7 and the Similitudes of Enoch, 4 Ezra 13 attributes to the Son of Man what Collins calls a "functional divinity." Boyarin, in an insightful essay on Jewish high Christology in the Second Temple period, makes the following comments on the divine attributes of the Messiah:

> Even more sharply—partly owing to its relative density—than in *1 Enoch*, the Ezra passage makes absolutely clear the combination of the Son of Man, divine figure, and the Redeemer, or Messiah, a high Christology indeed, and of course, one that is

30. J. Collins, "Son of Man," 462–63.
31. J. Collins, "Son of Man," 464.

independent of the Jesus movement entirely.... Once again, we see a simile become a Redeemer. And since the simile clearly refers to a divine figure (a divine warrior), the Redeemer, the Man is held to be divine.[32]

Further on, he highlights three features of the messianic figure in the Ezra passage that are specifically divine in nature: First, are the references to the "breath" and "word" that are applied both to God and the redeemer figure (13:4, 10). Second, the Son of Man is said to ride the clouds (13:3), which is something that only Yhwh does. Third, the reference to offerings in 13:13 parallels Isa 66:20, which states, "And they shall bring all your brethren from all the nations as an offering to the Lord." The fact that the Son of Man receives these offerings is indication that he is being thought of as divine.[33] Finally, John Collins notes that 4 Ezra 13 as a whole is reminiscent of traditional "divine warrior" theophanies where Yhwh is presented as a warrior at whose voice the mountains melt like wax (Ps 97:5), only here it is the enemies of the Son of Man who are caused to melt.[34]

Thus, Boyarin arrives at the same conclusion that has just been presented when he states of Daniel, the Parables, and 4 Ezra that "according to all of these traditions the Messiah is a kind of divine man or man-God."[35] It can be readily seen that the three documents partake of the same basic thought world and elaborate on the same ideas, albeit with different emphases.

CONCLUSION

Looking at all of the evidence contained in the selected Second Temple Jewish literature, one could arrive at some tentative conclusions about the nature of God and of the Messiah as it relates to New Testament Christology:

First, Second Temple Jewish conceptions of the nature of God allowed for more variety than later rabbinic Judaism would allow. Although the prevalence of such heterodox (by later standards) views is not as widespread as Boyarin makes them out to be in his writings, they are nevertheless present.

Second, the description of "one like a Son of Man" in Dan 7 prompted a development in messianic thought that led to a more exalted view of the

---

32. Boyarin, "Enoch, Ezra," 350.
33. Boyarin, "Enoch, Ezra," 350–51; Stone, *Fourth Ezra*, 387.
34. J. Collins, "Son of Man," 464.
35. Boyarin, "Enoch, Ezra," 337.

Messiah. Certain texts from the Second Temple period, such the Parables of Enoch, 4 Ezra, and certain documents from the Dead Sea Scrolls furnish evidence that the Messiah came to be seen, at least by some Jews, as an otherworldly figure, who existed long before his being revealed to humankind by God, and is afforded divine prerogatives, such as judgment over the whole world.

If all of this is the case, then that means that it is not so much that Christianity was pushing against the grain of a strictly non-trinitarian monotheistic Judaism, but, on the contrary, the reverse is true: It is quite likely that the shift in emphasis in rabbinic Judaism towards a strictly unitarian interpretation of the oneness of God was a reaction to the prevalence of binitarian and trinitarian modes of thought in Christian circles, as well as in various other Jewish sectarian groups that later became deemed as "heretical." Without making any dogmatic conclusions on the matter, Hurtado states:

> It does seem a very cogent possibility . . . that reaction against the Jewish-Christian form of binitarian monotheism (devotion to God and to the exalted Christ) may have had the effect of making any other such programmatic binitarian development unacceptable thereafter.[36]

These developments make sense in light of the recent impetus, as seen in the work of Collins and Boyarin, to see Christianity and rabbinic Judaism as two divergent religious streams, both of which ultimately spring from the same root, that is, Second Temple Judaism. Collins, in his essay on Messianism in the Qumran Community, comments on this way of looking at Christianity and Judaism as follows:

> It was precisely the pluriform character of Judaism that allowed the emergence of early Christianity as a Jewish sect, sharply at variance with other Torah-oriented groups. Consequently, it is legitimate to trace lines of continuity from the Scrolls to early Christianity as study [sic] their links to rabbinic Judaism. Second Temple Judaism was the extraordinarily fertile soil from which both rabbinic Judaism and early Christianity sprang.[37]

In support of this interpretation, Donald H. Juel points out that the break between rabbinic Judaism and Christianity belongs to a much later period in history, after the destruction of the second Jerusalem temple and beyond

---

36. Hurtado, *How on Earth*, 132.

37. John J. Collins, "What Was Distinctive About Messianic Expectation at Qumran?," in Charlesworth, *Bible and Dead Sea Scrolls*, 2:75.

the time of the New Testament. This explains neatly how early Christian beliefs regarding the divine nature of the Messiah could fit comfortably within the matrix of late Second Temple Judaism. Juel states:

> The various crises that resulted in a great sifting within the family of Israel and the eventual emergence of an "orthodox" expression were the same as those that resulted in the eventual break between the Palestinian Jesus Movement and others within the Jewish family and the formation of a "Christian" identity.... The literature of the New Testament belongs largely on the other side of the great watershed, before the break that led in such different directions.[38]

In sum, when examined in light of other contemporaneous literature, the New Testament presents a much greater continuity with first-century Palestinian Judaism than is often thought, particularly in the area of Christology. This continuity lends support to the assertions by Sommer and Boyarin about the Jewishness of what have heretofore been regarded as "Christian" ideas regarding God and the Messiah, and allows us to see New Testament Christology not so much as a rupture with the Jewish thinking of its time, but as a fulfillment of a certain type of Jewish hope and expectation regarding the nature and person of the Messiah. Jews can look at New Testament teachings regarding Jesus and see an element of their own religious heritage, an element that has been discarded and forgotten in later Jewish history but remains enshrined in the apocalyptic literature of the late Second Temple Period.

BIBLIOGRAPHY

Anglican Church of Canada. "39 Articles of Religion." Anglican Church of Canada, 1604. http://www.anglican.ca/about/beliefs/39-articles/.
Becker, Adam H. *The Fear of God and the Beginning of Wisdom: The School of Nisibis and Christian Scholastic Culture in Late Antique Mesopotamia*. Divinations: Rereading Late Ancient Religion. Philadelphia: University of Pennsylvania Press, 2006.
Boccaccini, Gabriele, ed. *Enoch and the Messiah Son of Man: Revisiting the Book of Parables*. Grand Rapids: Eerdmans, 2007.
Bock, Darrell L., and James H. Charlesworth, eds. *Parables of Enoch: A Paradigm Shift*. Jewish and Christian Texts. London: Bloomsbury, 2013.
Bond, Helen K., et al., eds. *Israel's God and Rebecca's Children: Christology and Community in Early Judaism and Christianity: Essays in Honor of Larry W.

---

38. Donal H. Juel, "The Future of a Religious Past: Qumran and the Palestinian Jesus Movement," in Charlesworth, *Bible and Dead Sea Scrolls*, 3:72.

Hurtado and Alan F. Segal. Library of Early Christology. Waco: Baylor University Press, 2007.

Boyarin, Daniel. *Border Lines: The Partition of Judaeo-Christianity*. Divinations: Rereading Late Ancient Religion. Philadelphia: University of Pennsylvania Press, 2007.

———. "Enoch, Ezra, and the Jewishness of 'High Christology.'" In *Fourth Ezra and Second Baruch: Reconstruction after the Fall*, edited by Matthias Henze et al., 337–62. SupJSJ 164. Leiden: Brill, 2013.

———. "Is Metatron a Converted Christian?" *Ancient Judaism* 1 (2013) 13–62.

———. *The Jewish Gospels: The Story of the Jewish Christ*. New York: New Press, 2012.

Charlesworth, James H., ed. *The Bible and the Dead Sea Scrolls: The Princeton Symposium on the Dead Sea Scrolls*. 3 vols. Waco: Baylor University Press, 2006.

———. "The Date and Provenience of the Parables of Enoch." In *Parables of Enoch: A Paradigm Shift*, edited by Darrell L. Bock and James H. Charlesworth, 37–57. T&T Clark Jewish and Christian Texts. London: Bloomsbury, 2013.

———. *Jesus' Jewishness: Exploring the Place of Jesus Within Early Judaism*. Philadelphia: American Interfaith Institute, 1991.

———. *The Messiah: Developments in Earliest Judaism and Christianity*. Minneapolis: Fortress, 1992.

Collins, Adela Yarbro. "How on Earth Did Jesus Become a God?" In *Israel's God and Rebecca's Children: Christology and Community in Early Judaism and Christianity; Essays in Honor of Larry W. Hurtado and Alan F. Segal*, edited by David B. Capes et al., 55–66. LEC. Waco: Baylor University Press, 2007.

Collins, John J. *The Scepter and the Star: Messianism in Light of the Dead Sea Scrolls*. 2nd ed. Grand Rapids: Eerdmans, 2010.

———. "The Son of Man in First-Century Judaism." *NTS* 38 (1991) 448–66.

Hamilton, Catherine Sider. *The Death of Jesus in Matthew: Innocent Blood and the End of Exile*. SNTSMS 167. New York: Cambridge University Press, 2017.

Henze, Matthias, et al. *Fourth Ezra and Second Baruch: Reconstruction After the Fall*. Supplements to the Journal for the Study of Judaism. Leiden: Brill, 2013.

Hurtado, Larry W. *How on Earth Did Jesus Become a God? Historical Questions About Earliest Devotion to Jesus*. Grand Rapids: Eerdmans, 2005.

Kohler, Kaufmann, and Emil G. Hirsch. "Articles of Faith." *Jewish Encyclopedia*, n.d. http://www.jewishencyclopedia.com/articles/1832-articles-of-faith.

Knibb, Michael A. *Essays on the Book of Enoch and Other Early Jewish Texts and Traditions*. Studia in Veteris Testamenti Pseudepigrapha 22. Leiden: Brill, 2009.

Neusner, Jacob, et al., eds. *Judaisms and Their Messiahs at the Turn of the Christian Era*. Cambridge: Cambridge University Press, 1987.

Nickelsburg, George, W. E. *Jewish Literature Between the Bible and the Mishnah*. 2nd ed. Minneapolis: Fortress, 2005.

Nickelsburg, George, W. E., and James C. VanderKam. *1 Enoch 2: A Commentary on the Book of 1 Enoch, Chapters 37–82*. Edited by Klaus Baltzer. Hermeneia. Minneapolis: Fortress, 2012

Olson, Daniel C. *Enoch: A New Translation*. North Richland Hills, TX: BIBAL, 2004.

Philo. *Philo*. Translated by F. H. Colson et al. 10 vols. LCL. Cambridge, MA: Harvard University Press, 1929–62.

Porter, Stanley E., ed. *The Nature of Religious Language: A Colloquium*. Roehampton Institute London Papers. Sheffield Academic, 1996.

Reid, Stephen Breck. *Enoch and Daniel*. Bibal Monograph Series 2. Berkeley, CA: BIBAL, 1989.

Segal, Alan F. *The Other Judaisms of Late Antiquity*. Library of Early Christology. Atlanta, GA: Scholars, 1987.

———. *Rebecca's Children: Judaism and Christianity in the Roman World*. Cambridge, MA: Harvard University Press, 1986.

———. *Two Powers in Heaven: Early Rabbinic Reports About Christianity and Gnosticism*. SJLA. Leiden: Brill, 1977.

Sommer, Benjamin D. *The Bodies of God and the World of Ancient Israel*. Cambridge: Cambridge University Press, 2009.

Stone, Michael Edward. *Fourth Ezra: A Commentary on the Book of Fourth Ezra*. Edited by Frank Moore Cross. Hermeneia. Minneapolis: Fortress, 1990.

Waddell, James A. *The Messiah: A Comparative Study of the Enochic Son of Man and the Pauline Kyrios*. Jewish and Christian Texts. London: T&T Clark, 2011.

Chapter 5

"You Are Gods"
Deification in Christianity and Judaism

Michael M. C. Reardon

WHEN DISCUSSING POTENTIAL INTERSECTIONS of Jewish and Christian theology, one might expect issues explicitly shared by both faiths, which to be sure, are rooted in a shared set of Scriptures, the Christian Old Testament/ Jewish Tanakh: commonalities in protology, anthropology, ethical norms, the role of a covenant defining the relationship between humankind and God, hermeneutic approaches, and so on. This volume's essays also illuminate potentially unexpected intersections of Jewish and Christian thought, such as closely aligned approaches to theodicy, unified ecclesiological possibilities, cooperative political arrangements, and the inclusion of Jewish sensibilities within the Christian New Testament. Yet even among these stimulating investigations, this chapter may appear to be a bridge too far. Several informal conversations I had with Jewish friends about the topic underscore this sentiment. Can deification—the possibility of humans becoming God, gods, or in some significant sense, divine—truly be an intersection of Jewish and Christian thought? This is what we set out to investigate in the ensuing pages.

To be sure, what follows is not a comprehensive analysis of deification in either faith. For Christian portrayals of deification, an ever-growing body of scholarship exists, of which I have contributed some insights.[1] Concerning

1. Reardon, "Becoming God"; Reardon, "You Adore a God"; Reardon and Copan,

the presence of deification within Jewish thought, able scholars such as Carl Mosser, Silviu Nicolae Bunta, M. David Litwa, and David Burnett have covered ample ground.[2] My singular aim, instead, is to place Christian and Jewish understandings of the doctrine in immediate proximity, and by doing so, demonstrate that a shared Jewish-Christian heritage of human beings being divinized exists (and further, that this heritage is not unidirectional in its trajectory—while Christians inherited an early Jewish exegetical tradition related to deification, Jews remained in contact with Christians beyond the first-century, and possibly assimilated Christian-adjacent ideas related to the intersection of anthropology and soteriology).

With this in mind, I have organized my essay as follows. Because deification is more readily understood to be part of the Christian tradition (though to be sure, is by no means universally affirmed by modern-day Christians), I do not present the *case* for Christian deification, which I have done in past publications. Instead, we begin the first section by examining key issues related to how deification is best expressed within a monotheistic framework: specifically, what deification *does* and *does not* entail. Though rooted in Christian theological reflection, issues and/or concerns raised in this section are equally relevant to the boundaries of deification in any monotheistic context, including Judaism. After briskly delineating differing understandings of the doctrine within Christianity, we turn to discussing scriptural bases for Christian deification, as this allows for easier comparison with Jewish midrashim.

The second section narrows its focus to examining key midrashim which articulate the notion of deification within the Jewish theological imagination. Care is taken to explicitly "make the case" for the presence of deification with Judaism. We conclude by synthesizing our findings, discussing both shared and dissimilar features of Christian and Jewish portrayals of deification, and by doing so, demonstrating that deification is indeed an intersection of Jewish and Christian thought.

CHRISTIAN DEIFICATION

The earliest definition of deification in the Christian tradition is offered by Pseudo-Dionysius: "The attaining of likeness to God and union with him so

---

Transformed into the Same Image. Also see the (currently) unpublished dissertation, Reardon, "So Also Is the Christ." The first four paragraphs of the next section are drawn from this latter work.

2. Mosser, "Earliest Patristic Interpretations"; Burnett, "So Shall Your Seed"; Bunta, *The Lord God of Gods*; Litwa, *Desiring Divinity*.

far as possible."³ This brief definition fails, however, to explicate numerous crucial dimensions—protological, anthropological, christological, pneumatological, ecclesiological, eschatological—and the (perhaps intentionally) vague phrase "union with him so far as possible" has been understood differently across time periods and theological traditions. Hence, in homage to Pseudo-Dionysius, the so-called father of the apophatic tradition, we begin by detailing what deification is *not*.

What Deification Does Not Entail

Against portrayals of the doctrine advanced by Mormonism and polytheistic mystical traditions, Christian deification disallows any notion of human beings becoming God in the Godhead. Fully deified human beings—whether presently or eschatologically—will never be exalted as objects of worship, and their deification never results "in any essential change in the Godhead, in the eternal, immutable, triune being of the one true and unique God."⁴ Additionally, deified human beings never share God's incommunicable attributes—i.e., his otherness, transcendence, omnipotence, omniscience, omnipresence, self-existence, or the ability to create ex nihilo.⁵

Moreover, humans cannot self-initiate the process of deification. Rather, as New Testament texts such as 2 Cor 5:21 and 8:9 indicate, it is only because God acted first via the incarnation that human beings now are enabled to partake of and participate in God.⁶ Last, humans are not, as Platonists and other Greco-Roman philosophical schools suggested, connatural with God—though by virtue of being created in the *imago Dei* there exists a close relationship.⁷ Rather, God is God according to "His very es-

---

3. Pseudo-Dionysius, *Ecclesiastical History* 1.3 AT. To be clear, this is the first *definition*—not expression or conception of deification. Numerous early Christian interpreters incorporated interchange statements and deification-imagery within their theologies. Irenaeus and Athanasius, for example, affirmed deification centuries earlier, stating that "the Word of God, our Lord Jesus Christ, who did, through His transcendent love, become what we are, that He might bring us to be even what He is Himself" (*Haer.* 5, preface) and "for He was made man that we might be made God" (*Inc.* 54) (Russell, *Doctrine of Deification*, 21).

4. Kangas, "Becoming God," 3.

5. Robichaux, "Can Human Beings Become God?," 40.

6. Compare to Gorman, *Participating in Christ*, 214–35. In 2 Cor 5:21 it is *because* Christ becomes sin that humans become righteousness; in 2 Cor 8:9, it is *because* Christ becomes poor that humans become rich; in patristic language, it is *because* God became flesh that humans can become gods.

7. For example, Plato and the neo-Platonist philosopher Plotinus believed that souls possess an uncreated portion, and thus, share kinship with the divine realm—for Plato,

sence" while "human beings are made gods by participation in the unique God."[8] The church fathers were unequivocally clear about these concerns; a common patristic description of deification was the unique God is God by nature while humans only become gods by grace.[9] For example, Augustine discusses the distinction between the unique God, deified human beings, and pagan idols:

> Our God, the true God, the one God 'stood in the assembly of gods,' that is of many gods, not by nature, but by adoption, by grace. There is a great difference between on the one hand the God who is, the God who is always God, the true God, not the only God, but indeed the god-making God, so to speak, the deifying God, the unmade God who makes gods, and on the other hand gods who become such—but not by a craftsman.[10]

While the Christian tradition near-universally affirms the above circumscriptions of deification, controversy emerges when promulgating cataphatic statements—that is, statements which positively describe with deification *is*.

What Deification Does Entail

Though many taxonomies of deification exist,[11] the limited scope of our discussion requires only a cursory introduction. For this, we turn to Norman Russell's watershed volume, *The Doctrine of Deification in the Greek Patristic Tradition*. Russell suggests that the early church held variegated conceptions of deification broadly aligned with three categories—nominal, analogical, or metaphorical—with metaphorical usage broken down into ethical and realistic categories, and the realistic category further divided between ontological and dynamic understandings.

Nominal deification involved attaching honorifics to notable persons and analogical usage pertains to assigning divinity to human beings without

---

with the realm of Forms; for Plotinus, with the transcendent One (Louth, *Origins of Christian Mystical Tradition*, 14–41). Additionally, Aristotelians, Cynics, Stoics, and Epicureans similarly argued for the kinship of humanity with the divine realm (see Jervis, "Becoming Like God Through Christ").

8. Robichaux, "Can Human Beings Become God," 37.

9. E.g., Cyril, Athanasius, Jerome, Augustine, Symeon the New Theologian.

10. Augustine, *Homily on Psalm 81*, in Casiday, "St. Augustine on Deification," 29.

11. E.g., Blackwell, *Christosis*, xxii–xxiii, 104–8; Popov, "Idea of Deification"; Borysov, *Triadosis*, 18–83, 195; Fairbairn, "Patristic Soteriology"; McGinn, "Love, Knowledge, and *Unio Mystica*."

an explicit transformative process. Metaphorical usage, on the other hand, is more important to our present concerns, as it is most often what readers assume when deification is discussed. "Ethical" portrayals of deification suggest that likeness with God is achieved through "ascetic and philosophical endeavor whereas "realistic" conceptions assume "that humans are in some sense transformed by deification." As noted, "realistic" approaches are further divided into "ontological" understandings, which posit that human nature is transformed by virtue of the incarnation, and "dynamic" understandings, where human nature is understood to be transformed via the sacraments.[12]

Even without further discussion of these possibilities, it is readily apparent that a wide range of Christian understandings of deification existed in the early church; subsequent traditions arising from each of these understandings further refined, reimagined, and systematized the notion of deification in response to adjacent doctrinal concerns (e.g., anthropology, soteriology). For example, in the Greek East, a strict distinction between God's essence and energies arose was identified and later formalized by Gregory Palamas. This view purports that humans only participate in God's energies, but never his essence. On the other hand, in the Latin West a desire to maintain divine simplicity persuaded many thinkers that humans participate in God's essence without *comprehending* his essence. Thinkers both within and apart from these traditions held (and continue to hold) their own particular outlooks concerning the extent to which human beings participate in the divine essence. The point here is not to get bogged down in metaphysical or philosophical categories, but rather to demonstrate a significant diversity of possibilities related to how deification is understood within the Christian tradition. This is especially noteworthy, as we will encounter a similar variability when examining Jewish portrayals of the doctrine.

Scriptural Bases for Christian Deification

It is now widely accepted that one of the most important verses related to deification for patristic Christians was drawn from the shared Scriptures of Jews and Christians—"I said, 'You are gods, sons of the Most High, all of you" (Ps 82:6 ESV). Carl Mosser notes that three of the most important ante-Nicene fathers—Justin Martyr, Irenaeus of Lyons, and Clement of Alexandria—comment on this verse multiple times, as well as on its surrounding context, not only to demonstrate its relationship to soteriology,

---

12. Russell, *Doctrine of Deification*, 1–3.

but also to trace the trajectory of the human creature—created in the *imago Dei* (image of God), damaged by the fall, and awaiting a promised eschatological restoration to godlikeness.[13] Below are sample quotes drawn from each of the three thinkers that link Ps 82 to deification:

> It is proved that all human beings are deemed worthy of becoming gods and of having the power to become sons of the Most High, and will be judged and condemned on their own account like Adam and Eve.[14]

> And again: "God stood in the congregation of the gods, He judges among the gods" [Ps 82:1]. He refers to the Father and the Son, and those who have received the adoption; but these are the Church.... Of whom He again speaks: "The God of gods, the Lord has spoken, and has called the earth" [Ps 50:1]. ... But who are these gods? Those to whom He says, "I have said You are gods, and all sons of the Most High" [Ps 82:6]. To those, no doubt, who have received the grace of the "sonship, by which we cry, Abba Father" [Rom 8:15].[15]

> It is time, then, for us to say that the pious Christian alone is rich and wise, and of noble birth, and thus call and believe him to be God's image, and also his likeness, having become righteous and holy and wise by Jesus Christ, and so far already like God. Accordingly this grace is indicated by the prophet, when he says, "I said that you are gods, and all sons of the Highest." For us, yea us, he has adopted, and wishes to be called the Father of us alone, not of the unbelieving.[16]

Equally important, insofar as it underscores the significance of the verse within the Christian imagination—is the fact that Ps 82:6 is restated by Jesus himself in John 10:34–35. The crux of interpretative possibilities related to this profound statement repeated twice in Christian Scripture, apart from

---

13. One of the first scholars to underscore the importance of this verse was Carl Mosser in a superb article entitled "The Earliest Patristic Interpretations of Psalm 82, Jewish Antecedents, and the Origin of Christian Deification." Mosser persuasively demonstrates that these three thinkers remained within a trajectory of Second Temple Jewish interpretations of Ps 82:6 that affirmed the doctrine of deification, as opposed to the past consensus advanced by Adolf Harnack and others who argued that patristic conceptions of deification relied upon the incorporation of Hellenistic philosophy in Christianity.

14. Justin Martyr, *Dialogue with Trypho* 124, quoted in Russell, *Doctrine of Deification*, 99.

15. Irenaeus, *Haer.* 3.6.1 AT.

16. Clement of Alexandria, *Protrepticus* 7.122.4–7.123.1, quoted in Mosser, "Earliest Patristic Interpretations," 55.

whatever emphases or nuances articulated by various interpreters, is fairly straightforward: it provides an indisputable basis to identify human beings as gods *in some sense*.

An elementary feature of New Testament studies is that this collection of twenty-seven epistles was not produced in a vacuum, and in fact, exhibits many features in line with Jewish theological reflection during the Second Temple period.[17] To be clear, being "in line" with such thought does not entail wholesale agreement with prior literature. The New Testament obviously contains *substantial* theological development beyond the boundaries of what might be considered "acceptable" Jewish thinking during the time period; but perhaps not. For example, speculation concerning prophecies related to the messiah and his identity was especially pregnant during the first century AD—a fact that is attested to within the New Testament itself by Gamaliel, the Pharisaic teacher of the apostle Paul (Acts 5:34–39). The point I wish to make here, without delving into particularities or alternative views at this time (due to lack of space and not desire!), is that there is a significant basis to understand the New Testament as a collection of texts extending from—as opposed to being entirely alien or contrary to—Jewish thought in the first century. This includes commentary about the possibility of human deification.

Second Peter 1:4 is a classic proof text utilized by Christians in support of deification, of which the most important phrase is quoted: "So that through them you may become partakers of the divine nature" (ESV). What may be surprising to many readers, however, is that Russell and others have conclusively demonstrated that this verse's popularity when discussing deification—so popular that, for example, it is the only Scripture cited in a host of venues ranging from the article on deification in Wiley's *Encyclopedia of Christian Civilization* to the lay level, but nevertheless highly regarded *OrthodoxWiki* on *theosis*—is a rather late development in church history.[18] Deification finds support in the Johannine corpus as well, including multiple passages in the Gospel of John which speak of the incorporative union and participation of believers in and with God, as well as an explicit reference in 1 John 3:2: "Beloved, we are God's children now, and what we will be

---

17. For example, the entire Sept. 2018 issue of the highly influential *JSNT* was devoted to "Reading the New Testament as Second Temple Literature." Moreover, numerous scholars such as Gerald McDermott have published volumes examining the intimate relationship between Jewish thought and Christian origins (e.g., McDermott, *Understanding the Jewish Roots of Christianity*—and in fact, I am a good friend of Gerald and have taught several courses examining the deep roots of Jewish influence in Christian origins. Other authors have published acclaimed volumes such as Brad Young's *Jesus the Jewish Theologian* and *Paul the Jewish Theologian*.

18. Kurian, "Divinization or Deification"; OrthodoxWiki, "Theosis."

has not yet appeared; but we know that when he appears *we shall be like him*, because we shall see him as he is" (ESV, emphasis added).[19]

However, as someone trained first in Pauline studies, I will leave the follow schematic below, with little comment, to articulate a fulsome Pauline understanding of deification::

1. Deification is predicated upon believers receiving a new life—i.e., the life of God (Phil 1:21; Gal 2:20; Col 3:4). Paul describes the reception of this new life with birth-imagery (Rom 8:22–23; Gal 4:19) and the language of sonship (Rom 8:14–17, 23; Gal 4:6; Eph 1:5), which implies both a familial and filial relationship between humans and God.

2. Deification is also predicated upon a perichoretic union between persons—

3. The mutual indwelling of Christ in human beings (Rom 8:10; 1 Cor 13:5; Gal 2:20) and human beings in Christ (Rom 12:5; 2 Cor 5:17; Gal 3:28).

4. Deification is effected by a pneumatic union and infusion of the Spirit with(in) human beings. Humans are "joined to the Lord" and made "one spirit" with Him (1 Cor 6:17). The Spirit infuses the life of God throughout the inward parts of human beings and secures the perichoretic union between Christ and human beings (and even, the entire triune God and human beings) (Rom 8:2–11; see also 1 Cor 12:12–13).

5. Deification is characterized by ongoing participation in Christ, his works, his attainments, and his obtainments. Human beings are enabled to participate in Christ's sufferings (Rom 8:17; 2 Cor 4:8–12; 12:1–10; Phil 1:29, 3:10), death (Rom 6:3–8; 2 Cor 4:10–11; Gal 2:20, 6:15), resurrection (Rom 6:5, 8:11; Phil 3:10; Eph 2:5; Col 3:1), and ascension (Eph 2:6). In this way Christ's life and works are not merely historical events, but present spiritual realities that formatively shape believers' lives.

6. Deification entails an ontological transformation whereby human beings are presently being transformed into the image of the glory of Christ (2 Cor 3:18; 4:4) and conformed to the image of the firstborn Son of God (Rom 8:29), who is the image of God (Col 1:15). This process consummates in the eschatological glorification of their bodies (Phil 3:21; 2 Cor 4:17; Col 3:4). Stated differently, deified humans undergo a process in which they progressively express God more fully

---

19. Two exemplary studies of deification in the Johannine corpus: Byers, *Ecclesiology and Theosis*; Gorman, *Abide and Go*.

(per Paul, from "glory to glory") over the course of their lives and to the greatest degree at the Parousia.

7. Aside from general statements about transformation, Paul expresses more specific claims. Believers are transformed not merely to imitate God and *be* righteous, but even to *become* righteousness (2 Cor 5:21; see also 1 Cor 1:30); not merely to imitate Christ, but even to inwardly possess and outwardly express him (1 Cor 2:16; Phil 2:5–8; 3:1–10). Thus, in addition to expressing God's glory and sonship, believers also possess and express Christ's divine nature.

8. Pauline deification has a telos—not individual transformation, which is merely the *means* God uses to accomplish his goal, but the corporate transformation (Rom 12:2; 2 Cor 3:18; 5:21) of believers into a unified (id)entity known as the body of Christ (Rom 12:5) and even Christ (1 Cor 12:12). The joining of individual believers with one another to form this (id)entity is actuated by the same pneumatic union that joins them to God and Christ (1 Cor 12:13; 6:17).

With the above depiction of Christian deification addressed, we move onto examining Jewish portrayals of the doctrine.

JEWISH DEIFICATION

As noted at the outset, Jewish friends of mine found it strange, bordering on absurd, that I would write a chapter about deification for this book. I nevertheless have done so—not to be outrageous or incendiary, but with humility, to explore a true, yet often overlooked, intersection between the two faiths. With this in mind, I open this section not by articulating my own claims, but an insight from Silviu Nicolae Bunta's superb exploration of Jewish literature spanning from the preexilic era to classical rabbinic teaching. Speaking on deification theology within Second Temple literature, Bunta contends that:

> The only limit is confusion—the deified gods can receive the entire treatment of God, even worship, but as *gods* and not as *God*. And indeed in these texts confusions are rare, so lessons in exclusion are rarely given. The point is theological: God is revealed as shared and unshared at once.[20]

The first half of this quote is a somewhat remarkable claim given that Judaism is often portrayed as advancing a stricter monotheistic framework than

20. Bunta, *Lord God of Gods*, 3; emphasis in original.

Christianity. Yet, it bears true. Qumranic texts such as 4Q491c and 4Q427 exhibit virtually no distinction between deified humans and God—though to be clear, they are exceptions and not the normative model of Jewish deification theology.[21]

The more salient point Bunta makes, however—i.e., that most Jewish thinkers reject any notion of confusion between the deified and God—is both highly significant and equally applicable to Christian proponents of the doctrine. Because the aim of this chapter is not merely academic, but focused upon demonstrating that deification is a genuine intersection of Christian and Jewish thought that can be utilized in modern-day dialogue, our ensuing discussion is limited only to portrayals of deification that are most plausible within the context of shared understandings leading to fruitful dialogue (i.e., I focus only on texts in which deified humans do not receive worship, which the vast majority of both Christians and Jews would reject out-of-hand as being entirely alien to their understanding(s) of God).

Scriptural Bases for Jewish Deification

Jewish portrayals of deification are not formally developed in the same manner or to the same degree as Christian articulations of the doctrine. Classic rabbinic texts do not employ specific technical terms for deification (e.g., Hebrew equivalents of *theosis* (Gk.) or *deificare* (Lt.)). Yet, we shall see that the absence of developed philosophical frameworks or specific vocabulary should not be equated with the absence of the *notion* of deification within Judaism. The potential for humans to be deified is, in fact, well attested in numerous Jewish texts. We begin with a Tannaitic interpretation of Ps 82, as it nicely parallels our previous discussion of Christian interpretations of the passage:

> R. Simai used to say further: Both the soul and body of creatures created from heaven are from heaven; both the soul and body of those creatures created from the earth are from earth, except for that one creature, man, whose soul is from heaven and whose body is from earth. Therefore, if man lives by the Torah and performs the will of his Father in heaven, he is like the heavenly creatures, as it is said, 'I said, Ye are godlike beings, and all of you are sons of the Most High (Ps. 82:6). But if he does not live by the Torah and does not perform the will of his Father in heaven,

---

21. For further reading, see Bunta, *Lord God of Gods*, 181–89.

he is like the creatures of the earth, as it is said, 'Nevertheless ye shall die like Adam' (Ps. 82:7).[22]

This passage contains two distinguishing features. First, the author explicitly demarcates humankind from the rest of God's creation—This, of course, hearkens back to Christian reflections which emphasize the significance of the creation of humankind in the image and likeness of God. Second, and most importantly, the author ties the faithful performance of individuals to the Torah as resulting in being divine *in some sense*—that is, being "like the heavenly creatures," and importantly like "godlike beings" spoken of in Ps 82. Intriguingly, it appears that Jewish *and* Christian interpretations of this passage (and as will be seen, several others) "share more features with each other than either one shares with a plain-sense reading" of this particular psalm.[23]

These two features—the link between the creation of humanity and deification, and the notion that the faithful observance of Torah results in human deification—is articulated by Jewish commentators elsewhere. In an important essay entitled "Theosis Through Works of the Law: Deification of the Earthly Righteous," Rabbi Jonah Steinberg identifies multiple midrashim from Genesis Rabbah, which taken together, illuminate a "distinctive rabbinic concept of divinization."[24] Genesis Rabbah 8:10, for instance, comments upon Gen 1:26 in a striking manner:

> Rabbi Hoshaya said: At the moment with the Blessed Holy One created the first human being, the ministering angels mistook him and sought to say before him, "Holy!" . . . What did the Blessed Holy One do? He cast a deep sleep upon him, and then all knew that he was the human being.[25]

Steinberg shrewdly notes that this passage demonstrates that the humankind was originally created as "a convincing likeness to God"—so much so that even angelic beings were utterly befuddled. Indeed, it was only through the "idleness" of sleep being cast upon Adam that humankind could eventually be identified as being dissimilar to God.[26]

---

22. *Sifre to Deuteronomy*, quoted in Russell, *Doctrine of Deification*, 73. Russell notes that this "is a Tannaitic on Numbers and Deuteronomy" and "was a product of the school of R. Akiba."

23. Kaminsky, "Paradise Regained," 17.

24. Steinberg, "Theosis Through Works of the Law," 50.

25. Quoted in Steinberg, "Theosis Through Works of the Law," 51.

26. Steinberg, "Theosis Through Works of the Law," 52.

Qumranic commentators similarly identified the significance of humankind's divine appearance (and divine attributes) during the Genesis narrative of creation:

> My eyes have gazed on that which is eternal,
> on wisdom and concealed from men,
> on knowledge and wise design (hidden) from the sons of men;
> on a fountain of righteousness and on a storehouse of power,
> on a spring of glory (hidden) from the assembly of flesh.
> God has given to them His chosen ones as an everlasting possession,
> and caused them to inherit the lots of the Holy Ones.
> He has joined their assembly to the Sons of Heaven
> to be a Council of Community,
> a fountain of the Building of Holiness,
> and eternal Plantation throughout all ages to come.[27]

This text is far more explicit than the midrash from Genesis Rabbah—it is not just a case of mistaken identity by angels, but rather, *the revelation of humankind's true identity as being at least equal to, if not greater than angels.* Humankind, according to the author, was chosen to have an everlasting possession, to inherit "the lots of the Holy Ones," to join the assembly of the "Sons of Heaven," and so on. There is a divinely ordered imbuing of characteristics of divinity such as immortality upon humanity and an identification of human beings as properly belonging to the celestial (and indeed, divine) realm.

Two additional midrashim from Genesis Rabbah are significant insofar as they expand upon the discussion of *how* humans are deified. The first resolves an apparent textual contradiction in Gen 18 related to Abraham and his three visitors:[28]

> "And he stood over them"—Here you say "he stood over them," but earlier it says "standing over him."
> Rather understand it thus: Until he had done right by them, *they stood over him.* One he had done right by them, *he stood over them.* The awe of him was cast upon them. The angel Michael trembled, the angel Gabriel trembled.[29]

This passage is important since it demonstrates how "Abraham achieves his superiority; it is not inevitable." Abraham is able to climb the 'cosmic

---

27. Qumranic text, quoted in Russell, *Doctrine of Deification*, 69.

28. In Gen 18:2, the text states the visitors stand "over" Abraham, but in Gen 18:8 it states that Abraham "stood over them."

29. Quoted in Steinberg, "Theosis Through Works of the Law," 52.

hierarchy,' so to speak, by performing a righteous act; so significant is his work of righteousness that even the chief angelic beings Michael and Gabriel are awestruck and tremble before him. While Adam's godlikeness was diminished by his "idleness" in Gen 1, Steinberg underscores a key lesson from Abraham's experience in Gen 18: "the human being can regain divine glory through righteous action."[30]

Another midrash, Gen. Rab. 68:12, comments upon a linguistic oddity in Gen 28:12. Though the verse speaks of Jacob's vision of a ladder, the noun is masculine in Hebrew, which allows it to be rendered as "him" as opposed to "it"—in other words, for *Jacob* to be a "ladder" joining heaven to earth. Though space disallows adequate treatment of this midrash, the passage contains three key statements which complete Steinberg's synthesis of classic rabbinic deification theology:

> As to the one who says, "Ascending and descending on Jacob"—
> They were extolling and disparaging him, poking him, prodding him, goading him, as it is said, *"Israel in who I [God] shall glorify myself."* (Isa. 42:1)
>   'You are he whose image is engraved on high!'
> They would ascend above and see his image; descend below and find him asleep.
>   The matter can be likened to a king, who sat and judged. Go up to the palace and one finds him judging. Go out to the outskirts and one finds him asleep.[31]

While the text at first glance appears to suggest that angels are diminishing or mocking Jacob, the passage underscores two significant items. First, Jacob's image is engraved in heaven, which in Jewish thought is suggestive of his image being linked to or even borne upon the throne of God. Second, the likeness of Jacob to this heavenly image is directly tied to his activity, or in this situation, his lack of activity while sleeping—which, we note, aligns with what we observed in Gen. Rab. 8:10—Adam possessed extraordinary godlikeness, yet an eventual dissimilarity from God through idleness. This is especially fascinating as it indicates that it was sufficient for Jacob to have a vision of heaven being joined to earth; as the author intimates, just as is the case with a king, his rulership and identity only have true utility when exercised through action. These two items allow Steinberg to round out his depiction of rabbinic deification theology in an especially illuminating manner: "It is not enough for the human being to envision or contemplate

---

30. Steinberg, "Theosis Through Works of the Law," 54.
31. Steinberg, "Theosis Through Works of the Law," 55.

connection with God; to realize divine identity one must stand up and act in the world."[32]

Though space constraints disallow investigating additional examples of Jewish deification, they are plentiful and include: (1) commentary in multiple Jewish texts (1 Enoch, Testament of Moses, 4 Ezra, 4 Maccabees) that affirm the belief that "in the resurrection or the afterlife the righteous were to in some sense become as the stars or angels";[33] (2) texts discussing the deification of Moses[34] and the deification of Daniel;[35] and (3) midrashic commentary related to Adam which speculates about the enormity of his created body filling the entire earth,[36] his created body being luminous or light itself,[37] and his omniscience prior to the fall.[38] For now, however, we conclude this section with a passage from Deuteronomy Rabbah, which as was the case with many of the passages examined thus far, dovetails with Christian understandings of deification:

> Rabbi Levi said: Just as one who serves idols becomes like them, as it is said, "Like them shall be their makers" (Ps 115:8), he who serves the Holy Blessed One will, all the more so, be like him.[39]

CONCLUSION

Christianity and Judaism possess a shared heritage of affirming deification. Much of the overlap between the two faiths in this regard is the result of interpreting deiform intentionality in texts such as Ps 82 and Gen 1:26, and thereafter, constructing theological frameworks which relate these texts to other scriptural narratives. Of course, differences in how deification is handled by Christians and Jews also exist. For our present purposes, I offer the briefest of outlines discussing the role of deification in the two faith traditions.

Deification looms large in the earliest centuries of Christianity. The doctrine's formative role during the patristic era gave rise to the creation of specialized technical terms such as *theosis, apotheosis, theopoiesis*, and

32. Steinberg, "Theosis Through Works of the Law," 58.
33. Burnett, "So Shall Your Seed Be," 231.
34. Bunta, *Lord God of Gods*, 131–55; 173–80.
35. Bunta, *Lord God of Gods*, 157–71.
36. Bunta, *Lord God of Gods*, 243–57.
37. Bunta, *Lord God of Gods*, 225–41.
38. Bunta, *Lord God of Gods*, 259–65.
39. Cited in Steinberg, "Theosis Through Works of the Law," 71.

many more in the Greek East; *deificare, deificatus*, and the like in the Latin West; and a plentitude of illustrations (e.g., iron in a fire; light rays from the sun) in both theological hemispheres. The development of the doctrine also required the creation of philosophical frameworks to square deification with an unabashed affirmation of God being utterly transcendent with no peers. We did not delve into these competing theological frameworks, but to be clear, they include a wide spectrum of possibilities: deification through sacraments or without them; deification via asceticism or not; deification through passive contemplation or active participation; deification being metaphorical, analogical, or ontological; and so on. While our present discussion did not necessitate examining these particularities, these issues surely warrants careful examination in other contexts.

Jewish deification, on the other hand, was not developed within especially robust philosophical frameworks nor is it identified within rabbinic texts with specialized or technical language. It is, nevertheless, a reality affirmed by numerous Jewish commentators and evident in numerous Jewish texts. In some passages, it aligns more with an increasingly utilized notion of "angelification" within modern scholarship; we did not examine such texts. In other instances, Jewish authors dissolved nearly all dissimilarity between God and human "gods," at least to the extent that the latter could receive worship and participate in attributes such as divine omniscience. Again, we did not examine such texts in this chapter. But in the texts *we did examine* we found strikingly similar interpretations of texts utilized by Christian proponents of the doctrine—as well as an overarching emphasis not found in Christianity. While Christian deification is primarily Christocentric—that is, prioritizing both of the incarnation of Jesus Christ and the glorification of his humanity actuated during his resurrection—Jewish portrayals of deification prioritize acts of righteousness in alignment with the observance of Torah. This, of course, is a significant and concrete difference in how deification is understood within the two faith traditions.

Yet, it need not short circuit dialogue between practitioners of the two faiths. Human beings are created in the image and likeness of God. Both Jews and Christians affirm this fact. Human beings may, through participation in God become divine in various aspects. Both Jews and Christian affirm this fact. Human beings who are in right relationship to the God of Abraham, Isaac, and Jacob may, by the mercy of God, attain to a status that elevates them above all other creatures, and in a significant sense, causes them to inhabit the same "species" as the God they worship. Both Christians and Jews affirm this fact. In the months and years ahead, there will be ample opportunities to dialogue about each faith tradition's particularities related to deification; indeed, this occurred during the first several centuries of the Common Era between Jewish and Christian contemporaries. But the key conclusion is this: deification, while prima facie an unexpected commonality between Christianity and Judaism, is a genuine basis for Jews and Christians to stand shoulder to shoulder with one another, to not view one another as the "other," but as kinfolk of the same olive tree (Rom 11). May it be so in the coming months and years as we know one another not according to the flesh, but in our corporate identities as the "seed of Abraham."

BIBLIOGRAPHY

Blackwell, Ben C. *Christosis: Engaging Pauline Soteriology with His Patristic Interpreters*. Grand Rapids: Eerdmans, 2016.

Borysov, Eduard. *Triadosis: Union with the Triune God—Interpretations of the Participationist Dimensions of Paul's Soteriology*. Eugene, OR: Pickwick, 2019.

Bunta, Silviu Nicolae. *The Lord God of Gods: Divinity and Deification in Early Judaism*. Perspectives on Hebrew Scriptures and Its Contents 35. Piscataway, NJ: Gorgias, 2016.

Burnett, David. "'So Shall Your Seed Be': Paul's Use of Genesis 15:5 in Romans 4:18 in Light of Early Jewish Deification Traditions." *Journal for the Study of Paul and His Letters* 5 (2015) 211–36.

Byers, Andrew J. *Ecclesiology and Theosis in the Gospel of John*. SNTSMS 166. Cambridge: Cambridge University Press, 2017.

Casiday, Augustine. "St. Augustine on Deification: His Homily on Psalm 81." *Sobernost* 23 (2001) 23–44.

Fairbairn, Donald. "Patristic Soteriology: Three Trajectories." *JETS* 50 (2007) 289–310.

Gorman, Michael J. *Abide and Go: Missional Theosis in the Gospel of John*. Didsbury Lectures. Eugene, OR: Cascade, 2018.

———. *Participating in Christ: Explorations in Paul's Theology and Spirituality*. Grand Rapids: Baker Academic, 2019.

Jervis, L. Ann. "Becoming Like God Through Christ: Discipleship in Romans." In *Patterns of Discipleship in the New Testament*, edited by Richard N. Longenecker, 143–62. McMaster New Testament Studies. Grand Rapids: Eerdmans, 1996.

Kaminsky, Joel S. "Paradise Regained: Rabbinic Reflections on Israel at Sinai." In *Jews, Christians, and the Theology of the Hebrew Scriptures*, edited by Alice Ogden Bellis and Joel S. Kaminsky, 15–43. SemeiaSt. Atlanta: Society of Biblical Literature, 2000.

Kangas, Ron. "Becoming God." *Affirmation & Critique* 7 (2002) 3–30.

Kurian, George Thomas. "Divinization or Deification." In *The Encyclopedia of Christian Civilization*. N.p.: Wiley Academic, 2012. E-book.

Litwa, M. David. *Desiring Divinity: Self-Deification in Early Jewish and Christian Mythmaking*. Oxford: Oxford University Press, 2016.

Louth, Andrew. *The Origins of the Christian Mystical Tradition: From Plato to Denys*. Oxford: Oxford University Press, 2007.

McDermott, Gerald R., ed. *Understanding the Jewish Roots of Christianity: Biblical, Theological, and Historical Essays on the Relationship Between Christianity and Judaism*. Bellingham, WA: Lexham, 2021.

McGinn, Bernard. "Love, Knowledge, and *Unio Mystica* in the Western Christian Tradition." In Moshe Idel and Bernard McGinn, *Mystical Union in Judaism, Christianity, and Islam: An Ecumenical Dialogue*, 59–86. Bloomsbury Academic Collections; Religious Studies: Comparative Religions. London: Bloomsbury Academic, 2016.

Mosser, Carl. "The Earliest Patristic Interpretations of Psalm 82, Jewish Antecedents, and the Origin of Christian Deification." *JTS* 56 (2005) 30–74.

OrthodoxWiki. "Theosis." OrthodoxWiki, last edited Apr. 9, 2012. https://orthodoxwiki.org/Theosis.

Popov, Ivan. "The Idea of Deification in the Early Eastern Church." In *Theosis: Deification in Christian Theology*, edited by Vladimir Kharlamov, 2:42–82. Eugene, OR: Pickwick, 2011.

Reardon, Michael M. C. "Becoming God: Interpreting Pauline Soteriology as Deification." *CurBR* 22 (2023) 83–107.

———. "'So Also Is the Christ: Ecclesial Deification in Pauline Soteriology." PhD diss., University of Toronto, 2023.

———. "'You Adore a God Who Makes You Gods': Augustine's Doctrine of Deification." *Hor* 51 (2024) 104–33.

Reardon, Michael M. C., and Paul Copan, eds. *Transformed into the Same Image: Constructive Investigations into the Doctrine of Deification*. Downers Grove, IL: IVP Academic, 2024.

Robichaux, Kerry S. "Can Human Beings Become God?" *Affirmation & Critique* 7 (2002) 31–46.

Russell, Norman. *The Doctrine of Deification in the Greek Patristic Tradition*. OECS. Oxford: Oxford University Press, 2004.

Steinberg, Jonah Chanan. "Theosis Through Works of the Law: Deification of the Earthly Righteous." In *Crossing Boundaries in Early Judaism and Christianity: Ambiguities, Complexities, and Half-Forgotten Adversaries; Essays in Honor of Alan F. Segal*, edited by Kimberley Stratton and Andrea Lieber, 41–73. Supplements to the Journal for the Study of Judaism 177. Leiden: Brill, 2016.

Young, Brad H. *Jesus the Jewish Theologian*. Peabody, MA: Hendrickson, 2008.

———. *Paul the Jewish Theologian: A Pharisee Among Christians, Jews, and Gentiles*. Peabody, MA: Hendrickson, 1997.

Chapter 6

Holiness That Does Not Separate

Bridging the Gap Between Christian Models of Sanctification and Jewish Approaches to Holiness

Rafael Bello

INTRODUCTION

APPEALS IN THE JEWISH and Christian traditions to the קְדֻשָּׁה (*qʾdushá*) word group as an approach to the doctrine of holiness or sanctification is common. To be "set apart" however, is only one dimension of what holiness is within the Christian and Jewish traditions. In this chapter, I retrieve some insights into the doctrine of holiness from the Jewish tradition in order to bridge the gap with the common division of models in the Christian tradition on the doctrine of sanctification. In the Christian tradition, the doctrine of sanctification is divided into *models*: Wesleyan, Keswick, Reformed, etc. These models describe different ways one becomes "devoted," or "separated" for the Lord.

In orthodox Judaism, despite some variegation, the concept of holiness and/or sanctification boasts common loci and explanations within the tradition, broadly construed. The Shema and Lev 20 enjoy regular acceptance within all theologies of holiness. The article will discuss some of the common talmudic commentaries explanations on these sections as they relate to being set apart, and thereafter, medieval commentaries authored by Maimonides as sources of interpretation of Jewish theology of holiness. It is through Maimonides's conception of holiness as virtue and moderation that I will sketch a common source for a theology of sanctification. Whereas many Christian models state that people ought to grow in the likeness of God, I believe that Maimonides's relation of virtue and the law generates a profitable pathway for the description of the mechanism of how one ought to be holy like God is holy. Maimonides's description serves as a bridge between the Christian models of sanctification and the Orthodox conception of holiness.

The disputes in Christian and Jewish traditions may hardly be reconcilable in their intramural debates, but by understanding the mechanism and the role of the law in devotion, specifically in Jewish theology, one may be able to find interesting parallels between the different Christian models of sanctification and the different approaches to "separateness" in Jewish talmudic readings. For example, there may be interesting parallels between a Reformed approach to sanctification as progressive (*duplex gratia*) and the Jewish restrictions of the law as enforceable. The article will not only trace these parallels but sketch a reason of tendencies in Christian and Jewish theologies that lead thinkers in these directions.

CHRISTIAN CONCEPTIONS OF HOLINESS

In the Christian tradition, the doctrine of sanctification/holiness is often discussed in terms of differing models. "Models" here is an important category, and should be distinguished from the notion of doctrines. Oliver Crisp states that a model is a "theoretical construction that only approximates to the truth of the matter, offering a simplified account of a particular data set."[1] Doctrines on the other hand are—or at the least, should be—reflections of Scripture. Assuming Scripture is the *norma normans* of all Christian

---

1. Crisp, "Parsimonious Model of Divine Simplicity," 561. Crisp cites Ian G. Barbour, *Religion and Science*, as saying, "Models and theories are abstract symbol systems, which inadequately and selectively represent particular aspects of the world for specific purposes. This view preserves the scientist's realistic intent while recognizing that models and theories are imaginative human constructs. Models, on this reading, are to be taken seriously but not literally; they are neither literal pictures nor useful fictions but limited and inadequate ways of imagining what is not observable. They make tentative ontological claims that there are entities in the world something like those postulated in the models."

reflection, doctrines are judgments of scriptural concepts and therefore exegesis of a larger scale, a movement of biblical reasoning.[2]

Therefore, discussions within the Christian tradition that try to encapsulate the vision of the holy life should not attempt to describe the totality of this living in the movement of man's relation to God and God's relation to man. These models are an approximate reflection upon the doctrine of holiness. Holiness per se lives within the happy land of *mystery*. It is an invitation to plunder into the deep life of God without exhausting that life. Such conception will be helpful when looking for the relationship between Christianity and Judaism.

So, the following models cannot be faulted for not being comprehensive in relation to the scriptural portrayal of sanctification. In each model there may be aspects not covered in the other that may represent a facet of the *doctrine* of sanctification. What is going to suffice as a critique of a preferred adopted *model* is not that it does not cover every aspect, since models cannot, by definition, do so. However, the problem is that a *model* of sanctification must at least account for the mechanism of change. Every single model described below should provide an account of how people change.

Andy Naselli suggests that evangelical Christians hold to at least five different *models* of sanctification: the Wesleyan model, the higher life (or Keswick) model, the Pentecostal model, the Chaferian model, and the Reformed model.[3]

Wesleyan Model

John Wesley (1703–91) is commonly known as one who created a chronology from salvation to sanctification. The idea of Christian perfectionism is developed in his theology. However, far from advocating total perfection per se, he qualifies it as a kind of perfection that is contrasted with Adamic or angelic perfection. Wesley does this to create levels of will and create a spectrum of transgression of law, so that a sin is usually connected to intention.

Perfection is then a second work of grace. This second blessing is akin to a realized eschatology, for it is in this second work of God's grace that we experience "salvation from all sin, entire sanctification, perfect love,

---

2. See Yeago, "New Testament and Nicene Dogma."

3. Naselli, "Models of Sanctification." The next five descriptions are adapted from this essay. I chose Naselli here, as his essay represents well the Reformed evangelical view at large.

holiness, purity of intention, full salvation, second blessing, second rest and dedication of your whole life to God."[4]

Keswick Model

The Keswick model takes its name from the Keswick convention center in England. Here a series of revival meetings were held, which gave rise to what is now known as the "higher life" movement. This is another type of "two works of grace." After the first grace of salvation, Christians are called to "let go and let God." When agency is in some sense given up, God can take care of the work of sanctification, where the person's will be inclined to godly things.

The concept of agency is connected to a gracious movement of God. The Keswick movement—although often caricatured—taps into an important issue discussed in my sketch: that although virtue formation are part of stability of character, we cannot miss the fact that some grace is infused for this purpose.

Pentecostal Model

Naselli states, "Pentecostalism, according to most church historians, began on December 31, 1900. According to Pentecostalism, believers should experience Spirit-baptism after conversion and initially demonstrate this by speaking in tongues."[5] He proceeds with a description of the baptism on the Spirit and the second and third blessings.

I do not disagree with Naselli's description, though it seems to me a bit reductionistic. From the perspective of someone who lived in a third world country most of his life, I think most functional "doctrines" of sanctification in Pentecostal families are similar to the Reformed view below.

The current levels of conversions to Pentecostalism in the Global South shows that they have a reach that most historical denominations do not have. Most conversions to Christianity in the margins of society—drug dealers, prostitutes, the extremely impoverished, etc.—are conversions to Pentecostalism. The appeal of a radically changed life that Pentecostalism proclaims seems to do a lot of work for those who are hopeless and at the margins. And it is my perception that this appeal has little to nothing to do

---

4. Naselli, "Models of Sanctification," s.vv. "The Wesleyan View of Progressive Sanctification," para. 2.

5. Naselli, "Models of Sanctification," s.vv. "The Pentecostal View of Progressive Sanctification," para. 1.

with second and third blessings, even though such conception may be what is emphasized in systematic treatments of Pentecostalism. Those in the margins crave stability in their lives. And although formal Pentecostal doctrine of sanctification states the reality of two or three works of grace, the material structure is that, on some level to those external to Christianity, they want to experience what they interpret as Christian growth. As I will demonstrate later, stability of character is the greatest mark of virtue formation and a feature that should be present in a persuasive model of sanctification.

The Chafer Model

The Chafer model is connected to Lewis Sperry Chafer (1871–1952). This model separates humanity into three categories: unconverted (natural), carnal Christians, and spiritual Christians. A plethora of debates emerged in Evangelicalism because of this model. It created lack of discipleship and a view of religion that was disconnected from ethics.

Lots of problems could be pointed out about this view. For now, if we are relating to the formation of virtues and stability of character, this view fails to account for the how is that one can be a Christian and not progress in his work towards maturity and bear the marks of their vocation.

Reformed Model

Naselli then goes on to describe the Reformed vision of sanctification. According to Naselli, the fundamental characteristic that distinguishes the Reformed view is that it does not divide Christians into two groups.

> Justification and progressive sanctification are distinct, but they are inseparable. Faith alone justifies, but the faith that justifies is never alone. God's grace through the power of his Spirit ensures that the same faith that justifies a Christian also progressively sanctifies a Christian.
>
> *All Christians are spiritual; none are permanently carnal* (1 Cor 2:6—3:4). Paul describes people as natural, spiritual, and carnal (or "of the flesh"). The issue is whether those are three distinct categories. *Natural* refers to "the person without the Spirit," and *spiritual* refers to "the person with the Spirit" (NIV).[6]

---

6. Naselli, "Models of Sanctification," s.vv. "The Reformed View of Progressive Sanctification," paras. 3–4; emphasis in original.

This *duplex gratia* view is never divorced in the Reformed tradition.[7] Upholding the unity of these two doctrines avoids creating "special categories" of Christians. For the grace of sanctification and the grace of justification are not two sequential movements of the grace of God, but just two different faces of the same grace. It is impossible to have one without the other. What we need to further this discussion is how can we talk about growth and development without overemphasizing human agency and de-emphasizing God's agency.

Concluding Remarks on Christian Conceptions of Holiness

These models described above state in some way how the human agent relate to the divine; aiming for some kind of stability in the three-way relation of God-law-human. The divine law is the perfect stable repetition of the divine will. Each model describes that relationship through a different prism.

For example, while the Wesleyan model is concerned with spectrum of transgression of law, the Reformed is concerned with growth for those already in covenant relation. Of course, there are points where there are mutual exclusive conceptions in these models. Nonetheless, they are all concerned with Christian growth and relation to the law. And what most commentators on models of sanctification really miss is the discussion on the nature of divine law.[8] For such discussion we turn to Jewish conceptions of holiness.

JEWISH CONCEPTIONS OF HOLINESS

Personal holiness is inextricably link with the law in Jewish understandings of holiness. This, however, is not the full story. Objects and institutions can be holy in Judaism. Still, for the purposes of this essay, we focus on the personal dimension.[9]

---

7. Garcia, "Imputation and Christology."

8. It seems like lots of New Testament studies have been preoccupied with this question since the rise of the new perspective on Paul. See Rosner and Carson, *Paul and the Law*; Schreiner, *Law and Its Fulfillment*; Wright, *Climax of the Covenant*; Eastman and Barclay, *Paul and the Person*; Barclay, *Paul and the Gift*. Nonetheless, in systematic theology, and especially discussions on the nature of the law, the discussion on the nature of the law is very much forgotten.

9. Alan Mittleman's recent volume *Holiness in Jewish Thought* explores holiness in the Bible, Midrash, Talmud, and medieval biblical commentary.

Jewish reflection on holiness actually comes from a common source of Christian reflection: Lev 19–20. This text's description of a "holiness code" roots the source of holiness in Godself ("be holy for I am holy"), while at the same time deriving its principal force within a plethora of ritualistic and ceremonial observances. Moreover, these two chapters ground holiness it its relation to the land of Israel. Alan Mittleman reflects on the ethical ramifications for theological speech:

> Whether the implications of divine holiness are recognizably moral in modern terms ("Love your fellow as yourself: I am the LORD" 19:18) or rather alien to modern sensibilities ("You shall not make gashes in your flesh for the dead, or incise any marks on yourselves: I am the LORD" 19:27), correct action enables and protects God's presence in the world. Unholy action banishes it.[10]

Holiness is not merely a reactionary movement to God's presence. Much rather, holiness displays God's presence.

The basic question is whether one should live up to the standards of the law or if true holiness is attained to by adding to the law's righteousness. Similar to Christian conceptions of holiness, possible responses to the query are variegated. Rabbinic ethics enshrined in the Talmud "aims at the education of enlightened persons who accept upon themselves, as individuals and as a people, the 'yoke of the kingdom of heaven.'"[11] Jews are always to err on the side of precaution and goodness rather than relying merely upon recognition of the law. Mittleman cites the Talmud's exemplification of this principle with a story:

> Our Rabbis taught: He who judges his neighbor in the scale of merit is himself judged favourably. Thus a story is told of a certain man who descended from Upper Galilee and was engaged by an individual in the South for three years. On the eve of the Day of Atonement he requested him, "Give me my wages that I may go and support my wife and children."
>
> "I have no money," answered he. "Give me produce," he demanded; "I have none," he replied. "Give me land."—"I have none." "Give me cattle."—"I have none." "Give me pillows and bedding."—"I have none."
>
> [So] he slung his things behind him and went home with a sorrowful heart. After the Festival his employer took his wages in his hand together with three laden asses, one bearing food,

---

10. Mittleman, *Short History of Jewish Ethics*, 16.
11. Mittleman, *Short History of Jewish Ethics*, 16.

another drink, and the third various sweetmeats, and went to his house. After they had eaten and drunk, he gave him his wages.

Said he to him, "When you asked me, 'Give me my wages,' and I answered you, 'I have no money,' of what did you suspect me?" "I thought, Perhaps you came across cheap merchandise and had purchased it therewith." "And when you requested me, 'Give me cattle,' and I answered, 'I have no cattle,' of what did you suspect me?" "I thought, they may be hired to others." "When you asked me, 'Give me land,' and I told you, 'I have no land,' of what did you suspect me?" "I thought, perhaps it is leased to others." "And when I told you, 'I have no produce,' of what did you suspect me?" "I thought, Perhaps they are not tithed." "And when I told you, 'I have no pillows or bedding,' of what did you suspect me?" "I thought, perhaps he has sanctified all his property to Heaven."

"By the [temple] service!" exclaimed he, "it was even so; I vowed away all my property because of my son Hyrcanus, who would not occupy himself with the Torah, but when I went to my companions in the South they absolved me of all my vows. And as for you, just as you judged me favourably, so may the Omnipresent judge you favourably."[12]

The law may even demand a certain type of action, but the law does not come divorced from the wisdom of God and the precaution it also requests. Therefore, going beyond the law is not an exercise in mere legalism. It is actually the purpose of the law itself.

Medieval Jewish ethics—especially as articulated by Maimonides (1138–1204), on the other hand, reflects upon holiness through philosophical and metaphysical accounts. His reliance on Aristotle mirrors Aquinas's own Aristotelian predilection in the Christian tradition.[13] By recounting the notion of virtues and a strong moral psychology that understands itself through different faculties and capacities, holiness is pursued via conformity to the divine knowledge. Some like Mittleman take Maimonides to be more asocial and intellectualist in his appropriation of Aristotle. However, Maimonides's moral psychology serves not to create intellectual aloofness, but rather structures moral reasoning. For example, in Maimonides commentary on *teshuvah* he states:

> Let not the penitent suppose that he is kept far away from the degree attained by the righteous because of the iniquities and sins that he has committed. This is not so. He is beloved by the

12. b. Shabbat 127b.
13. Miller, "Moses Maimonides and Thomas Aquinas."

Creator, desired by Him, as if he had never sinned. Moreover, his reward is great; since, though having tasted sin, he renounced it and overcame his evil passions. The sages say, "Where penitents stand, the completely righteous cannot stand." This means that the degree attained by penitents is higher than that of those who had never sinned, the reason being that the former have had to put forth a greater effort to subdue their passions than the latter. . . . Great is repentance, for it brings men near to the Divine Presence, as it is said, "Return, O Israel, to the Lord your God" (Hos. 14:2).[14]

Mittleman argues that the above reflection entails that holiness is, more than anything, an increase in moral discernment where ethics is a mere subordinate to metaphysics.

However, it seems to me that Mittleman is creating an unnecessary disjunction between metaphysics and ethics. Knowledge of reality (a contemplation of God as the *summum bonum*) will inevitably display God's presence through the good that we practice today in the journey to the source of all good.

Maimonides's theology of holiness is preoccupied in understanding the nature of things so that one can effectively align the law with self. "All the actions prescribed by the Law . . . moral habits that are useful to all people in their mutual dealings—that all this is not to be compared with this ultimate end and does not equal it, being but preparations made for the sake of this end."[15] Such fixation on habits is what we find in common descriptions of virtue ethics. Ethical accounts that depend on virtue ethics are not mere intellectualist endeavors, but relate the stabilization of character through habitual processes. "Having a virtuous character enables one to move to the ultimate contemplative good such that fixity is a good thing in terms of creating a potentially durable happiness."[16]

The genius of Maimonides parallels that of Thomas Aquinas here. By interrelating ethics and metaphysics, they can explain human action with view of their telos from the human source. Such move differs from Aristotelian naturalism, by inflecting human growth with the rubric of divine aid (here paralleling Aquinas's discussion of infused grace). In other words, for Maimonides, "goodness without God may not be good enough. Grace of sorts enables capacity to satisfy the demand for humans to be all that they

---

14. Maimonides, *Guide to the Perplexed*, 510–11.
15. Maimonides, *Guide to the Perplexed*, 638.
16. Miller, "Moses Maimonides and Thomas Aquinas," 75.

can be and attain the good life."[17] There is a clear notion, for Maimonides, that holiness is neither brought in a vacuum or that humans are mere vessels for divine action. Maimonides's moral psychology will not allow for such simplification. Ethical living brings about divine presence, because *good* has source relation with the ultimate Good (*Summum Bonum*).[18]

MOVING TOWARD A SYMBIOTIC RELATIONSHIP: JEWISH AND CHRISTIAN THEOLOGIES OF HOLINESS

When discussing Christian theology, I focused on various models of sanctification, and with Jewish theology, both talmudic and medieval interpretations. As stated in the beginning of the chapter, my goal is to retrieve some insights from the Jewish tradition to enhance and expand upon these Christian models.

Christian models of sanctification are great to explain the method(s) of spiritual growth, but in many ways, lack an explanation of mechanisms for this growth in holiness because of a neglected systematic treatment on the nature of the law.

Maimonides, like Aquinas, understands that the law is not a source of legalistic oppression. Rather, by having God as its very source, the law moves the human moral structure to conform to its telos. In many ways, the retrieval of virtue ethics in Christian circles is a welcome project. But Christians may go beyond Thomas Aquinas. Maimonides provides a great source for virtue ethics, precisely because of his focus on covenant and the law. Whereas Aquinas's moral philosophy provides some mechanism for how to think about anthropology and psychology, Maimonides's project dives deeper into the role of the law of God in stabilizing the character.

For example, in *Summa Theologiae* 1.2.69, Aquinas tries to establish virtue ethics with an exclusive look to Jesus's Sermon on the Mount and the Beatitudes. Jonathan Pennington has shown that the ethical demands of the Beatitudes, though having a "virtue ethics perspective," is firmly rooted in the law's *asherisms* (*ašrê*). It is the righteous one's pleasure in the law of the Lord that creates true ethical beatitude.

Maimonides, on the other hand, in "Eight Chapters," places the human condition under the extremes of good and bad. Human formation does not appear divorced from the precepts of God. He states:

---

17. Miller, "Moses Maimonides and Thomas Aquinas," 80.

18. "It is what gives man a perfection belonging to himself alone and permanence whereby man is truly man" (Maimonides, *Guide to the Perplexed*, 599–600).

> The perfect Law which leads us to perfection as one who knew it well testifies by the words, (Psalms 19:8) "*The Law of the Lord is perfect restoring the soul*; the testimonies of the Lord are faithful making wise the simple" recommends none of these things (such as self-torture, flight from society etc.). On the contrary, it aims at man's following the path of moderation, in accordance with the dictates of nature, eating, drinking, enjoying legitimate sexual intercourse, all in moderation, and living among people in honesty and uprightness, but not dwelling in the wilderness or in the mountains, or clothing oneself in garments of hair and wool, or afflicting the body.[19]

The evangelical models of sanctification would benefit from this account of virtue ethics in which divine law and metaphysics flow into human character formation.

The law's restoration of the human soul attributes a certain agency to the law and to the one practicing it.[20]

Maimonides's focus on both the perfection of the law and the "path of moderation" sketches a potentiality for symbiosis with a robust Christian account of sanctification. What we commonly call virtue ethics in Christian accounts tends to traffic mainly either on the New Testament or through natural theology. By focusing either exclusively in the Sermon of the mountain and its *macarisms* or by focusing on human capabilities, Christian virtue ethics relegates Old Testament precepts to mere biblical ethics. But that does not need to be the case. Maimonides on the other hand posits that moderation or stability in life can only come through contemplation of the divine law.

In conclusion, virtue ethics as presented by Maimonides shows the source and goal of the law in God. Evangelicals have long preferred an emphasis on models of sanctification because Aquinas' account of virtue tended to confuse justification and sanctification. The main reason for such confusion was his deep reliance on natural theology. Although Christians need to pay attention to natural theology, Maimonides provides the better bridge between the models of sanctification and a concept of the mechanism of growth in holiness.

19. Moses ben Maimon, "Eight Chapters," §4; emphasis added.

20. Strategies of personification have been pervasive in the tradition. Joseph Dodson has said: "it communicates in a way like no other in order to decorate or amplify, to educate or clarify, to motivate or manipulate, to expose the cause or to deflect attention away from an insufficient system—and possibly a combination of the above. Therefore, we shall investigate each personification in Wisdom and Romans in light of these purposes, and perhaps will discover others along the way. As part of rhetoric, personifications primarily serve as a tool to persuade" (*"Powers" of Personification*, 49–50).

Furthermore, as we established, the Christian models are not an in toto account of the doctrine of sanctification. Therefore, appropriating insights from Maimonides and his ethical formulation is possible, regardless of which tradition a Christian finds themselves attached to.

BIBLIOGRAPHY

Barclay, John M. G. *Paul and the Gift*. Repr., Grand Rapids: Eerdmans, 2017.

Crisp, Oliver D. "A Parsimonious Model of Divine Simplicity." *Modern Theology* 35 (2019) 558–73. https://doi.org/10.1111/moth.12520.

Dodson, Joseph R. *The "Powers" of Personification: Rhetorical Purpose in the "Book of Wisdom" and the Letter to the Romans*. BZNW 161. Berlin: De Gruyter, 2008.

Eastman, Susan Grove, and John M. G. Barclay. *Paul and the Person: Reframing Paul's Anthropology*. Grand Rapids: Eerdmans, 2017.

Garcia, Mark A. "Imputation and the Christology of Union with Christ: Calvin, Osiander, and the Contemporary Quest for a Reformed Model." *WTJ* 68 (2006) 219–51.

Maimonides, Moses. *The Guide to the Perplexed: A New Translation*. Edited and translated by Lenn E. Goodman and Phillip I. Lieberman. Stanford, CA: Stanford University Press, 2016.

Miller, Corey M. "Moses Maimonides and Thomas Aquinas on the Good Life: From the Fall to Human Perfectibility." PhD diss., University of Edinburgh, 2015. https://pure.uhi.ac.uk/en/studentTheses/moses-maimonides-and-thomas-aquinas-on-the-good-life.

Mittleman, Alan L., ed. *Holiness in Jewish Thought*. New York: Oxford University Press, 2018.

———. *A Short History of Jewish Ethics: Conduct and Character in the Context of Covenant*. Hoboken: Wiley-Blackwell, 2011.

Moses ben Maimon (Rambam). "Eight Chapters." Sefaria, ca. 1157–65. https://www.sefaria.org/Eight_Chapters.

Naselli, Andrew David. "Models of Sanctification." Gospel Coalition, n.d. https://www.thegospelcoalition.org/essay/models-of-sanctification/.

Rosner, Brian S., and D. A. Carson. *Paul and the Law: Keeping the Commandments of God*. New Studies in Biblical Theology 31. Downers Grove, IL: IVP Academic, 2013.

Schreiner, Thomas R. *The Law and Its Fulfillment: A Pauline Theology of Law*. Grand Rapids: Baker Academic, 1998.

Wright, N. T., ed. *The Climax of the Covenant: Christ and the Law in Pauline Theology*. Minneapolis: Fortress, 1993.

Yeago, David S. "The New Testament and the Nicene Dogma: A Contribution to the Recovery of Theological Exegesis." *STRev* 45 (2002) 371–84.

Chapter 7

Toward a Holy Disillusion in Qohelet
How the Uniqueness of Israel's God Positions Jews and Christians for Authentic Living Before Him

Jordan W. Jones

INTRODUCTION

JEWS AND CHRISTIANS TOGETHER affirm the uniqueness of the God of Israel.[1] He is incomparable in character and ability, a case the book of Ecclesiastes[2] makes masterfully by setting the realities of human death, ignorance, and futility against the infinitudes of God. This tactic is meant to combat the many delusions of control and permanence that plague humanity, delusions manifested by endless pursuits for great wealth, impressive wisdom, public acclaim, and worldly accomplishments—all frail attempts to subvert the painful realities of human weakness and impermanence. Qohelet objects to such attempts, not to the relative value of money, wisdom, and work, which he affirms, but to the fantasy that these things can save a person from the inevitable: forgottenness (1:11; 9:5–6). Instead, he believes that one day, every

---

1. This is consistently the doctrine of traditional Judaism concerning God—see Luzzatto, *Way of God*, 31. Faithful Christian theologians of all ages echo the sentiment—e.g., Williams, *God, the World*, 55–81.

2. In this essay, the term "Qohelet" is used to refer to the teacher of the book, while "Ecclesiastes" is used to refer to the book itself. When specific chapters and verses are referenced, however, the book is abbreviated "Qoh" as in Qoh 1:1.

human monument will break down and be reduced to sand, like the statue of Ozymandias in Percy Shelley's classic poem.³ Eventually, every landscape will become "boundless and bare" (Shelley), there being "no remembrance of former things" (Qoh 1:11), leaving God alone as the only immovable constant in a transient universe.

For Qohelet, life's brevity is not a call to build bigger, live larger, get wiser, and work faster for the sake of human glory but to enjoy the present with a soul at rest, receptive to the simple gifts of God (2:24–26; 3:12–13, 22; 5:18–20 [Heb. 5:17–19]; 8:15; 9:7–10; 11:7—12:1), and attentive to the fear of God (3:14; 5:1–6; 8:12–13; 12:13).⁴ *That*, Qohelet asserts, is the sacred alternative to the above-stated delusions. His joy statements⁵ appearing throughout the book are actually a call for *holy disillusion*, that is, for his pupils to reject common illusions of human strength and instead adopt a simplicity that acknowledges that the best things in life—one's food, drink, work, and spouse—are not the product of human ambition but come "from the hand of God" (Qoh 2:24; see also 3:13; 5:18–20 [Heb. 5:17–19]; 8:15; 9:9).⁶

---

3. Shelley, *Complete Poetry*, 326.

4. Some scholars argue that Qohelet's talk of fearing God should be understood not in the conventional, biblical sense of reverence and practical concern for divine judgment, but as actual terror, merely a utilitarian choice to stay out of trouble (Longman, *Book of Ecclesiastes*, 155; Sneed, *Social World of the Sages*, 256). However, there is insufficient evidence in the text to justify this atypical function of "to fear" (*yr'*, ירא) with respect to God (see discussions in Whybray, *Ecclesiastes*, 25, 75; Dell, "Wise Man Reflecting on Wisdom," 142; Krüger, *Qoheleth*, 110; Davis, *Proverbs, Ecclesiastes*, 193).

5. The label "joy statements" is preferred over "carpe diem statements" and reflects my understanding of Qohelet as a realist who offers a real solution rather than a sardonic critic who merely bemoans the sorry lot God has given humanity (contra Longman, *Ecclesiastes*, 106–10, who argues that the carpe diem statements are made "resignedly"). Whybray makes the point that Qohelet's use of the verb "enjoy" implies he is viewing things positively despite all of life's futilities: "It is just this series of positive statements, punctuating the book, which expresses Qohelet's true conclusions: that it is only the person who has taken full account of the vanities of this world and faced up to them who is free to receive the divine gift of joy in simple things" (*Ecclesiastes*, 25–26; see also 102).

6. The term "holy" (*qādôš*, קָדוֹשׁ) appears only in 8:10, and it is not Qohelet's term of choice to describe God or human allegiance to God (though he would not disagree with those notions). His chosen expression "fear God" is related (see Ps 34:9 [Heb. 34:10]—"Fear Yʜᴡʜ, [you] his holy ones!" [*yər' û ' et yhwh qədōšāyw*, יְראוּ אֶת־יְהוָה קְדֹשָׁיו]) and refers to the activity of people walking in keeping with their divinely appointed status as holy. Hence, the term is used in this essay to refer to the state of mind/soul that should accompany God-fearers, one that strips away all of life's superficialities (vanities) to embrace authentic living before God. Qohelet wants his readers to develop a deep disaffection for the false promises of earthly ambitions given how very empty these masters are—as Heim summarizes Qohelet's position: "The goals that humans

Qohelet's teaching contends with both pagan ideology and an absolutist view of the retribution principle within Israelite thought (as seen in Job's companions). Though most scholarship has focused on the latter, there are clues that Ecclesiastes was intended to be read by more than just those intimately familiar with the God of Israel. The lack of the divine name in Qohelet's teaching, sparse mention of Israel and Jerusalem, the universal appeal inherent in Qohelet's examples, and numerous similarities between Qohelet's words and analogous texts from the ancient Near East (ANE)[7] all point to a broader audience, or at the very least, a Hebrew audience with significant exposure to pagan thought. Qohelet is indeed a worshipper of

---

pursue to find happiness are mirages, optical illusions of the mind" (*Ecclesiastes*, 39). His pupils are to adopt instead a more sophisticated and spiritually coherent view of the world that would replace the delusions of life, whether they be delusions of material or spiritual grandeur.

7. In this essay, ANE stands also for the adjectival form: "ancient Near Eastern," which includes primarily Egypt, Canaan, and Mesopotamia, or basically "western Asia" (Snell, *Religions of Ancient Near East*, 2). The most frequently cited comparative text for Ecclesiastes is *The Epic of Gilgamesh*. This Babylonian legend comments on the futility of human ambitions and calls such pursuits "wind" (Akk. *saru*; Heb. *rûaḥ*, רוּחַ; see Qoh 1:14, 17; 2:11; etc.). In the course of his journeys, Gilgamesh is told that he will not succeed in attaining immortality because the gods have set a boundary for human life. Consequently, he is advised to accept the futility of his quest and determine to live life to the fullest now, embracing the simple pleasures of food, drink, and family. Numerous startling parallels emerge between a particular speech in *Gilgamesh* and the joy statements of Qohelet (2:24–26; 3:12–13, 22; 5:18–20 [Heb. 5:17–19]; 8:15; 9:7; 11:7–12:1; see Pritchard, *The Ancient Near Eastern Texts*, 90; Gilgamesh III:1–13), but the major difference emerging in Ecclesiastes is the repeated focus on God as Sovereign (1:13; 3:11, 14–15; 7:14), Creator (12:1), Judge (3:17; 5:1–7 [Heb. 4:17–5:6]; 8:13; 11:9; 12:14), and Gift-Giver (2:26; 3:13; 5:20 [Heb. 5:19]; 7:14), as well as the injunction that people must fear him (3:14; 5:7 [Heb. 5:6]; 8:12–13; 12:13). In their respective texts, both Qohelet and Job veer away from meaninglessness and hopeless ignorance (compare to the Mesopotamian theodicies) and toward a faith-centric resolve in the God of Israel. Some would argue that stories like *Gilgamesh* do end in a kind of hope, the hope found in living life to the fullest now while embracing the responsibilities before you (for him, the city of Uruk), but the directives in Ecclesiastes contextualize these simple pleasures as gifts from the God of Israel, who must be feared, making *him* the ultimate source of hope in life. Themes related to those found in the Gilgamesh excerpt above and in Ecclesiastes can also be found in the oft-labeled "pessimistic literature" of the ANE, including the Babylonian texts *A Dialogue About Human Misery*, *A Pessimistic Dialogue Between Master and Servant*, and the Egyptian *A Dispute Between a Man and his Ba* (Pritchard, *The Ancient Near Eastern Texts*, 438–9; Lichtheim, *Ancient Egyptian Literature*, 163). There is insufficient space here to survey each of these texts to demonstrate that the ideology of Qohelet, while bearing the marks of shared thinking with older Egyptian and Semitic texts, is distinctly Israelite. For purposes of this essay, it is sufficient to note here that Qohelet is speaking with these competing ideologies in mind and offering a substantive solution for addressing life's inequities and enigmas, one grounded in the fear of God and in the recognition that all good things come from him.

Yhwh, the God of Israel, but his presentation or pedagogic tactic is intentionally broad. He thereby positions himself as a teacher not only of Hebrew youngsters but of anyone in the hearing of his voice. Though scholars have primarily focused on Qohelet's adverse reaction to a dogmatic and absolutist adoption of the retribution principle (again, think Zophar, Bildad, and Eliphaz), the ideological contrasts drawn up in this essay will focus more on how Qohelet's views of the divine nature and proper human response to it compete with pagan views of the same, broadly speaking.

Since the gods of the ANE behaved capriciously, like humans, and were themselves subject to forces beyond their control, the peoples of the ANE responded by devising means of stability whereby they sought to order life's outcomes or at least curb the negative ones. They did this through ritual manipulation of the gods and other cosmic forces (see the following section). The Hebrew Scriptures, on the other hand, present the God of Israel as wholly other and not given to the fickle whims or finitudes of ANE pantheons. Though Qohelet does not expressly name particular ANE texts or peoples, his teaching reveals a familiarity with such texts as he seeks to contradict the mentality of ancient people living within that system.[8] To all his readers, Qohelet has this to say: "God is in heaven, and you are on earth" (5:2 [Heb. 5:1]). This statement sets human finitude against the infiniteness of God, a contrast meant to disabuse his readers of all-too-common delusions of control and permanence, beliefs rooted in paganism, and to propose instead the only legitimate alternative: authentic living in the fear of God.[9] This proposal engages first with the topic of Yhwh's (and Israel's) uniqueness in the ideological landscape of the ANE, then, for the sake of space, with just one of the several contrasts Qohelet draws up between humanity and God: the extent of knowledge.

---

8. For a brief but helpful overview of ANE texts related to Ecclesiastes and how their intertextual relationship may be understood, see Anderson, "Ecclesiastes in Intertextual Matrix."

9. The term "authentic living" is an attempt to summarize Qohelet's many joy statements wherein he instructs his pupils to embrace the simple gifts of God (eating, drinking, working, and loving one's spouse) as sufficient for joy while also admonishing them repeatedly to live their lives in the fear of God. Note also that this brief essay focuses solely on the teaching of Qohelet in his *ancient* context, which at the very least includes the broader conceptual world of the ANE, though many scholars will also argue for a Hellenistic influence (e.g., Heim, *Ecclesiastes*; Krüger, *Qoheleth*; etc.). But Ecclesiastes's universal and timeless nature provides relevance for the present as well, so this study could be extended to discuss how modern notions of human flourishing have errantly (according to orthodox theology within Judaism and Christianity) proposed a fixation on self and the self's ability to effect change apart from the sovereign design of God— e.g., Pinker, *Enlightenment Now*.

FINITE DEITIES, ANXIOUS SUPPLICANTS, AND THE UNIQUENESS OF ISRAEL'S GOD

In Exod 5, Moses and Aaron enter the palace of Egypt and stand before the Pharaoh with a message from the God of Abraham, Isaac, and Jacob. The Pharaoh's response is relevant for all discussions on the Bible in its ANE context: "Who is Yhwh?" (*Mî yhwh*, מִי יְהוָה) "I do not know Yhwh!" (*Lōʾ yādaʿtî ʾ et-yhwh*, לֹא יָדַעְתִּי אֶת־יְהוָה) (Exod 5:2). This admission is backed by the unsurprising absence of Israel's God throughout the extensive corpus of ancient Egyptian literature. The Mesopotamian and Canaanite texts likewise exhibit an unawareness of the divine nature presented in the Hebrew Scriptures. They had rather adopted an understanding of deity that appeared to emerge from their experiences of the phenomenological world around them, associating various elements of nature with the respective deities themselves and seeing divine causation in all natural processes.[10] Israel likewise saw natural causation in God, but they viewed his relation to the natural world as transcendent and the scope of his supervision as universal (Gen 1; Isa 55:8–9; Jonah 1:9; Ps 24:1–2; 2 Chr 2:6).

The Finite Nature of the Gods

To combat the anxieties of life in the ancient world, Israel were to turn to Yhwh, exercising faith in his plan and power to sustain them (Ps 9:10; 111:15). The peoples of the ANE turned to their gods as well, but that relationship looked quite different. Unlike the God of Israel, those gods had origins, and the peoples' arrangements with the gods were far more pragmatic. For example, the gods needed to be fed, housed, and cared for so they could attend to the higher matters of the cosmos, chiefly the maintenance of order.[11] In exchange, the gods may choose to bestow blessings on the people, often in the form of crops, fertility, and protection from evil. To be sure, they possessed a sophisticated understanding of social propriety and right living before the gods, often expressed through law collections, proverbs, letters, and royal monuments, but notions of personal holiness and a highly internalized righteousness were features unique to religion-proper in Israel (e.g., 1 Sam 15:22–23; Mic 6:8). ANE peoples and syncretistic

---

10. See Rom 1:22. Natural phenomena were all attributable, in varying degrees, to the activities of the gods. There was no clear bifurcation of spiritual and physical realms in the minds of ANE peoples, not even a separate notion of religion—the gods were involved in everything; See Nemet-Nejat, *Daily Life in Ancient Mesopotamia*, 178–82.

11. Snell, *Religions of Ancient Near East*, 62.

Israelites instead participated with the gods rather mechanistically to maintain cosmic order, and they did this through sacrifice and whatever forms of obedience their personal or city gods required. Unfortunately, though, that did not make life any more predictable for such peoples since their gods were themselves fickle and finite, subject to the dangers they posed to one another, the dangers posed to them by humanity, and the unstoppable nature of fate.[12] The gods are also portrayed through myth as deeply selfish, their concern for humanity often being limited to how human action might negatively impact their divine schemes or even their comfort levels, as in the Mesopotamian creation myth *Atra-Ḫasis* when the gods killed nearly all of humanity because people were being noisy and keeping them from getting good sleep.[13] Humans had been created in the first place to take on the forced labor that the lesser gods were tired of doing. With gods like these, one may ask, "Who needs enemies?" But the average ANE supplicant did not think ill of the gods (not usually, at least); rather, they simply lived in reaction to what they believed were finite heavenly beings. As a result, they were forced to take control into their own hands, manipulating the gods through sacrifice, curbing the power of evil through magic, and ascertaining hidden knowledge through divination.

While this reactive existence was an ordinary way of life for people, the world of religious ritual does betray the many anxieties that accompany an inability to access and perfectly please the gods. The tower of Babel story may demonstrate these very concerns. As was common in various ANE cities, the people of Gen 11:1–9 constructed a tower "to make a name" for themselves, as a measure of centralizing their identity and allegiance to the deity through the erection of a pyramidal monument, a common practice among ANE kings. Practically speaking, if this was anything like the ziggurats of Mesopotamia, then the monument would serve as a convenient stairway for the gods to descend to earth, be sustained by sacrifices, care for their worshippers, and access the underworld.[14] On a much smaller scale, the peoples of the ANE also attempted to supplement the deficiencies of the gods by learning the future through various forms of divination, whether

12. Snell, *Religions of Ancient Near East*, 17, 21. Not all gods were immortal, and no ANE god was omniscient nor omnipotent. Like humans, they could be "arbitrary and unfair" (in this case specifically referring to Enlil, though the descriptor is true for many others as well) (21). Concerning the finitude of the gods and their subjection to fate, see Oswalt, *Bible Among the Myths*, 58–9.

13. Foster, "Atra-Ḫasis."

14. See Walton's explanation of the tower of Babel episode in Gen 11 (*Ancient Near Eastern Thought*, 119–23). What stories like this and others across the ANE reveal is that in order to execute their divine duty of maintaining order and justice, the gods needed the help of humanity to provide temples, food, gifts, cooperation, etc.

studying the stars, reading the entrails of sacrificed animals through extispicy, or analyzing other natural phenomena. They believed that rightly understanding such things could provide precious insight into the future,[15] something Qohelet teaches is impossible for humans to know (Qoh 6:12). Ancient people also worked hard to coax the gods through ritual observance, drive away demons through incantation, and circumvent fate through magic, all efforts at producing favorable outcomes for humanity.[16] The impression left from reading extant ANE literature is that the people's connection to their gods was one of utility and lacked the profound spiritual depth found in the Hebrew Psalms or the calls for holiness and ethical living found in the Torah, all of which emerge from the holy character of Yhwh in relationship with his people.

The Infinite Nature of YHWH

The Jewish-Christian understanding of God's incomparable nature finds its bearing in many passages throughout the Hebrew Scriptures (too many to mention here, but see esp. Exod 15; Deut 33; Job 36–41; and various passages throughout the Psalms and prophets). For the psalmists, Yhwh is in a singularly occupied class of being, "exalted over all the earth, greatly elevated over all the gods" (Ps 97:9). In contrast to the gods of the nations, he does not need anything because he already owns and oversees everything— "If I became hungry I would not tell you, for the world and its fullness belong to me" (Ps 50:12; see also vv. 13–15; Acts 17:24–25). Sacrifice to Yhwh was, therefore, an expression of heart obedience rather than an attempt to feed the hungry belly of God.[17] People, after all, were not created by God for slave labor (see Gen 1–2), and their noisiness could not interrupt God's rest since he never sleeps (Ps 121). Unlike the tower of Babel, the Israelite temple was not required for the mobility of Yhwh but for the holiness of the people in community with him (see 1 Kgs 6:12–13; 8:27). As for knowledge, the mysteries of the God of Israel cannot be extracted through a complex ritual formula; rather, he worked through prophets with whom he spoke "face to face" (Gen 32:30; Exod 33:11; Num 12:8; 14:14; Deut 5:4; 34:10).[18]

15. Maul, *Art of Divination*, 20.

16. Hilber, "Prophecy, Divination, and Magic," 368; Maul, *Art of Divination*, 1–16, 219.

17. Though cross-culturally familiar language may include expressions like "pleasing aroma" (Gen 8:12; Exod 29:18; etc.).

18. In many places throughout the Hebrew Scriptures, individuals sought divine knowledge of future events (or advice for how to act) through prayer (Judg 13:8; 2 Kgs 19:14–34), by asking legitimate or illegitimate prophets (Judg 18:5; 1 Kgs 22:7;

Though there are parallels to divinatory practices (e.g., the use of Urim and Thummim, Gideon's fleece, etc.), they are remarkably few and contextually distinct from comparable ANE practices. The infrequency of these methods seems to cohere with the broader scriptural imperative to exercise faith whenever circumstances lack clarity (e.g., Hab 3:17–19). While any Israelite ritual could be twisted into an attempt to manipulate God (e.g., 1 Sam 13:9–13), the priestly system was not designed to work in a mechanistic way devoid of internalized loyalty to a God for whom animal sacrifices are insufficient—he requires also "a broken and contrite heart" (Ps 51:16–17; against attempts to manipulate God, see Qoh 5:1–7 [Heb. 4:17—5:6]).

The peoples of the ANE not only worked rituals to secure positive outcomes on earth but also engaged in delusions of permanence through the construction of monuments to themselves and the gods. These buildings were adorned with inscriptions testifying to the builder's incomparable attributes and impeccable righteousness before the gods, inscriptions that threatened curses against all who may be tempted to dismantle them.[19] By contrast to the gods of the nations and the ever-eroding monuments of men, the God of Israel is infinite in every good way, meaning that his knowledge is complete, his work is permanent, his life is eternal, and his status with respect to humanity is *Judge*.

HOW FINITE GOD-FEARERS RESPOND TO THE INFINITE GOD OF ISRAEL

Qohelet teaches that God-fearers must rightly respond to the infinitudes of Israel's God by recognizing that their knowledge is limited, that their worldly endeavors and very lives are transient, and that their status with respect to God is *judged*. Unlike the peoples of the ANE, God-fearers should not attempt to control the heavens. According to Qohelet, they must rather accept the realities of their finitude, including their vulnerability to the unpredictable things of life, and become disillusioned with tendencies toward control and permanence, accepting as sufficient the good gifts of God while

---

etc.), through forbidden divination (1 Sam 28; 2 Kgs 21:1–9; etc.), or by other approved means (e.g., dreams: Gen 40:8; Joel 2:28 [Heb. 3:1]; signs: 2 Kgs 20:8–11; Isa 7:11; casting lots: Lev 16:8). Ironically, even when God does reveal a bit of his knowledge for human good, it is often despised or ignored (Deut 31:20; Isa 1:2–3; Jer 32:2–3; Job 21:14–15; etc.).

19. E.g., an inscription of Sargon of Akade reads: "May Anu destroy the name and Enlil finish off the offspring, Inanna do [harm] . . . to whosoever destroys this inscription" (Pritchard, *Ancient Near Eastern Texts*, 268). See Qohelet's parody of the royal self-aggrandizement motif in Qoh 1:16; 2:1–10.

living in the fear of God. One pathway toward this kind of acceptance is through sober acknowledgment of the limited extent of human knowledge.

The knowledge and sovereignty of God expressed throughout Ecclesiastes form a backdrop against which the ignorance of humanity is set. This limitation is expressly stated by Qohelet in several places (cited below), admitted by Qohelet as a problem of his own (7:23–29), and is exemplified by Qohelet's own repeated use of the term *hebel* (הֶבֶל, pronounced "hevel"), a term meaning "incomprehensible" whenever it is used to describe the work of God in the world. Throughout the book, he applies the term *hebel* (1) to human endeavors, where it is best understood as "superficial/empty/futile" (1:2, 14; 2:1, 11, 15, 17; 4:4, 7–8; 5:7 [Heb. 5:6], 10 [Heb. 5:9]; 6:4, 9, 11; 7:6; 11:8, 10; 12:8) and (2) to the enigmatic ways of the world, which he attributes to God's works, where the term is best understood as "incomprehensible" (1:2; 2:19, 21, 23, 26; 3:19; 4:16; 6:2; 8:10, 14; 12:8).[20] These definitions of *hebel* are preferred to translations such as "meaningless," since Qohelet does indeed see meaning and consequence in human and divine actions, or "absurdity," which seems critical of the very God for whom Qohelet has such great reverence. To be sure, the negativities expressed by the term *hebel* are related to the imperfections and limitations of humanity, not God. With respect to God and his administration of the earth, Qohelet "does not mean that everything is meaningless or insignificant, but that everything is beyond human comprehension," writes C. L. Seow.[21] Arthur Keefer similarly asserts that while purpose and significance are important aspects of meaning, "'coherence' remains the book's unquestionable focus," noting that Qohelet "concentrates most on the (un)reliability and (in)comprehensibility of patterns in life."[22] Of the two major definitions provided above for *hebel*, it is the second that primarily concerns this essay since it pertains to humanity's inability to fully understand the ways and works of God.

20. A brief survey of how the term is rendered by commentators includes: "vanity" (Loader, *Ecclesiastes*; Ogden, *Qohelet*; Whybray, *Ecclesiastes*; Murphy, *Ecclesiastes*; Seow, *Ecclesiastes*; Davis, *Proverbs, Ecclesiastes*; Brown, *Ecclesiastes*; etc.), "meaningless" (Garrett, *Proverbs, Ecclesiastes*; Longman, *Book of Ecclesiastes*; etc.), "futility" (Crenshaw, *Ecclesiastes*; Krüger, *Qoheleth*; Fox, *Ecclesiastes*; Sneed, *Social World of the Sages*; etc.), "a breath" (Lohfink, *Qohelet*; Alter, *Wisdom Books*; etc.), "absurd" (Fox, *Qohelet and His Contradictions*; Schoors, *Ecclesiastes*; etc.), "evanescent" (Burkes, *Death in Qoheleth*), "mirage" (Heim, *Ecclesiastes*), "illusory" (Weeks, *Ecclesiastes and Skepticism*), "enigmatic" (Bartholomew, *Ecclesiastes*; etc.). This list is not an attempt to lock scholars into a single definition but to show the breadth of interpretation for *hebel*. Many will note that no one definition seems to work perfectly in every place throughout the book. For example, I suggest that Qohelet means something different when the term is applied to human endeavor than when it is applied to the mysteries of God.

21. Seow, *Ecclesiastes*, 59.

22. Keefer, "Meaning of Life in Ecclesiastes," 449.

The Reality of Human Ignorance:
They Cannot "Figure Out" (*MṢ'*, אצמ) or "Know" (*YD'*, עדי)

Qohelet begins by acknowledging God's sovereignty over the enigmatic world that human beings are desperately trying to figure out, and it is this "contemptible business" ('*inyan rā'*, עִנְיַן רָע) to make sense of things that Qohelet laments (1:13). What he discovers is that humanity is incapable even of figuring out one another (7:23–29), much less the mysteries of God's creation (3:11–15; 11:5). The verb "to find" (*mṣ'*, מצא) is introduced in 3:11 where it is used to convey that human beings cannot "figure out" what God has done in the past and cannot "figure out" what God will do in the future because he has set a boundary on human knowledge (human inability to know the future is an important, recurring theme in Ecclesiastes (3:22; 6:12; 7:14; 8:7; 9:12; 10:14; 11:2), a reality that ought to be contrasted with the practices of ANE peoples who sought this outcome through divination. The next time the verb appears is in 7:14, where, once again, Qohelet claims that God sovereignly oversees good things and bad things so that human beings cannot "figure out" the future, making every day of human life unpredictable (see also 10:8–11). After this comes 7:24, where again he claims that human beings cannot "figure out" all that has happened on earth. Every use of the term *mṣ'*, מצא in Ecclesiastes is for figuring out rather than searching to find a particular thing, including 7:25–28, where his mission is not to "find" an upright man or woman but to "figure out" people, a context set by vv. 23–24.[23]

The verb "to know" (*yd'*, ידע) is also scattered throughout the text. Part of Qohelet's mission was to "know" the inexplicable evils of the world

---

23. The majority view on Qoh 7:25–28 is that Qohelet is, in fact, speaking about how difficult it is to find a righteous person, asserting that he could find no righteous women and only one out of a thousand men. However, that would require understanding *mṣ'* (מצא) differently here than all elsewhere in the book, where it means "figure out." Whybray states regarding v. 28, "The commentators, in interpreting it, have failed to notice that it does not state what it is that the speaker has sought, and which he has, or has not, found" in his investigations (*Ecclesiastes*, 127). Furthermore, Qohelet notes elsewhere (9:9) that enjoying and loving one's wife is one of the simple, God-approved pleasures of life, a sentiment at odds with the interpretation that Qohelet was unable to find a single upright woman. If the context is set mainly by vv. 23–24 (rather than by v. 26), which I believe it is, then Qohelet could figure out not even one woman and could figure out only one out of a thousand men (an admission of Qohelet's ignorance rather than a general judgment against women). In this case, v. 26 is an interjection to note one of the only things he could figure out, that there's something worse than death. Verse 29 is not ordering the entire context as a quest to find upright people; rather, it is an explanation for why people are impossible to figure out—because they operate through "many schemes."

(1:17), but his results were disappointing. For example, no one can "know" whether their offspring will be foolish as adults (2:19), what exactly happens after death (3:21),[24] the times when they themselves are fools (5:1 [Heb. 4:17]), the present or the future (6:12; 8:7; 9:12; 10:14), deep wisdom (8:1), human emotions (9:1), how the ordinary things of life happen (11:5), when exactly disaster will strike (11:2), or whether any of their efforts will succeed (11:6). Some know less than most (10:15), and the knowledge humans think they have cannot protect them from unpredictable harm (9:11). Among the only things they can "know" for certain is that they will die (9:5) and then face God's judgment (11:9). Simply put, people cannot "figure out" the world, and what they do "know" amounts to very little.

The Object of Human Ignorance: The Work of God

Though his actions are not perfectly predictable nor perfectly understandable to humans, the God of Israel is not altogether unknowable. He has both described and shown his own character in Israel's history (e.g., Exod 20:2). He is clear about who he is and what he expects of his people (e.g., Lev 19:1-4). It is known, for example, that Yhwh is not fickle like the gods of the nations (Qoh 9:1 is a reference to human emotions, not divine).[25] The unknowability of the ANE gods is a frustration experienced by their people, one expressed by the so-called Babylonian Job, who could not ascertain what it took to please or enrage the gods.[26] On the contrary, Qohelet has already instructed his pupils to fear God and do what pleases him (2:26; 8:10-13; 3:14; 5:7 [Heb. 5:6]; 7:18; 8:12-13; 12:13), implying along with the rest of the Hebrew Scriptures that God can be sufficiently known by people. Nevertheless, the "work of God" (7:13; 8:17; 11:5)—that is, the *what* and *why* of everything that happens on earth—cannot be satisfactorily figured

---

24. Both Jews and Christians teach that there is life after death, but from Qohelet's limited perspective this information has not yet been fully revealed; accordingly, he writes, "Who knows?" (Qoh 3:21-22). In the Hebrew Scriptures, the repeated and dominant view is that there is only Sheol (e.g., Isa 38:18; Ps 6:5; 30:9 [Heb. 30:10]; 88:8-12 [Heb. 88:9-13]; Job 7:9; etc.). There are places that may represent glimpses into the afterlife, or at least a hope for it (e.g., Isa. 26:19-21; Ps 49:15 [Heb. 49:16]; Job 19:25-27; Dan 12:2-3; etc.), but most of these texts are debatable. Jesus explained to the Sadducees, citing Exod 3:6, that there is a resurrection because God is the God of the living, not the dead (Matt 22:32). But Qohelet speaks from a place of uncertainty; hence, he does not share the confidence of such later groups who absolutely reject life after death (Note: Qoh 12:7 is likely a reference to one's breath, not one's soul).

25. For Qoh 9:1 as referring to human emotions, see Seow, *Ecclesiastes*, 298; divine emotions: Fox, *Ecclesiastes*, 61. Seow's interpretation is preferred.

26. Foster, "Poem of Righteous Sufferer."

out by human beings. What God *has* revealed to humanity is his righteous character and his desire that humans live in accordance with that character, which Qohelet expresses to his disciples through admonitions to live wisely (7:1–13; 9:11—10:20) and reverentially (3:14; 5:1–6; 8:12–13; 12:13).

If one accepts a realistic understanding of human limitations, then one's pursuit of wisdom and knowledge can be a good thing (2:13; 10:2; etc.), but pursuing knowledge as an *ultimate* thing is delusional, like chasing the wind (2:15–17) since such a pursuit does not account for the boundaries God has set on humanity (3:11; 7:13–14). No matter how much effort a person applies to decode "the work of God" (7:13; 8:17; 11:5), they will not succeed. In the end, some may, through self-delusion, claim that they have solved such mysteries (8:17), but Qohelet gives us the inside track—actually, "they *cannot* figure it out" (*lōʾ yûkal limṣōʾ*, לֹא יוּכַל לִמְצֹא)! Acceptance of this fact better positions God-fearers to live authentic lives devoid of the kinds of manipulation and control that persist in the ideologies of ANE peoples, syncretistic Israelites, or those who think they can twist the arm of God through rote obedience.

CONCLUSION

The world of Qohelet featured systems of belief that contradicted the way of God taught in the Hebrew Scriptures. On the one hand, the religious ideologies of the ANE had worshippers futilely attempting to control life's outcomes through manipulation of the gods. On the other hand, certain Hebrews, like the interlocutors of Job, held to the similarly false belief that the outcomes of life could be predicted through ritual obedience to and right living before Yhwh. Qohelet, however, rejects these false systems by presenting the God of Israel as wholly other and in every good way infinite. Hence, the good things that come in life come from his hand, and God-fearers must receive such things joyfully and in reverential gratitude toward God. To do so, however, they must also reject delusions of permanence and control, recognizing that the realities of human finitude confound such vanities. Among the many human limitations exposed by Qohelet, such as powerlessness, mortality, fallibility, etc., humans are shown to be more ignorant than they realize, the boundaries of their knowledge having been set by God himself (3:11). He has done this so that people will "fear before him" (3:14)—indeed, the God who "made everything" has also made it impossible for human beings to figure it all out. By contrast, God fully understands the thoughts of humanity, "that they are futile," a mere breath (*kî-hēmmâ hābel*, כִּי־הֵמָּה הָבֶל [Ps 94:11]; ὅτι εἰσὶν μάταιοι [1 Cor 3:18–20]).

Given the besetting limitations of humanity, what is a faithful God-fearer to do? Indeed, one must choose: either (1) follow the pagan program of finite deities and the human delusions of control and permanence that emerge from it, or (2) embrace the holy disillusion taught by Qohelet, that is, the scriptural teaching of an infinite God and the opportunity provided by that God to live joyful, simple (that is to say, "authentic") lives in reverential obedience to him. There is a foundational similarity here for how Jews and Christians understand God, but how that plays out differently for each depends on one's view of proper Jewish observance, on the one hand, and adherence to the Christian gospel on the other. Nevertheless, Jews and Christians today would do well to sit at the feet of Qohelet, a teacher who points his pupils to joyful acceptance in the fear of God (3:14; 5:6; 8:12-13; 12:13).

BIBLIOGRAPHY

Alter, Robert. *The Wisdom Books: Job, Proverbs, and Ecclesiastes; A Translation with Commentary*. New York: Norton & Co., 2010.
Anderson, William H. U. "Ecclesiastes in the Intertextual Matrix of Ancient Near Eastern Literature." In *Reading Ecclesiastes Intertextually*, edited by Katharine Dell and Will Kynes, 157–75. LHBOTS 587. New York: Bloomsbury, 2014.
Bartholomew, C. G. *Ecclesiastes*. BCOTWP. Grand Rapids: Baker Academic, 2009.
Brown, William P. *Ecclesiastes*. IBC. Louisville: John Knox, 2000.
Burkes, Shannon. *Death in Qoheleth and Egyptian Biographies of the Late Period*. SBL Dissertation Series 170. Atlanta: SBL, 1999.
Crenshaw, James L. *Ecclesiastes: A Commentary*. OTL. Philadelphia: Westminster, 1987.
Davis, Ellen. *Proverbs, Ecclesiastes, and the Song of Songs*. Westminster Bible Companion. Louisville: Westminster John Knox, 2000.
Dell, Katherine J. "A Wise Man Reflecting on Wisdom." *TynBul* 71 (2020) 137–52.
Foster, Benjamin. "Atra-Ḫasis." In *The Context of Scripture*, edited by William W. Hallo and K. Lawson Younger Jr., 1:450–51. New York: Brill, 1997.
———. "The Poem of the Righteous Sufferer." In *The Context of Scripture*, edited by William W. Hallo and K. Lawson Younger Jr., 1:486–92. New York: Brill, 1997.
Fox, Michael V. *Ecclesiastes*. JPS Bible Commentary. Philadelphia: JPS, 2004.
———. *Qohelet and His Contradictions*. JSOTSup 71. Sheffield: Almond, 1989.
Garrett, Duane A. *Proverbs, Ecclesiastes, Song of Songs*. NAC 14. Nashville: Broadman and Holman, 1993.
Heim, Knut Martin. *Ecclesiastes: An Introduction and Commentary*. TOTC 18. Downers Grove, IL: IVP Academic, 2019.
Hilber, John W. "Prophecy, Divination, and Magic." In *Behind the Scenes of the Old Testament: Cultural, Social, and Historical Contexts*, edited by Jonathan Greer et al., 368–74. Grand Rapids: Baker, 2020.
Keefer, Arthur. "The Meaning of Life in Ecclesiastes: Coherence, Purpose, and Significance from a Psychological Perspective." *HTR* 112 (2019) 447–66.
Krüger, Thomas. *Qoheleth*. Hermeneia. Minneapolis: Fortress, 2004.

Loader, James A. *Ecclesiastes*. Translated by John Vriend. Grand Rapids: Eerdmans, 1986.
Lohfink, Norbert. *Qohelet*. CC. Minneapolis: Fortress, 2003.
Longman, Tremper, III. *The Book of Ecclesiastes*. NICOT. Grand Rapids: Eerdmans, 1998.
Luzzatto, Moshe Chaim. *The Way of God: An Essay on Fundamentals*. Translated by Aryeh Kaplan and Gershon Robinson. 6th ed. New York: Feldheim, 1998.
Maul, Stefan M. *The Art of Divination in the Ancient Near East: Reading the Signs of Heaven and Earth*. Translated by Brian McNeil and Alexander Johannes Edmonds. Waco: Baylor University Press, 2019.
Murphy, Roland E. *Ecclesiastes*. WBC 23A. Dallas: Word, 1992.
Nemet-Nejat, Karen Rhea. *Daily Life in Ancient Mesopotamia*. Peabody, MA: Hendrickson, 2002.
Ogden, Graham S. *Qohelet*. Readings, a New Biblical Commentary. Sheffield: JSOT, 1987.
Oswalt, John N. *The Bible Among the Myths: Unique Revelation or Just Ancient Scripture?* Grand Rapids: Zondervan, 2009.
Pinker, Steven. *Enlightenment Now: The Case for Reason, Science, Humanism, and Progress*. London: Lane, 2018.
Pritchard, James B., ed. *The Ancient Near Eastern Texts Relating to the Old Testament*. 3rd ed. with suppl. Princeton Studies on the Near East. Princeton, NJ: Princeton University Press, 1969.
Schoors, Antoon. *Ecclesiastes*. HCOT. Paris: Peeters, 2013.
Seow, C. L. *Ecclesiastes*. AB 18c. New York: Doubleday, 1997.
Shelley, Percy Bysshe. *The Complete Poetry of Percy Bysshe Shelley*. Edited by Donald H. Reiman et al. Vol. 3. Baltimore: Johns Hopkins University Press, 2012.
Sneed, Mark R. *The Social World of the Sages: An Introduction to Israelite and Jewish Wisdom Literature*. Minneapolis: Fortress, 2015.
Snell, Daniel C. *Religions of the Ancient Near East*. Cambridge: Cambridge University Press, 2011.
Walton, John H. *Ancient Near Eastern Thought and the Old Testament: Introducing the Conceptual World of the Hebrew Bible*. Grand Rapids: Baker, 2006.
Weeks, Stuart. *Ecclesiastes and Skepticism*. LHBOTS. London: T&T Clark, 2012.
Whybray, R. Norman. *Ecclesiastes*. New Century Bible Commentary. Grand Rapids: Eerdmans, 1989.
Williams, J. Rodman. *God, the World, and Redemption*. Vol. 1 of *Renewal Theology: Systematic Theology from a Charismatic Perspective*. Grand Rapids: Zondervan, 1996.

Chapter 8

Jewish and Christian Perspectives on the Problem of Suffering
Discerning the Ways of God in a Fallen World

Timothy S. Yoder

THE PRESENCE OF HUMAN suffering, especially in a world created and ruled by a transcendent and good God, prompts a perennial question. Why does evil, and in particular horrendous evil, persist in our world? No individual is free from the pain of suffering, and no thoughtful person is free to ignore the challenge posed by this condition. The challenge is heightened for those, like Jews and Christians, who hold to the belief in powerful and beneficent deity.

The history of responses to this perennial question is a long and significant one, with roots in the ancient world and continued debate up to the present day. In this chapter, I examine this history, with special attention to the ways that the Christian and Jewish traditions run in similar paths, as well as the distinctives offered by each tradition. I begin with some classic figures in the intellectual tradition of both religions—Saadiah Gaon and Moses Maimonides for the Jewish faith, and Augustine for the Christian church. The bulk of the chapter, however, is devoted to contemporary reflections on the problem of evil (hereafter, PoE) in both traditions. Jewish theologians and philosophers have wrestled deeply with the horrendous evils propagated by the Nazis (their "final solution") in a body of scholarship known as Holocaust theology. Around that same time, the Christian philosophical tradition experienced a renaissance and much of it contains commonalities, as well as some important distinctives, with Jewish reflections.

CLASSIC THINKERS: SAADIAH, MAIMONIDES, AND AUGUSTINE

Theistic responses to the PoE are a natural place for intellectual integration. The three individuals examined in this section moved freely within the disciplines of philosophy and theology. The starting point for all those who worship the God of Abraham, and who are troubled by evil in this world, is the Hebrew Bible—the story of Job, the laments of psalmists, and prophets like Habakkuk and Jeremiah. This reflection continued in the rabbinic tradition, and eventually into the theology and philosophy of both traditions.

One of the first well-known Jewish philosophers was Saadiah Gaon (882–942). Saadiah wrote a commentary on Job entitled *Book of Theodicy* in which he attempted a rational interpretation of Job's story that advanced beyond the existing rabbinic tradition, which tended to side with Job's counselors.[1] In keeping with the book's title (more literally, "the book which confirms justice"), Saadiah sought to defend both God and Job in his commentary. "Plainly, His bringing creation into being from nothing is the ultimate act of grace. For He created the entire world and settled it with human beings for their benefit."[2] Saadiah held that even when God brings suffering upon the world, it is an act of benevolence, since "He causes us to feel sufferings, so as to exercise goodness and grace when He saved us from these."[3]

These greater goods occur in three ways. First, some suffering is for discipline and instruction, concerning which Saadiah cites Prov 3:11–12 as support. A second way includes purgation and punishment. Although the suffering is punishment, it is restorative punishment. "Its object is grace."[4] The last case is that of trial and testing, and this is the situation of Job. Saadiah defended God's use of trials thus: "An upright servant, whose Lord knows that he will bear sufferings loosed upon him and hold steadfast in his uprightness, is subjected to certain sufferings, so that when he steadfastly bears them, his Lord may reward him and bless him. This too is a kind of bounty and beneficence, for it brings the servant to everlasting blessedness."[5] The

1. Leaman, *Evil and Suffering*, 50.
2. Saadiah, *Book of Theodicy*, 124.
3. Saadiah, *Book of Theodicy*, 125.
4. Saadiah, *Book of Theodicy*, 125.
5. Saadiah, *Book of Theodicy*, 125–26.

clear implication of this interpretation is that Saadiah held to an afterlife in which this bounty would be received.

Another aspect of Saadiah's position on these undeserved sufferings (which are clearly not discipline or punishment) is that they result in greater blessing than the nature of the suffering. Therefore, God cannot be held to be unjust, and neither is the sufferer to be held culpable for the evil that they endure. Lenn Goodman interprets Saadiah in this way:

> Recompense, as Saadiah employs the notion to explain the Book of Job, goes beyond restitution, to justify God's upsetting the moral balance by imposing sufferings where there was no prior desert of suffering. Ultimately—in the afterlife—victims of these "sufferings of love" will recognize that their lot has been improved over what it would have been otherwise.[6]

A towering figure in the history of Jewish intellectual life is Moses Maimonides (1138–1204), author of *The Guide for the Perplexed*. In this volume, Maimonides offers his thoughts both on the story of Job and the challenge of human suffering. He begins by noting that Job is described as a righteous, but not necessarily wise, man.[7] This ostensibly uncharitable remark is actually an important distinction that goes to the heart of Maimonides's interpretation of Job. The principal lesson that Maimonides derives from Job's narrative is that God should not be equated to us. "We should not fall into the error of imagining His knowledge to be similar to ours, or His intentions, providence, and rule to be similar to ours."[8] Thus, contra Saadiah, Maimonides does not assume that divine justice parallels human notions. He believed that Job acquired wisdom when he abandoned these traditional ideas of God and replaced them with true knowledge—that is, that God's ways are higher than ours. Job was naïve in expecting God to act like a kind parent, rewarding and punishing on the basis of justice. For Maimonides, God does not act this way. He is unconcerned with the material world and prizes instead the intellect, as it is the pathway to true knowledge.[9]

Regarding the nature of evil, Maimonides contends that all of God's works and actions are good, and, thus, evil is a privation. "It cannot be said of God that He directly creates evil or that He has the direct intention to produce evil; this is impossible."[10] The creation is material, and this fact opens the door to suffering, but nothing God made is evil. Evil, thus, is a

6. L. E. Goodman, in Saadiah, *Book of Theodicy*, 136.
7. Maimonides, *Guide for the Perplexed* 3.22, 297.
8. Maimonides, *Guide for the Perplexed* 3.23, 303.
9. Leaman, *Evil and Suffering*, 74–75.
10. Maimonides, *Guide for the Perplexed* 3.10, 266.

negation or corruption of the good of God's creation. Illness and poverty are evil because they reflect an absence of the good that was. They are negative properties, not the good that comes from God. Maimonides also objected to the position that the evil far outweighs the good, which he attributed to Al-Razi, though he likely also has Saadiah as a shadow target.[11] Ignorant people believe the world filled with evil, but this perspective only considers the human circumstance. When we include the angelic realm, the whole of the universe, and even the elements and atoms, we discover that suffering only occurs in very small percentage of the creation. The universe exists for God's sake, not our own, so our human perspective unjustifiably magnifies the PoE.[12]

Maimonides held that there are three kinds of evil which befall humankind. The first arises from our condition as people that come into existence and also pass out of it. Our "genesis and destruction" is a direct result of our material nature, which means we are subject to deformities, illnesses and other physical problems. The second kind of evil has to do the kinds of things that people do to each other. These "moral evils" include assault, murder, and various acts of war. The most numerous evils are found in the third class, which are the things that individuals do to harm themselves. Maimonides finds biblical support for the prevalence of these evils. Proverbs 19:3 proclaims, "A man's own folly ruins his life, yet his heart rages against the Lord," and in Eccl 7:29, the Teacher says, "This only have I found: God made mankind upright, but men have gone is search of many schemes." It is noteworthy that Maimonides does not engage in promotion of theodicies or explanations to PoE. This absence is due, of course, to his core conviction that true knowledge is found in recognizing that God's justice is not like human justice, so the task of justifying God is fundamentally misplaced. In addition, the problem of evil is frequently exaggerated, and an analysis of the kinds of evil in the world reveals that most of them are simply our fault. So, placing them at God's feet is to display a lack of wisdom. Although Maimonides experienced human suffering (his brother was lost at sea, which led to significant financial hardships for the family), no catastrophic evil like the Holocaust transpired during his lifetime. This fact is important to note, as some twentieth-century Jewish thinkers have argued that the gratuitous evils perpetrated by the Nazis elevated consideration of the PoE to a new level. An example is Emil Fackenheim, who held that the Shoah was unprecedented historically and unanticipated by all previous philosophy.[13]

11. Goodman, "Judaism and Problem of Evil," 199.
12. Maimonides, *Guide for the Perplexed* 3.12.
13. Fackenheim, "Holocaust."

Moving back in history to the great Catholic thinker Augustine (354–430), we find a number of interesting commonalities with Maimonides, not to mention the seeds of important contemporary Christian and Jewish reflections on the PoE—like Maimonides, Augustine began with the conviction that "everything that exists is good."[14] The creation is good, as the account in Gen 1 asserts six times. Nothing in creation was evil, so the introduction of evil meant that the good was corrupted, that is, that it now fails to be something that it was. This corruption Augustine described as a *privation*, a state of "a thing being *deprived* some good appropriate to the kind of being it is."[15] For instance, a blanket with a hole is now deprived of the integrity it once had. The hole is not a thing per se (it can't exist on its own), but it is a flaw, an imperfection, which is a mark of corruption. "Everything that exists is good, then; and so evil, the source of which I was seeking, cannot be a substance, because if it were, it would be good."[16] A privation is not a created thing that exists in its own right as a substance, but rather it is parasitic on the good substance, like a hole in a blanket, wrinkles on a shirt, or rust on a car.

For Augustine, the problem is not so much why does God allow evil to persist, but why does evil emerge in a perfect creation? The answer that he gave begins with the understanding that God made us as contingent being. Of course, he could do no other. A created being cannot be eternal or necessary, so as created beings, we are contingent. Contingent being as such are prone to corruption, and the culprit is taken to be our free will. Augustine reflected on this question in his book *On the Free Choice of the Will*, as his dialogue partner Evodius asked why God gave us the free will, since by it we do sinful things. Augustine's answer was "no one can act rightly except by that same free choice of the will, and I affirmed that God gave us free choice in order to enable us to act rightly." The will is the mechanism by which we love and do good things, however, sometimes we use our will poorly. The problem, as Cary explains, is not that we love evil, but rather that we love evilly. "We do choose things that we think will make us happy. And the point here is that our choices in this regard can go wrong."[17] For Augustine, it is a matter of disordered loves. We love something like food or money over some higher good like other people or God, and this upsetting of the order of good things produces evil. The ability to love is a good

---

14. Augustine, *Confessions* 7.12.18, 174.
15. Cary, "Classic View," 16; emphasis in original.
16. Augustine, *Confessions* 7.12.18, 174.
17. Cary, "Classic View," 20.

gift from God, but when it is deployed in an unbefitting manner, then the consequence is sin and evil.

HUMAN SUFFERING AND HUMAN SIN

The word "evil" is an ambiguous word. It is used as a synonym for "suffering" or "tragic," as in the evils of the recent coronavirus pandemic or the devastating 1755 Lisbon earthquake. The phrase *natural evil* refers to these instances of human suffering that are not the result of human causality. However, evil also refers to sin and lawlessness. Reformed Christian theologian D. A. Carson writes that "evil is evil because it is rebellion against God. Evil is the failure to do what God demands or the performance of that which God forbids."[18] This second sense of evil is sinful evil or *moral evil*. The Judeo-Christian tradition affirms that moral evils occur because of the rebellion of Satan and his demons and also the fall of Adam and Eve, as described in Gen 3. The curse imposed on Satan and the first two humans means that we live in a fallen world, characterized by natural and moral evils. Clearly, there is a strong connection between evil in the suffering sense and evil in the sinful sense. There was no evil or suffering in the world that God created (Gen 1–2), but post-fall, we live in a fallen world.

Orthodox Jewish theologian Abraham Joshua Heschel (1907–72) has made a strong case that considerations of the PoE need to commence with the understanding that the problem begins with our own sin: "The decay of conscience fills the air with a pungent smell. Good and evil, which were once as distinguishable as day and night, have become a blurred mist. But that mist is manmade. God is not silent. He has been silenced."[19] The silence of God will be examined more deeply below, but it is important to see the strong position that Heschel is taking about human sinfulness. In the classic PoE objection—raised by philosophers from Epicurus to David Hume to Friedrich Nietzsche—the challenge is addressed to God. Why does the omnipotent and omnibenevolent deity allow horrendous evils like the Shoah to occur? Heschel's reminder is that the ultimate fault is the human. Per Braiterman, "For his part Heschel refused to blame the God of History when the immediate responsibility for evil lay with human beings."[20]

Braiterman notes that in an earlier work, Heschel sided with God against Job's accusations.[21] However, Heschel is not echoing the conclusion

---

18. Carson, *How Long, O Lord?*, 42.
19. Heschel, *Man Is Not Alone*, 152.
20. Braiterman, *(God) After Auschwitz*, 69.
21. Braiterman, *(God) After Auschwitz*, 68.

of Job's counselors, who, in their many speeches, urged Job to confess his terrible sin. They held to a punishment theodicy—that is, that all suffering is the direct result of a specific sin (Job 4:7–8; 8:3–7; 11:13–20). But certainly, this conclusion is too simplistic and does not follow. Carson develops the conclusion that characterizes the evangelical position, namely that there is such a thing as innocent suffering. It is impossible to draw a tight causal connection between a sinful act and suffering. Sometimes the righteous suffer, and sometimes the wicked prosper. Carson notes that it is not the case that "all suffering is directly related to a specific sin; it means that some suffering in this world is not directly related to any sin."[22]

SKEPTICAL CHALLENGES

It is not only atheists and agnostics that raise skeptical challenges against God in the face of human suffering. When horrendous evils like the Shoah occur, the faith of the devout may be shaken. A prime example is Elie Wiesel, even who grew up in Poland in a very observant Orthodox family. Arrested by the Nazis and imprisoned in the camps, Elie, who was only a boy, was one the few in his family to survive. His famous book *Night* describes both the horrors of the Nazi tortures and the anguished disappointment of the Jews, who waited in vain for divine rescue. He also details the assault on his faith that these events provoked, even on the first night of his imprisonment. "Never shall I forget that night, the first night in the camp, which has turned my life into one long night, seven times cursed and seven times sealed." He continued, "Never shall I forget those moments which murdered by God and my soul and turned my dreams to dust."[23] But these words should not be interpreted to mean that Wiesel became an atheist or believed that God had truly died. In a later memoir, Wiesel clarified his position: "I have never renounced my faith in God. I have risen against His justice, protested His silence and sometimes his absence, but my anger rises up within the faith and not outside it."[24]

It is commonplace in philosophical circles to identify two kinds of skeptics that arise from the PoE. There are those who claim that evil in the word rules out a loving and powerful God. The conclusion is called the *logical conclusion*, as its adherents (like Nietzsche and Russell) reason that evil and God are mutually exclusive. The second group is a bit more cautious, and they prefer an inductive approach which concludes that the existence

22. Carson, *How Long, O Lord?*, 140.
23. Wiesel, *Night*, 32.
24. Wiesel, *All Rivers Run*, 84.

of God is unlikely, but not decisively ruled out, especially given the horrendous and gratuitous evils present in the word. Philosophers of religion like Paul Draper and William Rowe fit in this category, usually called the *evidential conclusion*.[25] I think that Elie Wiesel fits in a third category, which I call the *moral outrage conclusion* from evil. Those in this group are angry and disappointed with God, and frequently can find no plausible reason for God's inaction. However, they stop short of sharing the atheist or agnostic conclusion. According to Wiesel, there is no justifying God for allowing the horrific evil of the Holocaust, but there is also no disbelieving him either. Wiesel wrote, "Auschwitz is conceivable neither with God nor without Him. Perhaps I may someday come to understand man's role in the mystery Auschwitz represents, but never God's."[26]

Individuals like Rowe and Draper draw a different conclusion than Wiesel. Interacting with Christian philosophers and their theodicies, Rowe and Draper still find that the presence and extent of suffering in the world are difficult to square with an all good and supremely powerful deity. Thus, they conclude that it is more likely that there is no god. Rowe's most famous argument concerns gratuitous evils, those for which there does not seem to be a plausible or readily outweighing good. He proposes a thought experiment in which a fawn is trapped in a terrible wildfire. The deer is burned and injured, but survives the fire, only to die an agonized death of starvation and thirst, since the fire consumed or spoiled all available food and water. Rowe argues that the deity could have prevented this state of affairs but chose not to do so. If there is a greater good, such a choice could be justified—however, no such good seems apparent. When one factors in the vast variety of these kinds of pointless evils (like the Holocaust, natural disasters, and the like), it becomes increasingly difficult to come to a rational conclusion that a god like the God of Abraham exists. Rowe avers, "In the light of our experience and knowledge of the variety and scale of human and animal suffering in our world, the idea that none of this suffering could have been prevented by an omnipotent being without thereby losing a greater good or permitting an evil just as bad seems an extraordinarily absurd idea, quite beyond our belief."[27]

A prominent response to Rowe's argument was presented by Christian philosopher Marilyn McCord Adams, an ordained Episcopal priest and longtime professor at UCLA. Adams acknowledged that horrendous evils

---

25. William Lane Craig calls these the "logical version" and the "probabilistic version" of the internal problem of evil in his essay on the Molinist view, in Meister and Dew, *God and Problem of Evil*, 41.

26. Wiesel, *All Rivers Run*, 84.

27. Rowe, "Problem of Evil," 3.

seem to present prima facie evidence for doubting that someone impacted by such an evil could experience life as a great good and would instead consider their life a tragedy. In addition, it is difficult to see how the situation could be remedied. However, there is in the Christian worldview an answer. Following Anselm, God is a being who is himself greater than anything else, inclusive of good and evil. The promise of the Christian Scriptures is an eternity in the presence of God (Rev 21:3–4). Adams reasoned thus: "The good of beatific, face-to-face intimacy with God is simply incommensurate with any merely non-transcendent goods or ills a person might experience. Thus, the good of beatific face-to-face intimacy with God would *engulf*... even the horrendous evils humans experience in this present life here below, and overcome any prima-facie reasons the individual had to doubt whether his/her life would or could be worth living."[28]

The last of the three skeptical conclusions is the boldest of them all. Atheists claim that the presence and persistence of evil in the world rules out the existence of God. Evil and God are mutually exclusive. This is the so-called logical conclusion to the PoE. J. L. Mackie made this argument in the early 1960s, and his presentation of it was fodder for Christian philosopher Alvin Plantinga's response in his book *God, Freedom, and Evil*. At approximately the same time, Jewish philosopher (and Conservative rabbi) Richard Rubenstein published *After Auschwitz*, a book in which he developed a Jewish version of death of God theology. It created an immediate sensation and vigorous protests against its radical proposals. The "death of God" metaphor is, of course, most often associated with Friedrich Nietzsche's "Parable of the Madman." In the mid-1960s, there was a short-lived theological trend in liberal Protestant theology that promoted this position, which was hyped by a shameless *Time* magazine cover in 1966 (the Easter issue, no less) asking "Is God dead?"

Rubenstein's work produced two effects. It sparked more sustained Jewish intellectual reflection on the meaning and impact of the Shoah, and it invoked a Jewish version of the logical conclusion from the PoE:

> How can Jews believe in an omnipotent, beneficent God after Auschwitz? Traditional Jewish theology maintains that God is the ultimate, omnipotent actor in the historical drama. It has interpreted every major catastrophe in Jewish history as God's punishment of a sinful Israel. To see any purpose in the death camps, the traditional believer is forced to regard the most demonic, antihuman explosion in all human history as a

---

28. Adams, "Horrendous Evils," 379; emphasis in original.

meaningful expression of God's purposes. The idea is simply too obscene for me to accept.[29]

It should be noted that Rubenstein's position was not precisely as atheistic as that held by Nietzsche and Mackie. Rubenstein affirms that the death of God (a phrase he stopped using in the second edition of *After Auschwitz*) does not necessarily mean the death of all the gods. Rather, for Rubenstein is the demise of the omnipotent actor of the Judeo-Christian tradition. Instead, Rubenstein calls for an "insightful paganism" and a god who is a Holy Nothingness.[30] A deity after this manner cannot resolve the PoE, thus there is no possibility of theodicy.

Another revision of the idea of God that appears in both Christian and Jewish reflection is the legacy of process theology. Hans Jonas, a prominent Jewish philosopher, jettisoned the conclusion that God was omnipotent, and in its place argued for a suffering deity that lacks the majesty of El-Shaddai. Jonas suggested a god who is "a becoming God. It is a God emerging in time instead of possessing a completed being that remains identical with itself throughout eternity." In addition, Jonas says, this new version of God not remote and detached, but also caring. This state of affairs, however, means that God is dependent on others. "He is therefore also an endangered God, a God who risks something. Clearly that must be so, or the world would be in a condition of permanent perfection."[31]

RESPONSES TO THE CHALLENGES

An important response to the various challenges discussed above is the Jewish concept of *hester panim*, which refers to God hiding his face and it appears in two quite distinct ways in the Hebrew Bible. The first way God hides his face is as a consequence of anger and judgment. Deuteronomy 31:17–18 is a clear example, as the Lord says, "Then my anger will be kindled against them in that day, and I will forsake them and hide my face from them, and they will be devoured" (ESV). God turns his face away because of their sin. However, in many passages God's absence is noted, but it is not due to the sin of the individual to whom God is hidden. Consider Ps 44, in which the people lament their sufferings. However, it is not because they have lacked faith in God (v. 8) or forgotten the covenant (v. 17). Nevertheless, they are

---

29. Rubenstein, *After Auschwitz*, cited in Katz, *Wrestling with God*, 416.

30. Braiterman, *(God) After Auschwitz*, 92–95.

31. Hans Jonas, "God After Auschwitz," in Cohn-Sherlock, *Holocaust Theology*, 138–39.

humbled and rejected by God (v. 9), made a reproach to their neighbors (v. 13), crushed (v. 19) and led like sheep to the slaughter (v. 22). The psalmist cries out in despair, "Awake! Why are you sleeping, O Lord? Rouse yourself! Do not reject us forever! Why do you hide your face? Why do you forget our affliction and oppression?" (vv. 23–24 ESV). Clearly, in this psalm, the Lord is hidden and absent, but for reasons other than the sin of the people.

Steven Katz suggests that there are three conclusions that can be drawn from this second kind of hester panim. First, the sufferings of the death camps are not a divine punishment for their sins. Second, God is not the direct cause of the evils of the Holocaust. Rather, they are the work of sinful individuals. Third, despite the empirical evidence to the contrary, Hashem is still a God who saves his people.[32] But how does God save if he is absent from his people? This process is explained in a stirring passage from Orthodox Rabbi Eliezer Berkovits's *Faith After the Holocaust*. Berkovits asserts that if humans are to act on the basis of their own responsibility, then God must remove himself and hide his all-encompassing power and majesty. However, humans left to their own devices are capable of great evil. Thus, God must walk a fine line between over-awing and under-ruling. He proposes, "That man may be, God must absent himself; that man may not perish in the tragic absurdity of his own making, God must remain present. The God of history must be present and absent concurrently. He is present without being indubitably manifest; he is absent without being hopelessly inaccessible."[33] This balancing act of God leads to two implications—innocent people will suffer, and evil will not conquer the good.

This last point leads to perhaps the most significant theodicy in the Judeo-Christian tradition, which is the free will defense. Interestingly, two of the most articulate expressions of this long-standing argument (which first finds expression on the work of Augustine) were published within two years of each. There is the ground-breaking work of Alvin Plantinga in *God, Freedom, and Evil*, published in 1974, and Berkovits's classic *Faith After the Holocaust* a year earlier. I begin with Berkovits, who repeats the teaching of Rabbi Meir that whatever God created was made with its opposite. "There could be no mountains without valleys."[34] But these dialectics must be understood properly. The contrast is not absolute (God created good and evil both), but relative. Berkovits rejects Manichean dualism, holding instead that God creates the possibility of evil and good in humans. It is for this reason that God created human with freedom. In fact, "freedom and

---

32. Katz, *Wrestling with God*, 358.
33. Berkovits, *Faith After the Holocaust*, 107.
34. Berkovits, *Faith After the Holocaust*, 102.

responsibility are of the very essence of man."[35] If humans are to be able to love, obey, and exercise faith, they must also be able to hate, disobey, and reject God. If God exercised all his power to prevent the negative consequences, then humans could never be the beings that he made them to be.

A very similar line of thinking emerges is Plantinga's version of the free will defense. First, he takes on the logical conclusion to the PoE that the presence of evil in the world rules out the existence of God. Plantinga examines the claims of J. L. Mackie, and he finds that Mackie produced no explicit or implicit contradiction between God and evil. One of Mackie's fundamental principles is that there are no limits for what an omnipotent God can do, but Plantinga corrects that belief. There are things that God cannot do (he cannot lie or break his promises), and, in fact, there are possible worlds that God cannot actualize.[36] Plantinga shows that it is also the case that God cannot create a world in which people have significant freedom and there is no evil (or sin).[37] This conviction might seem to be a problem for theists, but Plantinga believes that the way out of the classic PoE is to understand that "God creates a world containing evil and has a good reason for doing so."[38] The good reason is that some evils are necessary for some goods. Without suffering, goods like heroism, patience, and grace cannot obtain. Therefore, a world containing humans with significant freedom is a more valuable world, even though it means that these humans will inevitably go wrong at many points in their lives.[39] With these simple strokes, the sting of the logical problem from evil is removed, and Mackie's robust challenge refuted.

CONCLUSION

Clearly, much more could be said regarding Jewish and Christian reflections on the PoE. Critical names on this issue have been left out, including Christian thinkers Eleanore Stump and Tim Keller, and Jewish intellectuals Primo Levi and Rabbi Shapira. Important issues, like the role of the afterlife, have not been addressed. What stands out from the discussion is the complementary nature of these reflections, both in the medieval world and the contemporary one. Jews and Christians wrestling with the challenge of evil bring their own distinctive perspectives to the conversation. Yet, important

35. Berkovits, *Faith After the Holocaust*, 105.
36. Plantinga, *God, Freedom, and Evil*, 16–17.
37. Plantinga, *God, Freedom, and Evil*, 45.
38. Plantinga, *God, Freedom, and Evil*, 26.
39. Plantinga, *God, Freedom, and Evil*, 27–30.

parallels and commonalities between Jewish and Christian reflections upon the PoE point to the enduring reasons to trust in a good and faithful God, even in the worst moments of human existence.

BIBLIOGRAPHY

Adams, Marilyn McCord. "Horrendous Evils and the Goodness of God." In *Philosophy of Religion: Selected Readings*, edited by Michael Peterson et al., 374–82. 5th ed. New York: Oxford University Press, 2014.

Augustine. *The Confessions*. Translated by Maria Boulding. 2nd ed. Hyde Park, NY: New City, 2012.

Berkovits, Eliezer. *Faith After the Holocaust*. New York: Ktav, 1973.

Braiterman, Zachary. *(God) After Auschwitz: Tradition and Change in Post-Holocaust Jewish Thought*. Princeton, NJ: Princeton University Press, 1998.

Carson, D. A. *How Long, O Lord? Reflections on Suffering and Evil*. 2nd ed. Grand Rapids: Baker, 2006.

Cary, Phillip. "A Classic View." In *God and the Problem of Evil: Five Views*, edited by Chad Meister and James K. Dew Jr., 13–36. Spectrum Multiview. Downers Grove, IL: InterVarsity, 2017.

Cohn-Sherlock, Dan, ed. *Holocaust Theology: A Reader*. Washington Square: New York University Press, 2002.

Fackenheim, Emil. "Holocaust." In *20th Century Jewish Religious Thought*, edited by Arthur A. Cohen and Paul Mendes-Flohr, 399–402. Philadelphia: JPS, 2009.

Goodman, Lenn. "Judaism and the Problem of Evil." In *Cambridge Companion to the Problem of Evil*, edited by Chad Meister and Paul K. Moser, 193–209. Cambridge Companions to Religion. New York: Cambridge University Press, 2017.

Heschel, Abraham Joshua. *Man Is Not Alone: A Philosophy of Religion*. New York: Farrar, Straus and Giroux, 1951.

Howard-Snyder, Daniel, and Paul K. Moser, eds. *Divine Hiddenness: New Essays*. Cambridge: Cambridge University Press, 2002.

Katz, Steven T. *Post-Holocaust Dialogues: Critical Studies in Modern Jewish Thought*. New York: New York University Press, 1983.

Katz, Steven T., et al., eds. *Wrestling with God: Jewish Theological Responses During and After the Holocaust*. New York: Oxford University Press, 2007.

Leaman, Oliver. *Evil and Suffering in Jewish Philosophy*. Cambridge Studies in Religious Traditions 6. Cambridge: Cambridge University Press, 1995.

Maimonides, Moses. *The Guide for the Perplexed*. Translated by Michael Friedlander. 2nd ed. New York: Dover, 1956.

Meister, Chad, and James K. Dew Jr., eds. *God and the Problem of Evil: Five Views*. Spectrum Multiview. Downers Grove, IL: InterVarsity, 2017.

Meister, Chad, and Paul K. Moser, eds. *Cambridge Companion to the Problem of Evil*. Cambridge Companions to Religion. New York: Cambridge University Press, 2017.

Plantinga, Alvin. *God, Freedom, and Evil*. New York: Harper and Row, 1974.

Rowe, William. "The Problem of Evil and Some Varieties of Atheism." In *The Evidential Argument from Evil*, edited by Daniel Howard-Snyder, 1–11. Indiana Series in the Philosophy of Religion. Bloomington: Indiana University Press, 1996.

Rubenstein, Richard L. *After Auschwitz*. New York: MacMillan, 1966.
Saadiah ben Joseph Al-Fayyumi. *The Book of Theodicy: Translation and Commentary on the Book of Job*. Translated by L. E. Goodman. New Haven, CT: Yale University Press, 1988.
Wiesel, Elie. *All Rivers Run to the Sea*. New York: Schocken, 1995.
———. *Night*. New York: Bantam, 1960.

Chapter 9

The Gift of the Human Body
The Physical Basis of Sexual Ethics in Judeo-Christian Thought

Jeff Yaneff

HISTORICALLY, WHY HAVE CHRISTIANS and Jews possessed a shared disapproval of same-sex erotic relationships, and what is the basis of this shared disapproval?[1] Conversely, what is the fundamental reason the alternative LGBTQ ethic views such sexual behavior as normative? This essay explores these questions and aims to uncover differences and similarities between these competing frameworks. While debate related to this issue will inevitably continue, clarification regarding *why* such differences exist may promote civil dialogue between proponents of each framework as they better understand the rationale of the opposing side.

There are three claims I wish to advance in this essay: (1) the reason Jews and Christians disagree with the LGBTQ ethic is because they jointly afford different levels of authority to physical rather than nonphysical elements of the human person; (2) the reason Jews and Christians agree on this subject is because they share the same reasoning process (i.e., prioritizing the outward reality of the body over inward desires) when formulating sexual ethics; (3) the reason Jews and Christians believe it is deeply problematic to

---

1. Of course, in recent decades some percentage of professing Christians and Jews have "affirmed" such sexual unions; hence, why this essay refers to the "historic" shared position of Christians and Jews.

prioritize unseen aspects of sexual identity such as feeling and passion *over* the outward physio-anatomical aspects of the body is because of a falsehood that is purported about human identity in the reasoning process.

This falsehood rejected by Jews and Christians alike, as I will demonstrate, ostensibly manifests when an individual presents themselves sexually to a member of their own biological category; this is because doing so involves the pretense that they are physically complementary and/or of the opposite sexual category when they are not. On this viewpoint, when identically bodied individuals present themselves to one another they fictitiously misrepresent themselves as if they were the sex they are not. We now turn to further explore my claims and thereafter, I discuss a handful of Jewish and Christian sources that substantiate them.

VISIBLE BODIES AND INVISIBLE INCLINATIONS

In answering the question of why one ethical system approves of same-sex intercourse while others do not, it is routinely overlooked that part of the answer boils down to which aspect of human identity is afforded ultimate worth—that is, whether one prioritizes the physical body (which is visibly paired for the opposite sex) or nonphysical emotions (which may incline one towards their own sex). It is readily apparent that human beings are a vast network of systems, both seen and unseen, yet somehow harmoniously functioning as a unified whole. The dilemma within sexual ethics is which *part* of oneself is granted final directive authority. With homosexual relationships there is an apparent conflict between the visible shape and structure of the physical human body and the invisible desires, beliefs, or passions. One of these competing phenomena must ultimately give way to the other; both cannot have simultaneous ultimate authority.

The reason the historic Judeo-Christian ethical system maintains the position it does is because it stubbornly insists that the material structure of human bodies is inherently valuable. All bodies of men and women are precious and purposeful exactly because they are created in the *imago Dei* (image of God). The historic Judeo-Christian position is one of complete affirmation and celebration of *the visible human body* (though not of all the invisible impulses housed within the visible body). From the Judeo-Christian vantage point, this means that same-sex couples are ultimately "incompatible" (visibly, regardless of any apparent invisible, emotional compatibility) because compatibility is foremostly defined in reference to the visible features of material sexual identity.

In affirming that the visible body is a divinely created and ordered gift, the Judeo-Christian position subordinates the significance of inclinations (whether they be feelings, senses, attractions, passions, or otherwise) that propel one away from embracing the objective goodness, beauty, and functionality of the visible structures present in the male-female binary.

Since the material world is created intentionally by a purposeful designer, the material bodies we possess are to be valorized and received as a gift—even if it is damaged either prior to or after its reception. For Jews and Christians alike, the body as gift is to be revered, and its shape, structure, function, and teleology are both authoritative and prescriptive in sexual-ethical conduct. Nonmaterial structures, such as inward inclinations, are secondary and subordinated. Indeed, they are to be interpreted, located, and even resisted in light of the primacy and totality of the material shape and function that life in the body involves from birth to death. Jews and Christians take seriously the biological reality that life is structured around the pairing of father and mother from beginning to end. Life begins at birth through such a pairing, and physical death can only be overcome through physical reproduction which involves the subsequent union of the same. Physical life either ends completely or continues based upon visible, material structures.[2]

Conversely, on the LGBTQ ethic, the internal sense of self and one's feelings, passions, and proclivities are instructive *despite* any possible cue offered by the material body or any understanding of how the body functions as the center of life in the world. Perhaps the clearest example of this hierarchy of values is the phenomenon of transgenderism—the physical body is not to be believed as ultimate because there is an inward self who "knows better." When a biological woman believes she is a man, an "inward sense" is granted the loudest voice, and it drowns out her physical identity. Any "voice" that her physical body possesses and communicate is silenced.

In this situation an inward mentality subdues the outward reality as "mind" is prioritized over "matter" and physical self-understanding is reshaped in light of an internal perception that is deemed ultimate. The reason the Judeo-Christian ethic disavows this move is because it results in a dismissal and rejection of the material world, which is inherently good. Such a move simultaneously says no to the gift of the body and instead tells a lie by advancing the proposition that one is what they are not.

For the Judeo-Christian view, when a teenager girl struggles with the thought that she may be male (transgenderism) or discovers an erotic

---

2. For the reader interested in questions of how human sexuality relates to life in its entirety, see Radner's recent volume, *A Time to Keep: Theology, Mortality, and the Shape of a Human Life*, pp. 87–100.

inclination for other girls (lesbianism), such feelings, while powerful, are not indicative of who she *is*, nor must they determine how she *acts*. Instead, they can be evaluated (and even disregarded) in light of more tangible embodied realities. Such feelings don't describe the truth about who she *is*. The person "deep down" is the true self. She should bravely "come out of the closet" to be faithful to her own self, because self *is* at its core, one's inner feelings.

Religious individuals often give the impression that the Judeo-Christian sexual ethic is rooted in a series of proof texts, and thus, much energy is expended debating the meaning of these texts. Yet all the while the undeniable realities of bodily existence are shouting out for acknowledgment, *and these very texts do, in fact point toward the empirical realm of the human body as the basis of their internal logic*. It is not textual analysis in isolation, but the body itself, and bodies themselves, that speak authoritatively regarding the intended function and complementary structure of physical sexual life. This ethic, therefore, is one rooted in the empirical world, which celebrates the goodness of the body, whereas the alternative ethic is rooted in the unseen realm, denies the body's instructive worth, and is a form of unfaithfulness to one's physical self.

Refusing the Gift and Accepting the Lie

For Christians, Jews, and others who prioritize visible, physical reality and afford ultimate dignity to the human body and its structures, practices that deny the worth of these realities will always be found wanting due to rejecting created realities and elevating invisible predilections. With same-sex practices and transgenderism, "impulse" is afforded a totalitarian position within the self so that one behaves because of how they feel rather than because of they *are*. Yet the Judeo-Christian framework does not define one's identity in terms of how they *feel*. A senior citizen may *feel* like a teenager, but ultimately, a senior *is not* a teenager. Grown adults may *feel* like they are infants, but this feeling does not indicate their true identity—even if they behave like one.

In daily life, the prioritization of inward claims over outward realities is the means by which lies are told. The reason same-sex partnerships espouse falsehood about physical human identity is because they claim that a member of the identical sex can function as one's legitimate *counterpart* despite being *identical*. Such an act involves falsely portraying oneself as the sex that they are not. It involves bearing false witness not about one's neighbor but about oneself *to* one's neighbor. Thus, the LGBTQ affirming ethic not only devalues the goodness of the body as a metaphysical category but demeans the value of truth as an epistemological category. On the Judeo-Christian viewpoint, when humans let their passions run wild (i.e., without regard for physical reality), truth is the foremost casualty. As adultery tells a lie about someone's social identity (the act essentially claims that someone is one's lawfully beloved partner when they are not), same-sex practice deceives about one's physical identity. Both adultery and same-sex practice are lies that betray the material world, which is the arena of human existence and the criterion for evaluating truth claims. While the Judeo-Christian position certainly *values* human feeling and sexual passion, such items are to be properly situated within the physical realities of bodily existence and are not afforded absolute power.[3] Each position, therefore, holds to a supremely different source of authority and differing conclusions are reached simply because of disagreement over the status that should be afforded to different parts of the self.

While it may be perplexing, for the Judeo-Christian ethic the experience of same-sex attraction is essentially meaningless with regards to identity formation. For the LGBTQ ethic, however, it is vitally important as it is the means by which one discovers and determines their true human identity, which in turn forms the basis for their choices and behavior. Each position demotes one aspect of human existence to favor the other. While people are certainly free to prioritize their emotions over their physiology—and I do not advocate against such freedom—it is inescapable that this hierarchy of the physical above the invisible or vice versa is in fact what is constructed, knowingly or not. We now turn to multiple Judeo-Christian texts and commentators to substantiate my contentions.

THE SHARED REASONING AND COMMON FOUNDATION OF SEXUAL ETHICS IN JUDEO-CHRISTIAN THOUGHT

In ethical-religious discussions about same-sex intercourse, somewhat "infamous" texts from Romans and Leviticus are near-universally discussed because of their crystal clear denunciations of the practice. Intriguingly, the focus of referencing these verses is usually placed upon the *fact* that the text condemns same-sex practice rather than examining what the text's underlying *rationale* of the condemnation is. Indeed, it is often completely overlooked that these texts do not appeal to a divine oracle, special revelation, or

---

3. See Gagnon, *Bible and Homosexual Practice*, 257–58; see also 264.

anything related to the spiritual realm. Nor are they arbitrary pronouncements by mere *fiat* that something is wrong. While these texts denounce and prohibit same-sex intercourse, they don't do so with a literary-revelatory appeal (as is often done by people who cite these very texts); instead they appeal to the tangible structures of the visible world and the empirical architecture of human bodies as they are observed and experienced. Texts like Rom 1 and Lev 18 presume that the physiological and anatomical features of human bodies, alongside their readily perceivable functionalities, are inherently authoritative, and in fact, are a revelation of the divine will and testimony related to ethical human behavior. These texts assume that the created world and the subset of physical bodies within this world are both visibly and inherently good, and thus, provide basic prescriptive data for sexual ethical conduct.[4] A great example of these claims (and of each item in my threefold contention stated above) is seen in Paul's Letter to the Romans.

A Text "Not About the Text"

Moving beyond the fact that Rom 1 denounces same-sex intercourse (both for female-female and male-male pairings), my aim here is to examine the *reason* it is denounced.[5] Paul's incrimination is part of the larger context in Rom 1:18–32 where Paul describes the journey human beings have freely embarked upon away from established reality into a world of hallucination where both their perception of God *and of self* have been sullied. To grasp Paul's point about same-sex intercourse it is valuable to realize that in the text each of these items (perception of both God and self) are connected and they contain parallel features to one another.

---

4. The visible quality associated with the term "good" is evident: "And God saw everything that he had made, and *behold*, it was very good" (ESV, emphasis added). There is also a suggested correspondence between what God sees as good and what the reader should recognize as good.

5. Longenecker correctly observes: "Paul's attitude toward homosexual behavior could hardly be more adversely expressed. For he condemns it totally—as did also all Jews and all Jewish Christians of his day" (*Epistle to Romans*, 217). After advocating for homosexual practice as normative, Sanders admits that Rom 1:26–27 "is a completely unambiguous condemnation of all homosexual activity" (*Paul*, 373). He later adds "Paul himself condemned homosexual activity . . . but he did not prohibit passion and desire within marriage" (747). This is because "passion and desire" are valuable when located within biological, anatomical, and social parameters.

The Twofold Mistake: Fantasies and Feelings

First, Paul states that the existence of God is plainly obvious to all humans by simple virtue of the fact that they are alive and exist in the world. Wherever they look within the physical universe, humans see indications of a carefully designed cosmos. God's very act of creating the world is explosively definitive evidence of his power at work and humans are equipped with an imbued intuition that can distinguish randomness from the results of intelligence. Humans, according to Paul, can easily infer that a powerful entity made the sun, the earth, and all living creatures. Like the psalmist who states that the golden sun and the lofty blue sky testify to the reality of God even while remaining silent (Ps 19:1–4), the point here is that the material realities we visibly observe speak to those who encounter them. Creation itself is not mute; it communicates, even if silently. This means that when humans fail to credit God for the gift of creation and refuse to give thanks for their daily existence (note the emphatic phrase "neither were they thankful" in v. 21) they do so by refusing to listen.

Based upon how clear it is that God has gifted those who are alive, failure to honor God leaves one "without excuse" (v. 20), meaning that the individual lacks evidential justification for their rejection of creation's message. It means that the individual has no possibility of providing a reason for refusing to give thanks to God that would meet the demands of a civil or legal court. Those who deny their design intuition and fail to live in light of it resultantly embrace a fantasy. The donative quality of life is so obvious to its beneficiaries that the only appropriate response should be a minimal heartfelt thank-you to a partially hidden Giver. Yet the tragedy of the human story is one where humans enjoy daily bread and draw moment-by-moment breath without acknowledgment or gratitude *to their Giver*. Every breath drawn by a living being is a marvelous gift from a generous Creator and each moment of time marks the passage of a gift received.

Paul is recorded elsewhere as having said that God provided a "witness" of himself to humanity "by giving you rains from heaven and fruitful seasons, satisfying your hearts with food and gladness" (Acts 14:17 ESV). Yet, the tragedy of much of humankind is that we harvest our crops, cut into our steaks, and accept many more gifts on a momentary basis without ever looking up. Paul's entire summary of his understanding of man's duty before God is this: "Give thanks in all circumstances; for this is the will of God in Christ Jesus for you" (1 Thess 5:18 ESV; see also Ps 107:8–9). Yet despite God's generosity and the clarity of his revelation, Paul says humans are not "thankful" (εὐχαριστέω)—they fail "to express appreciation for benefits or blessings."[6] Paul's catalog of chief vices involves the description of humans becoming "ungrateful" (ἀχάριστος [2 Tim 3:2]), a term "pertaining to a complete lack of thankfulness."[7]

This "new world" in which humans owe no obligation to acknowledge and thank God is a false version of reality; a fantasy in which humans presume to live in a godless universe where God is nonetheless present. Yet, in Rom 1 this denial of God is then bound up with *the denial of God's image*—the human creatures who were gifted by God as male and female.

After describing a situation where humans fail to respond appropriately to the observable data surrounding them, Paul introduces a second example, which parallels his first—another instance where a plainly obvious truth is encountered, then disregarded by fallen humankind. Humans reject the reality of God and the concomitant implication of endless thanksgiving (Rom 1:18-25). Additionally, Paul describes the rejection of the plain truth that God has made the human race as male and female, a reality that carries with it the acknowledgment that each category is clearly suited for the other and that they are complementary pairs suited for one another and created with a delicate balance of similarities and differences. Although each person comes into this world as a result of this complementary union, although the anatomical suitability of each primary sexual organ is obvious, and although this sexual pairing is the means of creating new life, God's engineering marvels are once again balked at by fallen human beings.

Combining Rom 1:20-25 with 1:26-27, the trajectory is one where humans, from time immemorial, first ignore visible evidence and reject the One they cannot see (the invisible God) and then similarly ignore the same visible evidence to reject what they can see (themselves). Rejection of the Giver is accompanied by the rejection of one of his most obvious gifts, the gift of each person's own body, the center of human life on earth.

As humans turn their eyes from the visible world—which should be the occasion of their thanksgiving to God—they also turn their eyes from the visible fact that God created humans as sexual pairs possessing obvious cues for functionality; they subsequently espouse that same-sex intercourse is praiseworthy. Paul describes this by saying that the "female, woman" (θῆλυς) exchanges the "natural" or "physical [φυσικός] function" for what is "against nature" (φύσις).[8] That Paul is referring to the "natural function" of the opposite sex is made clear in the next verse when he says, "In the

---

6. "ευχαριστέω," BDAG 415.

7. "αχάριστος," L&N 300.

8. I render φυσικός as "physical" in light of the Greek *physikos* and LSJ's definition: "the order of external nature, natural, physical" ("φύσις," LSJ 1964).

same way" (ὁμοίως) . . . "males, men" (ἄρσην) left the "physical function of females." Driven by desire (ὄρεξις), they turned "towards one another" (εἰς ἀλλήλους) with the result of "men in/with men" (ἄρσενες ἐν ἄρσεσιν). This behavior is described as inappropriate (ἀσχημοσύνη), a negative term often carrying a visual, observable quality.[9] While the physical world was supposed to provide parameters for sexual passion, here we see this relationship inverted for a scenario where passion becomes the master and body becomes the slave.

The Meaning of "Nature"

That the basis of Paul's sexual-ethical reasoning is not divine revelation or an apocalyptic appeal to the unseen realm is clear from his castigation of what is "against nature." Paul's term ("nature") is the Greek word *physis* (φύσις) from which is visibly derived words like "physics," "physique," and "physiology." It refers here to characteristics humans possess by birth and can describe our deepest constitution as living beings. Something possessed "by nature" does not describe an achievement accomplished during their lifetime—no one has a PhD or a criminal record "by nature." In accordance with "nature" humans put food in their mouths, grasp objects with their hands, walk upon their feet, and see with their eyes. In adolescence humans experience puberty as part of "natural" development. It does not refer *only* to what someone is born with—children are born without teeth and facial hair, items that are still natural—but the term includes "the nature of something as the result of its natural development or condition"[10] or "the natural form or constitution of a person or thing as the result of growth."[11]

In contrast to the human realm of nature, one can also speak of the nature of God, the "divine nature" (φύσις), which describes God as inherently immortal and incorruptible. God cannot die or cease to live, being eternal life itself. By nature, God possesses immortality (1 Tim 6:16) whereas humans do not. While humans can *inherit* immortality, it is another *gift* rather than something possessed "by nature."

What Paul means by "nature," in the context of describing the sexual behavior of male and females (vv. 26–27) could not be clearer. By "nature" individual humans exist as one entire half of a dual sexual spectrum—male or female. To act "against nature" in this context is to reject this visible

---

9. "ἀσχημοσύνη," BDAG 147.
10. "φύσις," L&N 584.
11. "φύσις," LSJ 1964.

binary—this complimentary gift—and is to despise the inherent goodness of both types of human bodies.[12] Paul thus vilifies sexual activity that disregards the constitutional categories of male and female and that denies their existence as anatomical, biological, and physiological counterparts. His critique extends to those who rewrite sexual norms independently of the discernible intention of physical bodies and its obvious parameters solely in favor of inward passions. Thus, one leading interpreter of Paul points out that Paul's use of the phrase "contrary to nature" (which may be a Stoic idiom) speaks of actions that are "contrary to the structure of created reality."[13]

Thus, we are presented here with the basis of Paul's reasoning on sexual behavior as he reveals the basis for his negative description of same-sex behavior. Since God has established human nature to consist of male and female who are obvious sexual counterparts, the attempt to present one's sexual self to a person of the same sex is to proclaim the lie that "identicals" are "complements." This act bears false witness about human identity, and the man who willfully presents himself sexually to the same sex effectively makes the claim that he is the opposite, complimentary sex. He imagines and portrays himself to be the opposite sex, thus falsely claiming to be what he is not.[14] Therefore, when Paul castigates humans for "exchanging the truth of God for the lie" this statement does not only refer to the first item described above (the denial that God is owed credit and thanksgiving) but to the second one as well—the lie is that individuals of the same gender can function as complementary sexual counterparts.[15]

Embodied Deception

The truth that is "exchanged for the lie" (v. 25) is not only the fact that God's reality is instantly detectable through rational reflection upon the created order, but also refers to the instantly detectable truth that God created humanity as two distinct sexes that can unite in sexual intercourse. "The lie" is not only the denial of God as being worthy of thanks, but the lie told by men who falsely perceive themselves as the sexual counterpart of other

12. According to Pew Research, women globally are more accepting of homosexual practice than are men (Poushter and Kent, "Global Divide on Homosexuality," s.vv. "Varied levels of acceptance for homosexuality across globe," para. 11). This is ironic since a man's rejection of the opposite sex involves a despising of the female form.

13. Gorman, *Romans*, 85.

14. This key insight is advanced ubiquitously by Robert Gagnon.

15. That these two points are actually related is also evident from Paul's repetition of the verb "exchanged" (μεταλλάσσω) in v. 25, "exchanged the truth of God for a lie," and again in v. 26, "exchanged the natural use for that which is contrary to nature."

men, meaning, as if they were female. Same-sex practice involves presenting oneself and treating another as if they *were* the sex they are not. This lie about human nature told through same-sex pairing is bound up with a rejection of the body as a gift; a good gift intended by God to be received with thanksgiving. Since this knowledge is obtained through observation and reflection, Paul assumes that human beings can know that same-sex intercourse is both a falsehood and gift rejection even if the Bible had never been written. Such knowledge is written into and onto the body itself.

THE GENESIS CREATION ACCOUNT

Paul's use of the Greek words "male" and "female" (rather than the more generic "man" and "woman") emphasizes both the component of biological sex in human beings[16] and their respective sexual differences.[17] His word choice also signals that the text of Gen 1 underlies the discussion since the creation account states "And God made humanity, according to his image he made him, male [ἄρσην] and female [θῆλυς] he made them" (Gen 1:27 ESV). When God created people, he made them as they continue to exist, as a sexual binary that is "very good" (1:31 ESV). It is, therefore, *not* good when the sexual constitution of the human race is denied and two identical, physically incompatible members of the same-sex attempt to "complement" one another or "complete" what the other lacks.

In Gen 2, after God says it is "not good for the man to be alone" (v. 18 ESV), there is a curious episode where the animals are brought before Adam in the process of finding him a companion. The reader—acquainted with the basics of physiology and anatomy—is to think "certainly God, Adam, and the writer of Genesis (Moses) know full well that this attempt to find an appropriate candidate to pair with Adam from among the animal kingdom is in vain!" And this is the point, for v. 20 makes plain "but to Adam, a companion was not found which was like him" (ὅμοιος αὐτῷ). Just like Adam did, the reader is to appreciate that there is far too much *difference* between Adam and the animals, which is why he cannot find a companion "like himself." What Adam needs is a partner *similar* to himself, but not *identical* to himself. The gift God provides is a companion who is a perfect balance of similarity and difference. A human being, to be sure, "flesh of his flesh," but not a *replica* of Adam since that would be too similar (see 1

---

16. *BDAG* says the term ἄρσην places a "strong emphasis on the sex" (135).

17. LSJ states that θῆλυς and cognate terms like θηλύτερος indicate "opposition rather than comparison" (798). LSJ adds, "In mechanics, those parts were called female into which others fitted."

Cor 15:39). The animals are too different to be a suitable counterpart, but an identical man is far too similar. The divine opinion, therefore, is that the woman is the perfect physically suitable counterpart for the man who should be perceived and received as a gift. Through her, the twin ditches of "too far" and "too close" are navigated.

Adam celebrates the double truth that this companion is "like him" ("this is now bone of my bone and flesh of my flesh") but not the *same* as him. As v. 23 reads: "She [not he] was received *out of man*" (emphasis added) and is thus *not* a man. When Adam looked upon Eve, he did not gaze upon the maleness he already possessed, nor did he behold a creature of such difference in kind that he could not relate to it. This term "companion" describes one who corresponds to the man, which involves her possessing certain traits the man lacks. Another man could not *correspond* to Adam since he would be physically identical to him. Adam's body can be properly understood only in light of the complementary female body since both were designed with the other in mind.

If the first man were paired with a duplicate of himself, he would still be "alone" in the sense described in 2:18a. He would be staring at himself as in a mirror and rather than seeing another he would effectively view himself. This all means that when a man presents himself to another man *as if he were that man's sexual counterpart* he is portraying himself as female—the man's actual counterpart. He is also treating the other man as if he were female, resulting in a double deception of identity. In fact, when the man presents his body to be sexually penetrated by another man, he is pretending to possess female anatomy and is presenting a part of his body as if it were something it is not.[18] This logic is also apparent in the prohibition against same-sex intercourse in the book of Leviticus.

LYING "WITH" . . . AND "TO" A MAN

The Levitical prohibition "You are not to go to bed with a man *as with a woman*" (Lev 18:22 Stern; emphasis added) does not simply condemn same-sex intercourse. Rather, it condemns same-sex intercourse *because* it involves treating a man *as if he were a woman*, which he both physically and visibly is not. This prohibition thus forbids a male from fraudulently treating another male *as if they were female*. Such falsehood devalues the other person's status as "very good" but it also denies what they are.[19] When the

---

18. On this, see Gagnon, *Bible and Homosexual Practice*, 169.

19. Gagnon observes "the primary concern" involves "behaving toward another man as if he were a woman by making him the object of male sexual desires" (*Bible and Homosexual Practice*, 136; see also 142).

text prohibits treating another man "like a woman" when he is *not* a woman, it means there is deliberate *deception* involved in the act as one pretends a female is interchangeable with another male.

The Septuagint translators' choice of the adjective γυναικεῖος (like women) emphasizes the point that the man should not be treated like the gender he is not.[20] The act of substituting a man for a woman in sexual matters is described in Hebrew as "abomination" (תּוֹעֵבָה) and Greek as "disgusting" (βδέλυγμα), a term often referring to something that is visibly grotesque. Theologian John Hartley explains that "such sexual unions are confusing and repulsive" because "they destroy rather than enhance human dignity before God."[21] Nearly one thousand years ago, the philosopher-commentator Ibn Ezra said such an act is an abomination "by the laws of nature."[22] Jacob Milgrom observes that "the difference between the biblical legislation and other Near Eastern laws must not be overlooked. The Bible allows for no exceptions: all acts of sodomy are prohibited, whether performed by rich or poor, higher or lower status, citizen or alien."[23] This is because the biblical position is rooted in physical-anatomical considerations rather than sociological ones.

Rabbi Chaim Rapoport emphasizes that Jewish thinkers have long distinguished between these sorts of laws that can be arrived at through natural observation and those that cannot be—and he underscores the significance of the former. He writes, "Rabbinic literature tends to divide the commandments of the Torah into three categories," which are (1) rational commandments, (2) suprarational commandments, and (3) symbolic commandments. Neither the symbolic or suprarational commandments can be

---

20. Josephus relays the story of a certain Ammonius who was to be put to death for betraying the Syrian King Alexander and who died "as a woman" (ὡς γυνή). What does this phrase mean? The context states that Ammonius sought to hide himself by disguising himself in women's clothing (στολῇ γυναικείᾳ), thus he pretended to be a woman when he was not, and was apparently still dressed like a woman when he was executed (*Jewish Antiquities*, 13, 108). While the manner in which women socially present themselves changes across regions and over history, the anatomical structure of their bodies as being suited for a male does not. The writer Lucian can use the term to describe Tiresias who lived "as a woman" for seven years after being instantly turned female by Zeus's wife. Since Tiresias is the only person thought to have lived both "as a man" (ἀνήρ) and "as a woman" (γυναικεῖος) the question is posed to Tiresias of which life is easier. For Tiresias, despite the pain of childbirth, being a woman is much easier because "women control men" (δεσπόζουσι τῶν ἀνδρῶν αἱ γυναῖκες) and they don't have to "fight in war or stand on battlements" (οὔτε πολεμεῖν ἀνάγκη αὐταῖς οὔτε παρ' ἔπαλξιν ἑστάναι) or "argue in parliament" (ἐν ἐκκλησίᾳ διαφέρεσθαι) or be "cross-examined in court" (ἐν δικαστηρίοις ἐξετάζεσθαι) (Lucian, *Dialogues of the Dead*, 9, 1).

21. Hartley, *Leviticus*, 299.

22. Ibn Ezra, *Leviticus/Va' Yikra*, 148.

23. Milgrom, *Leviticus*, 207.

deduced from observation and reflection; furthermore, they are not "ethical imperatives" even though the former can be grasped as being meaningful (such as Sabbath observance and inscribing Scripture on doorposts) whereas the latter are not (such as laws forbidding certain food or garments or elements of sacrifice).

The rational commandments, however, refer "to those commandments that may be described as logical or moral imperatives. Commandments such as honoring one's parents, honesty, and having concern for the property of others all fall under this rubric." Such commands "may well have been mandated by the intelligent and sensitive human being, as part of a non-divine logical structure." "A conglomeration of pragmatism, consequentialism, and utilitarianism, coupled with the dictates of human conscience, would have in all probability brought man to implement such laws."[24] In rabbinic thought, Rapoport explains, the symbolic and suprarational commandments can be broken in certain situations: "Generally speaking where human life is at risk, the commandments of the Torah are over-ridden. Thus, one may desecrate the Sabbath, eat pork, or consume leaven on Passover if life-threatening situations warrant."

Sexual immorality, on the other hand, belongs to the "rational commandments" and "is one of three categories of transgression where a person is obliged to forfeit his life rather than sin" (along with murder and idol worship).[25] Sexual transgression is not committed just because someone lacks access to written commandments, because it involves a violation of the basic structures of human life and thus constitutes one of the three "cardinal sins of Judaism."[26]

Rapoport goes on to say, "Without recourse to exaggerated analogies, we may simply say that the most superficial study of human biology and the details of the male and female sexual organs demonstrate that they were created to interact with one another. Consequently, any other sexual use of these organs may be described as 'unnatural.'"[27] This statement also demonstrates that the reasoning of Paul in Rom 1:26–27 is identical to the method of determining sexual propriety in Judaism.

---

24. Rapoport, *Judaism and Homosexuality*, 5.
25. Rapoport, *Judaism and Homosexuality*, 1.
26. Rapoport, *Judaism and Homosexuality*, 1.
27. Rapoport, *Judaism and Homosexuality*, 167n61.

THE MOSAIC-PAULINE POSITION IN SECOND TEMPLE JUDAISM

Rapoport's claims about the manner of reasoning in Judaism is corroborated by various Jewish texts contemporary with Paul. For instance after condemning men who "have intercourse with men" in the Letter of Aristeas (152) the author observes that Israel's law was not "drawn up at random" but on the basis of "right reason" (162). In the Testament of Naphtali the author states that the order of the sun, moon, and stars (which do not alter their course) are an example for humans, who should not depart from "the order of nature" through homosexual practice (3:2–5).

Additional references include Josephus, who describes marriage between one man and one woman as "according to nature" (κατὰ φύσιν);[28] Philo, who describes men who throw off "from their necks the law of nature" (φύσεως νόμον) and mount one another without respect for their common sexual identity, thus treating other men as women;[29] and Pseudo-Phocylides, who describes men who have sex with men as a transgression of the "limits set by nature."[30] Commenting on three of these texts, Martti Nissinen explains that "Philo, Josephus, and Pseudo-Phocylides argue against homoeroticism by traditional Jewish reasoning," which is an ethical position arrived at through basic empirical observation and lived experience in its most concrete form.[31] The late Rabbi Lord Jonathan Sacks has stated that one of the fundamental beliefs of Judaism is in a "deep congruence between the life we are called to lead . . . and the universe in which we are called to live it." "Nowhere," writes Sacks, "is this more apparent than in Judaism's understanding of sexuality."[32]

---

28. Josephus, *C. Ap.* 2.24 AT.

29. Philo, *Abr.* 35 AT.

30. Pseudo-Phocylides, sentence 192, trans. P. W. van der Horst, *Old Testament Pseudepigrapha*, 581. While Van der Horst translates εὐνὰς φύσεως as "the limits set by nature," the term itself is more literally "the beds of nature" and therefore emphasizes the sexual limitations provided by nature. In line 191, the writer states, οὐδ' αὐτοῖς θήρεσσι συνεύαδον ἄρσενες εὐναί (for not even male animals share beds together). This further shows his attempt to ground the prohibition in the natural world. While Van Der Horst describes this claim as an ancient zoological error, the general point he makes is clearly valid with regard to lifelong patterns in the animal kingdom. When the writer denounces sexual interactions between humans animals in sentence 188, his description of ἀλόγοις ζώοισι ("irrational animals") emphasizes the imbalance and extreme difference as the basis for the prohibition.

31. See https://vialogue.wordpress.com/2016/05/24/homoeroticism-in-the-biblical-world-notes-critical-review/.

32. Jonathan Sacks, in Rapoport, *Judaism and Homosexuality*, vii.

CONCLUSION

This essay has sought to move the discussion forward by presenting an explanation regarding why there is fundamental disagreement between historic Judeo-Christian sexual ethics and modern-day LGBTQ pronouncements. It should be apparent that the Judeo-Christian position is not rooted in bigotry or in hate but in a commitment to the value of the human body and a celebration of its inherent goodness. Those who engage in reasoned debate on this subject should recognize the disagreement is not primarily a matter of "love" and "hate" but a matter of *prioritization*, either of the physical, observable realm or of non-materialist considerations. The Judeo-Christian ethic is a materialist one where matter *matters*, and it remains committed both to the goodness of the body and to its reception as a gift.

BIBLIOGRAPHY

Gagnon, Robert A. J. *The Bible and Homosexual Practice: Texts and Hermeneutics*. Nashville: Abingdon, 2001.

Gorman, Michael J. *Romans: A Theological and Pastoral Commentary*. Grand Rapids: Eerdmans, 2022.

Hartley, John E. *Leviticus*. WBC 4. Dallas: Word, 1992.

Ibn Ezra, Abraham ben Meïr. *Leviticus/Va' Yikra*. Edited and translated by H. Norman Strickman and Arthur M. Silver. Vol. 3 of *Ibn Ezra's Commentary on the Pentateuch*. New York: Menorah, 1988.

Josephus. *Jewish Antiquities*. Translated by Ralph Marcus. Vol. 5. LCL 365. Cambridge, MA: Harvard University Press, 1943.

Longenecker, Richard N. *The Epistle to the Romans: A Commentary on the Greek Text*. NIGTC. Grand Rapids: Eerdmans, 2016.

Lucian. *Dialogues of the Dead. Dialogues of the Sea-Gods. Dialogues of the Gods. Dialogues of the Courtesans*. Translated by M. D. MacLeod. LCL 431. Cambridge, MA: Harvard University Press, 1961.

Milgrom, Jacob. *Leviticus: A Book of Ritual and Ethics*. CC. Minneapolis: Fortress, 2004.

Poushter, Jacob, and Nicholas Kent. "The Global Divide on Homosexuality Persists." Pew Research Center, June 25, 2020. https://www.pewresearch.org/global/2020/06/25/global-divide-on-homosexuality-persists/.

Radner, Ephraim. *A Time to Keep: Theology, Mortality, and the Shape of Human Life*. Waco: Baylor University Press, 2018.

Rapoport, Chaim. *Judaism and Homosexuality: An Authentic Orthodox View*. London: Vallentine Mitchell, 2004.

Sanders, E. P. *Paul: The Apostle's Life, Letters and Thought*. Minneapolis: Fortress, 2015.

Stern, David H., ed. *Complete Jewish Bible: An English Version of the* Tanakh *(Old Testament) and* B'rit Hadashah *(New Testament)*. Clarksville, MD: Jewish New Testament, 1998.

PART III

Jewish-Christian Rapprochement, Reconciliation, and Unity

Chapter 10

Οἱ Ἰουδαῖοι and the Gospel of John
Grappling with Anti-Judaism in the New Testament

Brian K. Gamel

> Another story told of three Jews who were determined to convert to Christianity. Outside a church they drew lots to choose which of the three should go first and then return to tell the other two what happened. When the one came out of the church, the other two ran to him, asking, "How did it go?" He replied, "Get away from me, you Christ-killers!"[1]

INTRODUCTION

JOHN'S USE OF THE phrase οἱ Ἰουδαῖοι (*hoi Ioudaioi*), often translated "the Jews," is a theological problem disguised as a linguistic one.[2] While some interpreters have tried to offer more precision to the referent behind this phrase—whether through innovative translations, historical context, and appeals to its symbolic meaning—the full weight of its problematic nature is often unacknowledged. A failure to recognize this dangerous and hurtful

---

1. Sandmel, *Anti-Semitism in the New Testament?*, 155.
2. John Dominic Crossan calls the passion narratives the "seedbed for Christian anti-Judaism" (*Who Killed Jesus?*, 35). Likewise Jon Meachem notes that "the roots of Christian anti-Semitism lie in overly literal readings—which are, in fact, misreadings—of many New Testament texts" ("Who Killed Jesus?," para. 6).

translation issue in the Fourth Gospel is both an impediment to contemporary Jewish-Christian dialogue and an evasion of Christian responsibility to name and confess sin in the interest of apologetics. This paper explores a way to both acknowledge this problem within John while still regarding the text as authoritative Scripture through the method of content criticism or *Sachkritik*.

JOHN'S USE OF ΟΙ ΙΟΥΔΑΙΟΙ

The presence of anti-Jewish features in the Gospel of John has been long noted.[3] Most interpreters discuss whether John's anti-Judaism arises only in its *Wirkungsgeschichte* or is located within the author's own intent. While interpreters debate the extent to which anti-Judaism exists in John, or at which level it appears—whether in its reception, within the text itself, or from the author himself—nearly all agree that anti-Judaism finds a firm orbit around the Fourth Gospel.[4]

Behind these claims is the rather totalizing manner in which John refers to the opponents of Jesus in his gospel as οἱ Ἰουδαῖοι (*hoi Ioudaioi*), usually translated as "the Jews."[5] Commentators have long observed the oddity of this phrase considering that nearly everyone in the Johannine narrative is a Jew.[6] The lame man tells "the Jews" that Jesus made him well, even though both he and they are Jews, and Jesus, whom they are discussing, is also Jewish (John 5:10–11). Likewise, Jesus tells the disciples that they cannot follow where he is going, "as I said to the Jews" (13:33). He refers to Torah as "your law" (8:17; 10:34) even though he is regarded as a rabbi and prophet (1:38, 49; 3:2; 4:31; 6:25; 9:2; 11:8, 29; 13:13–14; 20:16). The Jews are part of "the world," and as a result they will die in their sins (8:21–24). Indeed, they are

---

3. A distinction has often been made between concepts that are "anti-Jewish" and "anti-Semitic." Although these distinctions can be helpful, I will continue using the term "anti-Jewish" and "anti-Judaism" for both terms to encompass the broadest possible meaning. For a discussion of anti-Semitism vs. anti-Judaism (and supersessionism), see Kim, *Polemic in Book of Hebrews*, 3–7; see also Donaldson, *Jews and Anti-Judaism*, 13–29.

4. Bieringer et al., "Wresting with Johannine Anti-Judaism," 5–15.

5. There are almost seventy references to "the Jews" (οἱ Ἰουδαῖοι) in John, compared to five each in Matthew and Luke and six in Mark.

6. There are only a handful of characters in John that are clearly non-Jewish: the Samaritan woman (4:7) and the Samaritans from her village (4:39); the Greeks who come near the end of Jesus's ministry (although these characters do not speak or play any role in the narrative [12:20]); Pilate (18:28); and the Roman soldiers who carry out Jesus's execution (19:1). The "royal official" mentioned in 4:46 is ambiguous and could be a Jew or a non-Jew.

not from God since whoever is from God hears the word of God in Jesus (8:47). Nicodemus, as a leader of the Jews, does not believe in Jesus because he "loves darkness" since "his deeds are evil" (3:19–20).

The Gospel of John consistently uses "the Jews" to "other" opponents of Jesus: "the Jews" inquire of John the Baptist (1:19) and are identified other than John even though he is a Jew (3:25); Passover and other festivals are marked as being "of the Jews" (2:13; 5:1; 6:4; 7:2; 11:55; 19:42) as well as burial customs (19:40) and rites of purification (2:6). At many points the author goes further and uses "the Jews" to designate the enemies of Jesus: the Jews question Jesus after he heals a crippled man (5:10), look for an opportunity to kill Jesus (7:1), take up stones to kill him (8:59), are identified as those having tried to kill Jesus (11:8), and prevent Jesus from walking about openly (11:54). The followers of Jesus are threatened with being expelled from the synagogue by the Jews (9:22; 12:42; 16:2), and after Jesus's death the disciples meet behind closed doors on account of their "fear of the Jews" (19:38; 20:19). Most infamously, Jesus at one point tells the Jews that their father is not God but the devil (8:44) and that they are not from God (8:47).[7]

John's peculiar use of οἱ Ἰουδαῖοι (*hoi Ioudaioi*) highlights the paradox of how John is both the most Jewish of all the documents in the New Testament in its conceptuality and the most anti-Jewish. John's ideas and concepts are firmly rooted in Second Temple Judaism and cannot be understood apart from this thought world, and yet it is precisely those symbols and concepts that John rejects in light of Jesus. The result is a Judaism without the Jews. Raimo Hakola sees the basic problem as the Johannine Jesus's ambivalence towards Jewish identity. Jesus is presented as a Jew in the gospel, even the Messiah of Jews, of whom Moses wrote. He appeals to Moses and Abraham, yet is ambivalent towards the temple, Sabbath, circumcision, the revelation at Sinai, Moses, and the law.[8] "The knowledge and use of various Jewish traditions in John in no way excludes the conclusion that these traditions are, more often than not, used to underscore the faith in Jesus as a superior alternative to Jewish beliefs and practices. This shows how originally Jewish elements may well have contributed to the emergence of an identity that was not based on central matters of Jewishness but was, at least at some points, created in conscious opposition to them."[9] "John's symbolic universe is Jewish in so far as it is based on the rendering of diverse

---

7. There are neutral examples of John's use of "the Jews" (11:31, 33, 36). Some Jews are said to have believed in Jesus (8:31; 11:45; 12:11), and there is even a positive usage where Jesus exclaims, "Salvation is from the Jews" (4:22). But these examples are rare in comparison to explicitly negative uses.

8. Hakola, *Identity Matters*, 215–18.

9. Hakola, *Identity Matters*, 220.

Jewish traditions . . . [but] at the same time, non-Jewish in the sense that matters that were essential parts of Jewish identity are no longer relevant to the Johannine Christians."[10] "Jesus finally became a black hole into which all their Judaism disappeared."[11]

In light of Christendom's long history of anti-Judaism, and especially in the shadow of the Holocaust, nearly all modern interpreters have recognized that problematic nature of John's unique and pervasive usage of the phrase οἱ Ἰουδαῖοι (hoi Ioudaioi). A disagreement exists, however, over how to render this phrase in translation and how to understand its referent.

PROPOSED SOLUTIONS FOR JOHN'S ΟΙ ΙΟΥΔΑΙΟΙ

There are three prevailing possibilities for understanding whom John intends to identify by οἱ Ἰουδαῖοι (hoi Ioudaioi) in his gospel: all Jews, some Jews, or non-Jewish Christian opponents of the author.[12] We can consider these possibilities in reverse order. The most idiosyncratic is a proposal advanced by Henk Jan de Jonge and B. W. J. de Ruyter—that when John refers to οἱ Ἰουδαῖοι (hoi Ioudaioi) he is referring not to Jews, but rather to Christian opponents whom he considers heterodox. These authors contend that the two-level drama presented in John makes the most sense if Jesus's opponents represent other Christians who possess an inadequate Christology (that is, as understood by the Johannine community). In order to provide a modicum of historical verisimilitude, however, John has retroactively labeled these opponents as "the Jews" as "this was the only way they could be identified in a story about Jesus" since the historical Jesus did not interact with heretical Christians.[13] This proposal has not garnered much acceptance. The thrust of John's Gospel certainly contains strong christological elements, but the text does not seem to display any masked debate over the nature of this Christology. It also is not clear why John would change the opponents of Jesus from Pharisees, Sadducees, and chief priests as in the Synoptic Gospels if the author was concerned with historical fidelity. Finally, even if we were to grant this argument its full weight, John's use of "the Jews" as a blanket term for Jesus's theological interlocutors would be careless at best since it paints all Jews as opponents of Jesus, and thus opponents of the truth, by the sole virtue of them being Jews.

10. Hakola, *Identity Matters*, 221.
11. Gaston, "Lobsters in Fourth Gospel," 4:122.
12. For a full summary of these options, see Thatcher, "John and the Jews," 13–24.
13. De Jonge, "'Jews' in Gospel of John," 139.

A more promising thesis argues that when John writes about οἱ Ἰουδαῖοι (*hoi Ioudaioi*) he is referring not to the entirety of the Jewish race but only particular groups within it. Some argue that this term is really a circumlocution for the religious authorities. Indeed, in many of the pericopes in the Synoptics where the Jewish leaders are listed as opponents of Jesus John has substituted οἱ Ἰουδαῖοι (*hoi Ioudaioi*) instead.[14] Others insist that it is a geographical reference and denotes not the Jews as a people but those from Judea and should thus be rendered "the Judeans."[15] In either case these interpreters argue that John's term should not be translated as "the Jews" into English to avoid the implication that he is referring to all of the Jewish people.

Although there is some merit to these novel readings, neither are ultimately convincing. It is true that John often uses οἱ Ἰουδαῖοι (*hoi Ioudaioi*) *to* refer to the religious authorities, but he also uses the term to refer to the crowds (2:18; 6:52; 11:31), those believing in Jesus (11:45; 12:11), and the festivals, rites, and customs of a whole people rather than just religious leaders (2:13; 5:1; 6:4; 11:55). Furthermore, what sense does it make to say that "salvation is from the religious authorities" (4:22) or that Jesus is mocked as being the "King of the religious leaders" (19:20) rather than of all the Jews? Likewise, translating οἱ Ἰουδαῖοι (*hoi Ioudaioi*) as "Judeans" makes even less sense as Jesus himself is called a Ἰουδαῖος (*Ioudaios*) even though he is from Galilee (7:41), and John's explanation that Samaritans and Jews do not share things in common (4:9) does not make sense if he is only referring to Judeans. The fact that John has sometimes substituted references to religious leaders in the Synoptics with a blanket description of "the Jews" demonstrates that John is not anymore more concerned with geographical issues than the Synoptic Gospels.[16] The gospel does not seem any more particularly concerned with the inhabitants of Judea (as opposed to Galilee or other Jews of the diaspora) than the other gospels.[17] These translations

14. Wahlde, "Jews in the Gospel of John," has championed this view most forcefully.

15. Lowe, "Who Were the Ἰουδαῖοι?"; and Ashton, "Identity and Function of the Ἰουδαῖοι" have been two of the most prominent voices for this view.

16. "Even if Ἰουδαῖοι once denoted Judeans or Jewish authorities, the Gospel of John generalized and stereotyped those who rejected Jesus by its use of the term" (Culpepper, "Anti-Judaism in the Fourth Gospel," 66).

17. The gospel was written and circulated in the diaspora, not Israel, and has broader sense of the national, religious, political identity that was already current. Adele Reinhartz points out that the feasts of Jews mentioned are not defined by geographical location but identity of participants; the customs are not unique to Judea (2:6; 19:40); being children of Abraham is the identity of all Jews, not just Judeans; and being king of the Jews is not implausible for a man from Nazareth (2:19–21) ("Jews in Fourth Gospel").

can be sustained only by cherry-picking certain passages as representative of this interpretive strategy while dismissing a host of counterexamples that are hard to explain away.

The final, and most common, rendering of οἱ Ἰουδαῖοι (*hoi Ioudaioi*) is to interpret it as it seems: as a blanket term for all Jewish people. Even then, however, there are multiple variations of how this should be understood. J. Louis Martyn and Raymond Brown have suggested that John's Gospel embodies a "two-level drama" that tells the story of the Johannine community as it tells the story of Jesus. This community's own experience being expelled from the synagogue for their belief in Jesus as Son of God has fostered an alienation from Jewish life and identity while still operating within a Jewish matrix of thought.[18] Others have suggested that John is operating from a similar position as the community at Qumran who deeply criticized the Jewish leadership in Jerusalem and saw themselves as the true heirs of Israel's heritage. In this rendering, John's use of and critique of "the Jews" is part of the broader history of Jewish figures and movements engaging in fierce debates about the nature and practice of Jewish identity and belief (e.g., Jubilees, 4 Ezra, and 1 Enoch as examples of Second Temple Jewish texts engaged in such debates). In this way we can understand John (and other NT authors) in conflict with other Jews based on mutual frustrations with each other: frustration with Jesus leading people astray (for Jews) and frustration with the refusal to accept Jesus as Messiah (for Christians). This interpretation, of course, would absolve the New Testament of anti-Judaism.[19]

The argument that John's criticism of "the Jews" was representative of intra-Jewish critique fails to account for the fact that "Jesus' clash with his opponents in John is not over esoteric or marginal beliefs of a particular kind of Judaism, but over matters shared among many Jewish groups."[20] Faith in Jesus is expressed in John in such a way that anything uniquely Jewish is discarded.[21] This contrasts with, for example, the community at Qumran, who held onto basic Jewish ideas while still segregating themselves from society.[22] Furthermore, it is significant that Christians, not Jews, preserved all the documents cited above.[23] Finally, "It is noteworthy that the fourth gospel had no impact among those Jewish-Christian groups that continued

---

18. See Martyn, *History and Theology in Fourth Gospel*, 17–41.

19. See, e.g., Evans, *New Testament Anti-Judaism*, 82.

20. Hakola, *Identity Matters*, 228.

21. Hakola, *Identity Matters*, 233.

22. Hakola, *Identity Matters*, 224; see also 225.

23. As Marshall: "Jews did not preserve [4 Ezra], and I think that the very things that made it attractive to Christian readers . . . likely made it unattractive for long-term preservation by Jews" ("Apocalypticism and Anti-Semitism," 77).

to flourish well into the fourth and even fifth century. . . . It is significant that John was used especially by those on the Christian side, Origen, John Chrysostom and others, who wanted to secure the border between a Jew and a Christian."[24]

Many writers have noted that proposals which attempt to contextualize John's use of οἱ Ἰουδαῖοι (*hoi Ioudaioi*) seem like an effort to eliminate (or at least minimize) the problematic nature of translating the phrase as "the Jews."[25] In other words, all of these arguments seem driven by apologetic purposes to safeguard the text from saying what interpreters do not want it to say. As Adele Reinhartz notes,

> New Testament scholars' efforts to limit the meaning of Ἰουδαῖος and to explain John's comments on Jews and Judaism as a response to Jewish exclusion are not primarily dispassionate academic interpretations but rather attempts to defuse the Gospel's anti-Judaism and make its expressions more acceptable to a post-Holocaust audience without undermining its status as an authoritative and sacred text.[26]

The problem, then, is the seemingly undeniable presence of anti-Jewish sentiments in a canonized text of Scripture.[27] While acknowledging this problem, some interpreters choose to put "the Jews" in quotes to highlight the problematic nature of this referent, while others leave the term entirely untranslated as οἱ Ἰουδαῖοι (*hoi Ioudaioi*). While there is merit to these impulses, they create as many problems as they solve. Leaving the term untranslated erases Jesus from his Jewish context,[28] it complicates the task of a translator in making the text say what we want rather than what it seems to say,[29] and it often falls flat with Jewish audiences who view this maneuver as ultimately hollow.[30] Arguing that "the Jews" are a symbol in the gospel for

---

24. Hakola, *Identity Matters*, 235, 237.

25. "The chief means to this apologetic end is the placement of the early Christian writings within particular historical contexts that explain their anti-Jewish polemic without recourse to the hypothesis of anti-Semitic prejudice" (Marcus, "Epilogue," 291). Marcus insists that "merely acknowledging the historical factors behind early Christian polemic against Jews does not totally erase the problem that such polemic poses when it becomes part of the church's sacred Scripture" (294).

26. Reinhartz, "Jews in Fourth Gospel," 213.

27. Marcus also notes that this problem stems in part from the "eschatological chasm" between Christians' claims and the reality of the world ("Epilogue," 296).

28. "In removing the 'Jews' as Jesus' opponents, we also remove Jesus from Judaism" (Greenspoon, "Translating *Jesus* and *the Jews*," 24).

29. Blenkisopp, "Contemporary English Version," 51.

30. "I confess my discomfort with the quotation marks around 'the Jews' and all that they imply" (Reinhartz, "Jews in Fourth Gospel," 213).

all human misunderstanding and rejection is a helpful acknowledgement, but "it is Jews specifically who were spoken of, scorned, and pilloried."[31] Addressing this problem requires the admission it *is* a problem, and looking for resources that can directly address the problem at hand. "The root problem is that of deciding if one can accept the presence of an anti-Jewish approach in John's Gospel without abandoning the authority of Scripture."[32]

SACHKRITIK AS A TOOL FOR JOHN AND ΟΙ ΙΟΥΔΑΙΟΙ

It seems beyond dispute that John contains anti-Jewish elements that are unacceptable from a Christian point of view, and it is impossible to eliminate them from the text. We must interpret John honestly and responsibly. Many scholars writing on this topic admit the central problem in this dilemma: "If divine revelation is considered as the divine message to human beings by means of a sacred text, the problem will not go away . . . revelation is not simply identical with the sacred text."[33] Among the steps necessary to "de-antisemitize" the New Testament, another argues, is acknowledging a distinction between God and the text by seeing its authors as human and subject to bias, prejudice, and human error.[34] These are precisely the kinds of issues that *Sachkritik* attempts to address.

The twentieth-century theologian and biblical scholar Rudolf Bultmann responded to Karl Barth's insistence on *Sachexegese* (exegesis of the content/subject matter of Scripture) by insisting that interpreters must also, sometimes, exercise *Sachkritik* on the text in question.[35] While Bultmann later abandoned this term in favor of his larger project of demythologizing, *Sachkritik* has continued to play a vital role in theological interpretation of Scripture.[36] I will here offer a brief introduction to *Sachkritik* and then an example of its use by another author in a different text also dealing with anti-Judaism before applying it to John and his use of οἱ Ἰουδαῖοι.

The *Sache* of *Sachkritik* "refers to the revelation of God in Christ in the gospel, and so presupposes a Christian account of the subject matter of the

---

31. Sandmel, *Anti-Semitism in the New Testament?*, 118.
32. Beutler, *Judaism and the Jews*, 156.
33. Beutler, *Judaism and the Jews*, 157.
34. Freudmann, *Antisemitism in the New Testament*, 303–5.
35. Bultmann, "Problem einer theologischen Exegese." See also Congdon, *Mission of Demythologizing*, 49–50, 104–6, and esp. 723–27.
36. For the reception history of *Sachkritik* as a method of interpretation, see Morgan, "*Sachkritik* in Reception History."

Bible."[37] It is not criticism *of the content* of Scripture, but rather criticism of the text of Scripture *by its own content*. *Sachkritik* understands a difference between the kerygma—the living, active message of the gospel that confronts humans here and now—and the text itself, even though that kerygma arises from and is only heard through those biblical witnesses.[38] It is not the cutting away of bits of theology because it conflicts with a modern view of reality, but because it conflicts with the understanding of the core New Testament message. In this way it is an attempt to preserve the Protestant dependence on Scripture as a norm while also being open to modern critical thinking about those biblical witnesses.[39] The words of Scripture testify to the kerygma (which for Bultmann is always enshrouded in human words while never being fully identified with them), which then offers correction, and sometimes critique, of the words of Scripture itself.[40]

Sachkritik is thus distinguishable from Martin Luther's canon criticism and Ernst Käsemann's canon within a canon in which an arguably scriptural theological idea norms the canon of Scripture, as well as an honest and complete rejection of Scripture from other criteria entirely.[41] *Sachkritik* arises from interpretation of a text itself and uses the results of that interpretation to then weigh the words.[42] "*Sachkritik* accepts both the authority of the gospel heard in scripture and the necessity of sometimes criticizing a scriptural formulation."[43] The subjective nature of this enterprise has understandably made many interpreters nervous about its use, which is something I will address in the conclusions below; but here it is sufficient to note that no method is free of subjective tendencies and that no exegesis is presuppositionless.[44]

37. Morgan, "*Sachkritik* in Reception History," 177.

38. "*Sachkritik* is always based on the distinction between the biblical texts and the gospel itself, but that gospel, heard only through these biblical witnesses, finds different theological expression in different theologians" (Morgan, "*Sachkritik* in Reception History," 180).

39. Morgan, "*Sachkritik* in Reception History," 184.

40. "If we are not to conflate deity and humanity, kerygma and culture, then a critical hermeneutic, a method of *Sachkritik*, is necessary if we are genuinely to hear the voice of *God*" (Congdon, *Mission of Demythologizing*, 227; emphasis in original).

41. Congdon, *Mission of Demythologizing*, 185–89.

42. Barrett, "John and Judaism," 244.

43. Morgan, "*Sachkritik* in Reception History," 186.

44. Levenson argues that Christians and Jews do not read the same Scripture even when they formally share the same texts—and words—of their respective Bibles. The "polydoxy" of Scripture, he argues, must be flattened by Christian interpretation, a feature that Jewish interpretation tolerates, if not embraces ("Why Jews Are Not Interested").

As an example of how *Sachkritik* can address anti-Jewish passages in Matthew, let us look briefly at how Ulrich Luz uses this method to both name and own a problem in that text as well as offer a response to how interpreters should engage with those passages. There are two places in Matthew where, like John, anti-Jewish readings have long been a problem: the pronouncement of the woes on the scribes and Pharisees in ch. 23 and the cry of the crowd at Jesus's crucifixion, "Let his blood be on us and our children" (27:25). Although Luz stops short of calling Matthew anti-Jewish in itself or at its inception, he insists that its canonization by the gentile Christian church "was then the final step in making it an anti-Jewish book."[45]

Luz charges that the woes leveled against the scribes and Pharisees in Matt 23 is both historically unjust and contradicts the central teaching of Jesus in the gospel itself. Intra-Jewish sniping between competing groups was common in the Second Temple period, and even heated, Luz admits, but the depiction of the Pharisees goes beyond those conventions.[46] That "Pharisee" became in Christian parlance synonymous with hypocrite demonstrates how deeply problematic Matthew's portrayal of his enemies has been.[47]

Luz insists that the only response to this kind of deep polemic and historical injustice is the explicit and public exercise of *Sachkritik* on the text—that is, criticizing Matthew on the basis of what Matthew says elsewhere. The prohibition against judging, at all (7:1–2) seems violated in this chapter, as well as the warning to not prematurely pull the weeds in the parable of the wheat (13:29–30).[48] But how would one choose one of these texts over the other? Why elevate, for example, Matt 7 over Matt 23 and not the other way around? Luz insists that the commandments of the risen Jesus is the standard by which Matthew himself measures all theological proclamations, commandments which are embodied in the Sermon on the Mount.[49]

The center of Matthew's theology—and indeed, the standard by which he judges all things—is the teaching of Jesus epitomized by the Sermon on the Mount, where the love for one's enemies can be understood as the

---

45. Luz, *Matthew 21–28*, 173.

46. All polemics, Luz admits, are designed "to enlighten the readers by means of sharpened formulations" that work with hyperbole and caricature (*Matthew 21–28*, 137). Matthew's case, though, "exceeds in its contents what can be documented from other Greek and Jewish polemical texts" (138). See also 170.

47. In Germany, he notes, "Pharisee" became the name for a coffee with liqueur covered entirely with whipped cream so that one does not smell what is in the cup, and thus a "hypocritical" coffee (Luz, *Matthew 21–28*, 136).

48. Luz, *Matthew 21–28*, 175.

49. Luz, *Matthew 21–28*, 175, 633; compare to Luz, *Matthew 1–7*, 176–77, where he argues for the centrality of the Sermon on the Mount in Matthew's understanding.

very heart of Jesus's instruction.[50] Yet the message of Matt 23 seems to directly violate the command to "love your enemies and pray for those who persecute you" (5:44). Luz argues that not only does Matt 23 represent a betrayal of Jesus's command to love one's enemies, but also "a betrayal of Jesus's proclamation of God's unearned and limitless love that according to Jesus applies especially, and almost exclusively, to Israel."[51] When weighed against the central thrust of Jesus's message as Matthew himself articulates it, the overly polemical language of Matt 23 comes up short.

Turning to Matt 27:25 yields a similar discussion. The history of interpretation of the blood-curse of the crowd has wrought destruction and death for Jews for centuries who have been seen by Christians as guilty of the murder of Jesus.[52] Luz argues that as a text in the canon, we cannot make a sharp distinction between "its interpretation in the church that derive from it with some consistency, and its anti-Jewish applications that today everyone regrets . . . the basic biblical and ecclesiastical conviction that Israel's no to Jesus leads to God's judgment on Israel was the continuity of meaning that made this mixture possible."[53] Here Luz recapitulates his prior remarks on Matt 23, arguing that *Sachkritik* would critically evaluate this text, found only in Matthew among the gospels, on the basis of Matthew's own, better, insights located in the Sermon on the Mount.

In both cases the response of *Sachkritik* is not to deny the damning meaning of texts nor to ignore texts by claiming that such readings are not historical or should be conditioned by contextualization. They must be explicitly acknowledged and interpreters must come to terms with them—publicly and critically. *Sachkritik* "involves openly acknowledging both a text's own assertion and one's own criticism of it."[54] Indeed, Luz argues that "Matthew 23 is an important theological text even today not because it reveals God's truth but because it *exposes human reality—yes, human sin.*"[55] Evaluating the *words* of Matt 23 and 27:25 by the *content*, or the *Sache* of Matthew's central message—embodied in the Sermon on the Mount and supremely the command to love one's enemies—allows Luz to both honestly

---

50. Luz, notes that Matthew has given this command the "favored position in his last, conclusive antithesis" (*Matthew 1–7*, 285), and by calling it "perfect" insists that it "is not one demand among others but he center and apex of all the commandments" (290; see also 392 and the centrality of love for the teaching of Jesus).

51. Luz, *Matthew 21–28*, 175.

52. For a brief history of this interpretation, and its effects, see Luz, *Matthew 21–28*, 507–8.

53. Luz, *Matthew 21–28*, 508.

54. Luz, *Matthew 21–28*, 508.

55. Luz, *Matthew 21–28*, 177; emphasis in original.

interpret, own, and condemn the anti-Jewish impulse arising from these texts.⁵⁶ For Luz, "We must say, therefore—and we must do it openly and publicly—with the words of Martin Luther: this text does not 'promote Christ.'"⁵⁷

Having examined *Sachkritik* in both theory and example, let us now attempt to perform a similar technique on John's use of οἱ Ἰουδαῖοι (*hoi Ioudaioi*).⁵⁸ We have already outlined above the problematic nature that John's repeated, regular usage of this term entails, most acutely with his placing in the mouth of Jesus the declaration that "the Jews" come from the devil (8:44).⁵⁹ Is this the heart of John's Gospel? Where would we turn to find the central message—the *Sache*—of John? A good argument can be made for the pivotal role of the prologue (1:1–18).⁶⁰ Unlike the other gospels that begin with reports about the birth of Jesus or the start of his ministry, John offers a cosmic perspective that informs the story he is about to share. Because the reader, unlike the characters in the narrative, knows the truth about Jesus's identity and origin, the prologue serves not only as an introduction to the story but also as a lens through which every encounter with Jesus should be seen.⁶¹ As both introduction and lens, then, the prologue of John is a good place to find the central intent of John's message.

---

56. Compare Luz's approach with Anthony J. Saldarini's suggestions for dealing with the same passage in Matthew, which include contextualizing the passage and replacing "Jews" with Jewish leaders. Although helpful, this approach fails to explicitly acknowledge Matthew's own anti-Judaism as Luz's interpretation does, and thus fails to fully condemn it. See Saldarini, "Reading Matthew Without Anti-Semitism," 182–84.

57. Luz, *Matthew 21–28*, 138.

58. I am not, of course, the first to suggest this method for interpreting John's problematic passages. Barrett contrasts the message of John 4:22 (that salvation comes from the Jews) with 8:44 ("John and Judaism," 245), although it is not clear why one of these passages should be considered more central to the other in his analysis. Beck observes that many NT texts from the 1611 version have already been reduced to footnotes in most modern translations, and reducing the most virulent anti-Semitic texts to the same status affects a much smaller number of texts. He suggests doing the same for those passages in John, which could be considered similar to *Sachkritik* (*Mature Christianity in 21st Century*, 324n3).

59. "It is fair to admit, then, that the author of the Fourth Gospel is not free of anti-Jewish sentiments. The three Louvain authors quote my observation that the word of God has its human aspect, becomes flesh and can be infected with human sin" (Beutler, *Judaism and the Jews*, 147).

60. The question of the prologue's relationship to the rest of John is necessarily bound up with theories about the compositional history of the gospel. For an overview, see Ashton, *Understanding the Fourth Gospel*, 76–90. For the present essay it is sufficient to consider the function of the prologue in the gospel's final form.

61. For the Johannine prologue as a lens for reading all of John, see Kysar, *John*, 14–15; Neyrey, *Gospel of John*, 41; but esp. Culpepper, who maintains that the "plot"

I want to offer three ways in which the prologue implicitly critiques John's use elsewhere of οἱ Ἰουδαῖοι (*hoi Ioudaioi*): (1) the presence of careful nuance in the prologue that becomes noticeably lacking later in the gospel, (2) the prologue's insistence on the Word's power to enlighten all people over against the inability of the Jews to hear God's word, and (3) the centrality of the claim that anyone who believes has the power to become children of God in direct conflict with the assertion that Jews (or anyone else, for that matter) could have the devil for their father.

First, the narrator interrupts his train of thought in 1:6 when he introduces John the Baptist. After calling John a witness to the light, he clarifies that "this one was not himself the light, but [he came] in order to testify concerning the light" (1:8).[62] The author composes this section painstakingly, explaining the positive, and preparatory role of John the Baptist while also curtailing his influence and position; this kind of nuance is lost when the author later discusses "the Jews." In fact, there is so much repetition, qualification, and concern for absolute clarity here that becomes particularly excruciating when compared to 8:44.[63] If John (the evangelist) means only the religious leaders, or the Judeans, or any other subset within "the Jews," he could nuance this as easily as he does when discussing the precise role of John the Baptist vis-à-vis Jesus. If this kind of nuance is present just a few verses into the gospel then we might arguably claim nuance is at the heart of John's proclamation about Jesus, a nuance that should be extended throughout the rest of the story.[64]

Second, John proclaims that the Word which brought all things into being was "life" and that life was "the light of all people. And the light shines in the darkness and the darkness has not overcome it" (1:4–5). This light that has entered hostile territory "enlightens all people" (1:9).[65] It is tempting for some interpreters to make distinctions between the different appearances of πάντα (*panta*, all) in the prologue, insisting that when the author says

---

of the prologue is recapitulated in every scene of the gospel so that "each episode has essentially the same plot as the story as a whole" which is given already in the prologue (*Anatomy of Fourth Gospel*, 88–89). See also Culpepper, "Prologue as Theological Prolegomenon"; and Phillips, *Prologue of the Fourth Gospel*, 17–55.

62. Here and following represent my own translations. Novakovic notes the careful use of ἀλλ (*all*) and ἐκεῖνος (*ekeinos*) to carefully provide contrast and correction (*John 1–10*, 7).

63. I owe my personal correspondence with Julie Engebretson for this insight and language.

64. For a longer exposition of this careful nuance in the prologue, see Brown, "John the Baptist," 148–54.

65. Thompson stresses the "soteriological" aspect of the light, which brings salvation, life, and blessedness, and "shines" equally on all (*John*, 29–31).

that the Word creates "all things" we should take this at face value, but that when he proclaims that this Word as light enlightens "all" people we should read that with only potential value (i.e., all are able to be enlightened, or all are potential receptacles for enlightenment).[66] But this interpretation serves to introduce a discrepancy into the text not present there. John's proclamation that the light entering the world enlightens all people conflicts with his depiction of the Jews as from the devil and incapable of hearing the things of God.[67]

Finally, John notes that the Word "came to his own things, but his own people did not welcome him, but to the ones receiving him—to the ones believing in his name—he gave the power to become children of God, who were born not from blood nor from the will of the flesh nor from the will of a man but from God" (1:12–13). Here no distinction is made between the Word's own people who do not παρέλαβον (*parelabon*, welcome, accept) and anyone who ἔλαβον (*elabon*, receives) him, defined appositionally by the phrase τοῖς πιστεύουσιν εἰς τὸ ὄνομα αὐτοῦ (*tois pisteuousin eis to onoma autou*, those believing in his name).[68] The latter are given, in turn, the power to become children of God.[69]

This passage (1:12–13) clearly contrasts the notion of human, fleshly, patrilineal descent with the concept of God's own parenthood. The idea that "the Jews" are identifiable as a group by their opposition to Jesus (and thus to God for the evangelist) contradicts the claim made in the prologue about the possibility of changing one's own familial identifiers through belief. The suggestion that the Jews have the devil for their father is likewise nullified when read in light of this power that turns humans into children of God, for static labels of identity and relation have no place in the symbolic world of the prologue where existential possibility reigns supreme. This part of the prologue is the clearest renunciation of the language in 8:44 labeling Jews as children of the devil.

---

66. See Novakovic for the distributive aspect of the adjective πάντα (*panta*) (*John 1–10*, 8).

67. As a point of clarification I must add that I do not believe the prologue supports the thesis that all people will attain salvation or enlightenment simply by being "shined" on by the light; that undermines that gospel's central message to "believe." Rather, the stress of the light shining on all critiques the idea that a certain group of people—the Jews—are constitutionally incapable of believing or hearing by their very identity, as 8:44 suggests. This is nicely summarized by Frey: "[John 8:12] thematizes in a conditional formulation—wooing and appleative and yet primarily promising—the 'gain' of discipleship" (*Glory of the Crucified One*, 133).

68. See Novakovic, *John 1–10*, 10; Barrett, *Gospel According to John*, 163.

69. Culpepper, "Pivot of John's Prologue," 16.

An argument against this critique is that John himself sees the world in predetermined, predefined categories, and that some people are "from above" and others "from below," that those who "hear God" will receive Jesus and those who do not will reject him. These interpreters might argue that John reinforces, at least in certain places, a kind of metaphysical determinism.[70] In response I would argue, first, that it is not clear this is the case in John and this view of the gospel must be argued for, rather than an obvious position from which to argue. The centrality of the call to "believe" with its existentially open meaning is far more pervasive and central than its deterministic parts.[71] Further, I think it is possible, and even likely, that the cosmic dualism present in John that reinforces this view is a symbolic, and secondary, feature of John's deeper human dualism that centers human response to Jesus.[72]

Thus, we can see that the prologue, the "lens" for reading John's Gospel, offers sharp critique of John's own use of the phrase "the Jews" elsewhere in his story, a phrase that, perhaps tellingly, never appears in the prologue itself, especially where it might have been theologically expedient. This short examination of John offers a criticism of John's wording and phraseology with respect to "the Jews" from the heart of what John himself wants to say. This criticism of what John *says* by what John *means* is precisely what *Sachkritik* is designed to highlight. *Sachkritik* allows us to name and own the problematic usage of John's words in some places without confusing those instances with John's ultimate aims overall.

There are, of course, limits to *Sachkritik*, and its application to John's use of "the Jews" is not a panacea. Jewish scholars have been skeptical of approaches to John that attempt to interpret unflattering pictures of the Jews by positive ones.[73] Others offer a kind of reverse *Sachkritik*, as it were, and locate a center to John's theology that most Christians would find unsettling. "My own, more pessimistic reading is that the Fourth Gospel's polemic against Jews," Adele Reinhartz writes, "undermines its declarations of

---

70. See Kysar, *John*, 70–74.

71. The call to believe, implying movement from one location to another and not static identity, is central to John. See Loader, "Significance of the Prologue," 55.

72. "The Gospel makes the point primarily that humans are faced with two inescapable possibilities, and that cosmic dualism enters into its language for two reasons: [it] reinforces the importance of human dualism, [and] . . . [it] introduces the cosmic dualism to tie the bipolarity of life to Christology" (Kysar, *John*, 64).

73. Hakola is skeptical of efforts to deconstruct John's anti-Jewish bias by appealing to some other features of text (like 4:22) (*Identity Matters*, 241), although I would argue this is fundamentally different than *Sachkritik*.

God's boundless love for the world."[74] Hakola insists that, "What is needed is a search for new ways to define Christian identity in relation to Judaism."[75] As a tool and a way of reading, *Sachkritik* is not a comprehensive solution to a complex problem. It is offered here as contributing to this conversation, not providing a reason to end all dialogue.

CONCLUSIONS

John's use of οἱ Ἰουδαῖοι (*hoi Ioudaioi*) is a theological problem, for it maligns and denigrates not just any people-group (which is problematic in itself) but the very socio-religious matrix out of which Christianity and Jesus himself arises. Attempts to neutralize this issue by appealing to alternative translations (e.g., "the Judeans"), meanings (e.g., "the religious leaders") or minimizing its effect (e.g., situating John within internecine Jewish conflict) are both unconvincing and unhelpful in promoting genuine dialogue between modern Jews and Christians. Acknowledging this error as a problem for Christians is the first step towards healthy conversation with Jews and spiritual maturity with themselves.

While not a total solution to a complex problem, the interpretive method of *Sachkritik* offers a way for Christian interpreters to both acknowledge John's problematic use of οἱ Ἰουδαῖοι (*hoi Ioudaioi*) and insist on the theological, indeed authoritative, nature of John's Gospel as part of the church's canon of Scripture. *Sachkritik* is not an attempt to deny or reduce the problematic elements of the text but rather the application of the kerygma that arises from the text organically—but is not identified *with* the text absolutely—to the words of the text itself where the text fails to embody the kerygma. Thus, *Sachkritik* is not a rejection of John but an attempt to hear more clearly the heart of John's own message.

Interpreters who hold to a view of Scripture characterized by inerrancy will undoubtedly find much to criticize and reject with the application of *Sachkritik* to John's use of "the Jews" (or, indeed, any part of the Bible). While this a priori assumption about the text cannot be addressed or resolved in this conclusion, I would respond that this method is a self-conscious effort to provide some controls on a tendency that is not materially at odds with the "spiritual interpretation" favored by the church for centuries, whether the "allegorical" interpretation of the early church or the "typological" approach of the later Reformers. Origen explains that sometimes the literal, historical meaning of the text is devoid of meaning and one must seek only

---

74. Reinhartz, "Jews in Fourth Gospel," 217.

75. Hakola, *Identity Matters*, 241.

its spiritual interpretation. There are for him impossibilities in Scripture that yield no "bodily meaning."[76] He cites as examples the creation of light before the sun, moon, and stars, the idea that God would plant a magical tree that would offer life by eating its fruit (or knowledge by the eating of the fruit of another), that Cain could leave God's presence, or that Jesus would be taken to a high mountain and shown all the kingdoms of the world by the devil.[77] All these things Origen considers impossible, and they should spur readers to discern a meaning "worthy of God," i.e., a principle derived from Scripture but not identical to the words of Scripture itself. "For our position is that with respect to the whole of the divine Scripture all of it has a spiritual meaning, but not all of it has a bodily meaning, for there are many places where the bodily is proved to be impossible."[78]

Likewise, Augustine, who also maintains a distinction between the spiritual and fleshly levels of Scripture,[79] outlines his rules for interpreting commands as follows: "If the sentence [of Scripture] is one of command, either forbidding a crime or vice, or enjoining an act of prudence or benevolence, it is not figurative. If, however, it seems to enjoin a crime or vice, or to forbid an act of prudence or benevolence, it is figurative."[80] It is "charity" that ought to lead the interpreter to understand that heaping coals of fire on the head of another is a benevolent, not spiteful, act. Here Augustine seems also to have identified a key locus arising from Scripture and then applying it critically to the interpretation of other passages. Similarly, Luther seems more than happy to prioritize the parts of Scripture that show Christ plainly (e.g., John, Paul's letters—especially Romans, Galatians, and Ephesians—and 1 Peter) at the expense of others that, in his estimation, do not (like James, which he famously calls "an epistle of straw").[81]

In this way *Sachkritik* can be seen as a modern version of an ancient approach to Scripture that seeks both spiritual truth as well as intellectual honesty. Such a posture, one would hope, would produce better dialogue partners for Jewish-Christian conversations.

---

76. Origen, *On First Principles*, 2:4.2.9. For what follows I credit the spring 2023 Baylor University Faculty Interdisciplinary Colloquy on Patristics (BUFICOP) for my insights and sources.

77. Origen, *On First Principles*, 2:4.3.1; 4.2.9.

78. Origen, *On First Principles*, 2:4.3.5.

79. See Augustine, *Civ.* 17.16 (*NPNF*[2] 1:808), where Augustine offers his interpretation of Ps 45, arguing that no one is so stupid "as to believe that some poor woman is here praised."

80. Augustine, *Doctr. Chr.* 3.24 (*NPNF*[1] 2:1282).

81. Luther, *Prefaces to New Testament*, 9–10.

BIBLIOGRAPHY

Ashton, John. "The Identity and Function of the Ἰουδαῖοι in the Fourth Gospel." *NovT* 27 (1985) 40–75.

Barrett, C. K. *The Gospel According to St. John: An Introduction with Commentary and Notes on the Greek Text.* 2nd ed. Philadelphia: Westminster, 1978.

Barrett, C. Kingsley. "John and Judaism." In *Anti-Judaism and the Fourth Gospel*, edited by Reimund Bieringer et al., 231–46. Louisville: Westminster John Knox, 2001.

Beck, Norman A. *Mature Christianity in the 21st Century: The Recognition and Repudiation of the Anti-Jewish Polemic of the New Testament.* Rev. ed. New York: American Interfaith Institute, 1994.

Bennema, Cornelis. "The Identity and Composition of οἱ Ἰουδαῖοι in the Gospel of John." *TynBul* 60 (2009) 239–63.

Beutler, Johannes. *Judaism and the Jews in the Gospel of John.* SubBi 30. Rome: Editrice Pontificio Istituto Biblico, 2006.

Bieringer, Reimund, et al. "Wrestling with Johannine Anti-Judaism: A Hermeneutical Framework for the Analysis of the Current Debate." In *Anti-Judaism and the Fourth Gospel*, edited by Reimund Bieringer et al., 3–37. Louisville: Westminster John Knox, 2001.

Blenkisopp, Joseph. "The Contemporary English Version: Inaccurate Translation Tries to Soften Anti-Judaic Sentiment [Point]." *BRev* 12 (1996) 42–51.

Brown, Sherri. "John the Baptist: Witness and Embodiment of the Prologue in the Gospel of John." In *Characters and Characterization in the Gospel of John*, edited by Christopher W. Skinner, 145–64. LNTS 461. London: Bloomsbury T&T Clark, 2013.

Bultmann, Rudolf. "Das Problem einer theologischen Exegese des Neuen Testaments [1925]." In *Anfänge der dialektischen Theologie*, edited by Jürgen Moltmann, 2:27–72. Theologische Bucherei: Neudrucke und Berichte aus dem 20. Jahrhundert 17; Systematische Theologie. Munich: Kaiser, 1963.

Chilton, Bruce. "Jesus and the Question of Anti-Semitism." In *Anti-Semitism and Early Christianity: Issues of Polemic and Faith*, edited by Craig A. Evans and Donald A. Hagner, 39–44. Minneapolis: Fortress, 1993.

Congdon, David W. *The Mission of Demythologizing: Rudolf Bultmann's Dialectical Theology.* Minneapolis: Fortress, 2015.

Crossan, John Dominic. *Who Killed Jesus? Exposing the Roots of Anti-Semitism in the Gospel Story of the Death of Jesus.* New York: Harper Collins, 1995.

Culpepper, R. Alan. *The Anatomy of the Fourth Gospel: A Study in Literary Design.* Philadelphia: Fortress, 1983.

———. "Anti-Judaism in the Fourth Gospel as a Theological Problem for Christian Interpreters." In *Anti-Judaism and the Fourth Gospel*, edited by Reimund Bieringer et al., 61–82. Louisville: Westminster John Knox, 2001.

———. "The Pivot of John's Prologue." *NTS* 27 (1980) 1–31.

———. "The Prologue as Theological Prolegomenon to the Gospel of John." In *The Prologue of the Gospel of John: Its Literary, Theological, and Philosophical Contexts; Papers Read at the Colloquium Ioanneum 2013*, edited by Jan G. van der Watt et al., 3–26. WUNT, 1st ser., 359. Tübingen: Mohr Siebeck, 2016.

De Jonge, Henk Jan. "'The Jews' in the Gospel of John." In *Anti-Judaism and the Fourth Gospel*, edited by Reimund Bieringer et al., 121–40. Louisville: Westminster John Knox, 2001.

Donaldson, Terence L. *Jews and Anti-Semitism in the New Testament: Decision Points and Divergent Interpretations.* London: Society for Promoting Christian Knowledge, 2010.

Evans, Roger Steven. *Issues of New Testament Anti-Judaism: Son of Man, Deicide, and Divine Predetermination.* Lanham, MD: University Press of America, 2008.

Freudmann, Lillian C. *Antisemitism in the New Testament.* Lanham, MD: University Press of America, 1994.

Frey, Jörg. *The Glory of the Crucified One: Christology and Theology in the Gospel of John.* Edited by Wayne Coppins and Simon Gathercole. Translated by Wayne Coppins and Christoph Heilig. Baylor-Mohr Siebeck Studies in Early Christianity. Waco: Baylor University Press, 2018.

———. "Toward Reconfiguring Our Views on the 'Parting of the Ways': Ephesus as a Test Case." In *John and Judaism: A Contested Relationship in Context*, edited by R. Alan Culpepper and Paul N. Anderson, 221–42. RBS 67. Atlanta: SBL, 2017.

Gaston, Lloyd. "Lobsters in the Fourth Gospel." In *Approaches to Ancient Judaism*, edited by Jacob Neusner. Religious and Theological Studies, new ser., 4:115–23. Atlanta: Scholars, 1993.

Greenspoon, Leonard. "Translating *Jesus* and *the Jews*: Can We Eradicate the Anti-Semitism Without Also Erasing the Semitism?" In *Soundings in the Religion of Jesus: Perspectives and Methods in Jewish and Christian Scholarship*, edited by Bruce Chilton et al., 11–28. Minneapolis: Fortress, 2012.

Hakola, Raimo. *Identity Matters: John, the Jews and Jewishness.* NovTSup 118. Leiden: Brill, 2005.

Heschel, Susannah. "Historiography of Antisemitism Versus Anti-Judaism: A Response to Robert Morgan." *JSNT* 33 (2011) 257–79.

Kampen, John. "The Gospel of Matthew and the Challenge of Antisemitism." *Mennonite Quarterly Review* 92 (2018) 548–70.

Kim, Lloyd. *Polemic in the Book of Hebrews: Anti-Semitism, Anti-Judaism, Supersessionism?* Princeton Theological Monograph. Eugene, OR: Pickwick, 2006.

Kysar, Robert. "Anti-Semitism and the Gospel of John." In *Soundings in the Religion of Jesus: Perspectives and Methods in Jewish and Christian Scholarship*, edited by Bruce Chilton et al., 113–27. Minneapolis: Fortress, 2012.

———. *John: The Maverick Gospel.* Rev. ed. Louisville: Westminster John Knox, 1993.

Lamp, Jeffery S. "Is Paul Anti-Jewish? *Testament of Levi* 6 in the Interpretation of 1 Thessalonians 2:13–16." *CBQ* 65 (2003) 408–27.

Levenson, Jon D. "Is There a Counterpart in the Hebrew Bible to New Testament Antisemitism." *JES* 22 (1985) 242–60.

———. "Why Jews Are Not Interested in Biblical Theology." In *Judaic Perspectives on Ancient Israel*, edited by Jacob Neusner et al., 281–307. Philadelphia: Fortress, 1987.

Levine, Amy-Jill. "First Take the Log Out of Your Own Eye: Different Viewpoints, Different Movies." In *On "The Passion of the Christ": Exploring the Issues Raised by the Controversial Movie*, edited by Paula Fredriksen, 197–210. Berkeley: University of California Press, 2006.

Loader, William R. G. "The Significance of the Prologue for Understanding John's Soteriology." In *The Prologue of the Gospel of John: Its Literary, Theological, and Philosophical Contexts; Papers Read at the Colloquium Ioanneum 2013*, edited by Jan G. van der Watt et al., 45–55. WUNT, 1st ser., 359. Tübingen: Mohr Siebeck, 2016.

Lowe, Malcolm. "Who Were the Ἰουδαῖοι?" *NovT* 18 (1976) 101–30.

Luther, Martin. *Prefaces to the New Testament*. Translated by Charles M. Jacobs and E. Theodore Bachmann. Cabin John, MD: Wildside, 2021.

Luz, Ulrich. *Matthew 21–28: A Commentary*. Translated by James E. Crouch. Hermeneia. Minneapolis: Fortress, 2005.

Marcus, Joel. "Epilogue." In *Soundings in the Religion of Jesus: Perspectives and Methods in Jewish and Christian Scholarship*, edited by Bruce Chilton et al., 291–96. Minneapolis: Fortress, 2012.

Marshall, John. "Apocalypticism and Anti-Semitism: Inner-Group Resources for Inter-Group Conflicts." In *Apocalypticism, Anti-Semitism and the Historical Jesus*, edited by John S. Kloppenborg and John Marshall, 68–82. JSNTSup 275. London: T&T Clark, 2005.

Martyn, J. Louis. *History and Theology in the Fourth Gospel*. 3rd ed. NTL. Louisville: Westminster John Knox, 2003.

Mash, S. David. "Anti-Semitism in the New Testament: New Scrutiny of a Chronic Notion, Part 1." *BSac* 178 (2021) 143–62.

Meachem, Jon. "Who Killed Jesus?" *Newsweek*, Feb. 15, 2004; last updated Mar. 13, 2010. https://www.newsweek.com/who-killed-jesus-131113.

Morgan, Robert. "*Sachkritik* in Reception History." *JSNT* 33 (2010) 175–90.

Nanos, Mark D. "Paul's Reversal of Jews Calling Gentiles 'Dogs' (Philippians 3:2): 1600 Years of an Ideological Tale Wagging an Exegetical Dog?" *BibInt* 17 (2009) 448–82.

Neyrey, Jerome H. *The Gospel of John*. New Cambridge Bible Commentary. Cambridge: Cambridge University Press, 2007.

Novakovic, Lidja. *John 1–10: A Handbook on the Greek Text*. Baylor Handbook on the Greek New Testament. Waco: Baylor University Press, 2020.

Origen. *On First Principles*. Edited and translated by Jon Behr. 2 vols. Reader's ed. Oxford Early Christian Texts. Oxford: Oxford University Press, 2018.

Patte, Daniel. "Anti-Semitism in the New Testament. Confronting the Dark Side of Paul's and Matthew's Teaching." *Chicago Theological Seminary Register* 78 (1988) 31–52.

Phillips, Peter M. *The Prologue of the Fourth Gospel: A Sequential Reading*. LNTS 294. London: T&T Clark, 2006.

Pippin, Tina. "'For Fear of the Jews': Lying and Truth-Telling in Translating the Gospel of John." *Semeia* 76 (1996) 81–97.

Reinhartz, Adele. "'Jews' and Jews in the Fourth Gospel." In *Anti-Judaism and the Fourth Gospel*, edited by Reimund Bieringer et al., 213–17. Louisville: Westminster John Knox, 2001.

Saldarini, Anthony J. "Reading Matthew Without Anti-Semitism." In *The Gospel of Matthew in Current Study: Studies in Memory of William G. Thompson, S.J.*, edited by David E. Aune, 166–84. Grand Rapids: Eerdmans, 2001.

Sandmel, Samuel. *Anti-Semitism in the New Testament?* Philadelphia: Fortress, 1978.

Sheridan, Ruth. "Identity, Alterity, and the Gospel of John." *BibInt* 22 (2014) 188–209.

———. "Issues in the Translation of οἱ Ἰουδαῖοι in the Fourth Gospel." *JBL* 132 (2013) 671–95.

Standhartinger, Angela. "Paul, the Jews, and the Thessalonians: New Observations on Thessalonians 2:14–16." In *Thessalonica*, edited by James R. Harrison and L. L. Welborn, 249–67. First Urban Christians 7. Atlanta: SBL, 2022.

Thatcher, Tom. "John and the Jews: Recent Research and Future Questions." In *John and Judaism: A Contested Relationship in Context*, edited by R. Alan Culpepper and Paul N. Anderson, 3–38. RBS 67. Atlanta: SBL, 2017.

Thiel, Nathan. "'Israel' and 'Jew' as Markers of Jewish Identity in Antiquity: The Problems of Insider/Outsider Classification." *JSJ* 45 (2014) 80–99.

Thompson, Marianne Meye. *John: A Commentary*. NTL. Louisville: Westminster John Knox, 2015.

Tomson, Peter J. "'Jews' in the Gospel of John as Compared with the Palestinian Talmud, the Synoptics, and Some New Testament Apocrypha." In *Anti-Judaism and the Fourth Gospel*, edited by Reimund Bieringer et al., 176–212. Louisville: Westminster John Knox, 2001.

Wahlde, Urban von. "The Jews in the Gospel of John: Fifteen Years of Research (1983–1998)." *ETL* 76 (2000) 30–55.

Chapter 11

Lindbeck and Kinzer on the Church
Israel and Gentiles "Mutually Dwelling" in Christ as One People of God?

Axel Kazadi

THE RESURRECTION OF CHRIST has challenged Christian scholars to reexamine the relationship of Israel to Christ, of Israel and the church, and of gentile Christians to the promises of God declared in Christ.[1] The reason this challenge persists is Christ's messiahship—which is sealed by his resurrection—demands one to (re)think how Jews and gentiles are now related to and in Christ. Christ's disciples and the apostle Paul, for example, clearly wrestle with what this revelation meant for Jews and gentiles in their various epistles as well as conversations recorded in the book of Acts. Should

---

1. See Frymer-Kensky et al., *Christianity in Jewish Terms*. In this anthology, there are discussions between Jewish, Messianic, and Christian scholars on theological issues related to Jewish and Christian relations. This work is one of the examples that illustrates the wrestling with issues with which Jews, Messianic Jews, and Christians are typically involved, except these exchanges are taking place on a more scholarly level. Also see Kortner, "Lost Fragment." Kortner comments on how Jewish Christianity is a lost fragment which is often overlooked in Christian ecumenical dialogues. In this work, Kortner draws attention to the relation between Jewish Christianity and gentile Christianity. For other discussions on the relation between church and Israel, see Kinzer, *Postmissionary Messianic Judaism*; Kinzer, *Searching Her Own Mystery*; Radner, *Church*.

believing gentiles circumcise themselves?[2] Should gentiles be required to observe the Mosaic law? These are some of the questions the early Jewish Christians had to come to terms with in light of Christ's resurrection. The formation of new gentile gatherings caused the apostle Paul to discuss how Jews and gentiles relate to the divine promises in Christ—which were first given to Israel in Torah—in the book of Romans. While some have historically understood the gentile church as a new gathering that supersedes Israel, I will demonstrate in this chapter that George Lindbeck's Israel-like concept of the church satisfactorily affirms the *single* peoplehood of Jewish and gentile believers.[3] Moreover, I also take Mark Kinzer's concerns related to bilateral ecclesiology into consideration. Israel and church are used interchangeably because Israel and the church were "one people for the early Christians. There was no breach in continuity."[4] In order to advance this argument of the single peoplehood of Israel and church in Christ, it will be important to (1) first show the distinction between Jews and gentiles and (2) demonstrate how Israel and the church are one people in Christ. The retrieval of the Israel-like concept of the church is significant because it brings the church one step closer to confronting her historical sins against the Jews and repairing her relationship with the Jews.

THE DISTINCTION BETWEEN JEWISH AND GENTILE BELIEVERS

The development of gentile Christianity and its popularity around the globe may give the impression that Christianity was a gentile movement at the outset. Christianity, however, was primarily a Jewish movement in its earliest years. Before Rome became the center of gentile Christianity in the fourth century, Jerusalem was the center of the "Yeshua movement" in the first century. Mark Kinzer notes that "Luke's concern for the temple shows that he shared the widespread Jewish conviction that the Jerusalem sanctuary

---

2. Betz, "New Testament Canon," 42. For example, on early Jewish Christians wrestling with whether gentiles should get circumcised, Betz records that there was a "trend which argued that all Gentile Christians should be circumcised as full proselytes and integrated into Judaism." While the Jerusalem Council decided to have separate missionary strategies towards Jews and gentiles respectively, it was still a moment of serious reflection for early Jewish Christians in light of revelation of the risen Christ.

3. For other discussions on the church as Israel or the Israelhood of the church, see Lindbeck, "Confession and Community"; Lindbeck, "Church"; Lindbeck, "Postmodern Hermeneutics and Jewish-Christian Dialogue"; Lindbeck, "What of the Future?"; Radner, *Church*, 115–43; Brown, *George Lindbeck and Israel*.

4. Lindbeck, "Church," 150.

constituted the *axis mundi*, the meeting place of heaven and earth."[5] Israel was thus primarily regarded as the people of God.[6] The early Jewish Christians, however, recognized that God's power was also at work among gentile believers. Gentile believers were welcomed to fellowship and worship with Jewish believers in Christ because God granted them "repentance unto life" (Acts 11:18 NIV).

Though Jewish and gentile gatherings were different from each other, there was a spiritual communion between these two gatherings during the early period of Christianity. Thus, the push to define the church as primarily the people of God is on the right trajectory because this configuration of the church has "the greatest prima facie claim to ecumenical catholicity."[7] George Lindbeck states that the Old Testament story of Israel characterized and consolidated the "communal self-understanding" of early Christian communities as *ekklesia*.[8] In ancient Greece, an *ekklesia* technically meant an assembly of citizens in a city-state. Early Christians appropriated it to refer to their own assembly or gathering. The term itself generally means an assembly of people. Commenting on the story of Israel in OT shaping the early Christian self-understanding as an *ekklesia* or assembly of God's people, Lindbeck writes,

> All the categories they [Jewish Christians] possessed for their communal self-understanding were derived from the Hebrew Scriptures (usually, to be sure, in the Greek Septuagint version). These were their only inspired text, and they interpreted it as Jews. It was natural that they should understand their communities as *ekklésia*, as *qahal*, the assembly of Israel in the new age. Thus the story of Israel was their story. They were part of the people of God who lived in the time between the times after the messianic era had begun but before the final coming of the kingdom.[9]

The notion of the church as an assembly of people is more concrete and accurately depicts the formation of *ekklesias* in the first century. Jewish

---

5. Kinzer, "Bilateral Ecclesiology," 153.

6. For formulations that characterize the church as a people of God, refer to Lindbeck, "Church"; Lindbeck, "Confession and Community," 8; Radner, *Church*, 53–68.

7. Lindbeck, "Church," 147.

8. Lindbeck, "Church," 149.

9. Lindbeck, "Church," 149. For Radner, the ordering of the church as a people has a divine origin. Radner explains, "The Church is truly a people who can be a place and a person at the same time, because God makes it so. More fundamentally, the Church is truly a people, only because God makes peoples, and that divine making is what underlines everything a people is" (Radner, *Church*, 70).

and gentile *ekklesias* were both together considered people of God by early Jewish Christian believers. The Christian fellowship was maintained by a differentiated unity between Jewish and gentile *ekklesias*. While they shared the love of Christ with each other, the distinction between two groups was clearly acknowledged and defined.

Lindbeck conceptualizes the assembling structure of these people groups within the framework of communities. The Old Testament story of Israel is central to the organizing structures of their communities, though they are different from each other. Although Lindbeck recognizes the difference that exists between them, he stresses the unity of Jewish and gentile Christians as one people of God.[10] Lindbeck's commitment to retrieve the Israel-like concept of the church reinforces his focus on the single unity of Jewish and gentile believers as one people shaped by Israel's story. In other words, he does not drive any wedge between the two groups. Though the two groups are ethnically distinct from each other, it seems as though Lindbeck is less concerned with Kinzer's driving impulse to preserve Jewish customs. However, Lindbeck is clear that the gentiles, who are a fragment of the *ekklesia*, cannot "expropriate" Israel.[11] Commenting on the error of expropriation and its assumptions, Lindbeck expounds,

> Christians who expropriate the identity of Israel assume that to remain in covenant with God, Israel must be without fundamental error. They conclude that because Israel was errant, it was not worthy of being God's covenant partner. God consequently transferred all of God's promises to the church. In the expropriator's view, therefore, it was Israel's sin that made God revoke the covenant. But if the church is to endure until the end of ages, as the New Testament promises, it must be incapable of comparable unfaithfulness; it must be truthful and holy in a way that Israel was not. The error in this view is the conviction, essential to supersessionism, that God's patience is exhaustible and his covenant conditional. The Bible itself corrects the error of expropriation, for it informs us that God keeps his promises no matter how errant his people.[12]

Supersessionism assumes that the replacement of Israel by the church is deeply legitimated by the failures or sins of Israel. It portrays a divine image of God as one who is impatient. Yet, God does not forsake his people in the Old Testament when they break the covenant, nor will he ever forsake

10. Lindbeck, "Church," 150.
11. Lindbeck, *Church in a Postliberal Age*, 110.
12. Lindbeck, *Church in a Postliberal Age*, 110–11.

them in the future. His covenant with Israel is eternal. The gentile faction, as much as it gained traction in the Roman Empire, cannot present itself as the whole of Christianity nor can it assume that it has replaced Israel. Supersessionism does not make space for diversity as Lindbeck's Israel-like understanding of the church does. According to the supersessionist view, there is no differentiated unity of gentiles and Jews. One must completely replace and eliminate the other. Lindbeck's Israel-like concept of the church, on the other hand, recognizes the two fragments (Jews and gentiles) that make up the people of God.[13] The gentile fragment, through its incorporation in the people of God, does not expropriate Israel, but appropriates Israel and "claims to be Israel without replacing the Jews."[14] The gentiles can identify with Israel's story, and Israel's story becomes theirs through Christ.

The unity of Jews and gentiles has potential dangers if understood improperly. For example, the loss of hermeneutical identity is a possibility. It is only in this context where Lindbeck's ideas of maintaining the distinction between the two groups' particularities are more pronounced. Assimilation cannot be an option for both hermeneutically. Warning against assimilation, Lindbeck writes,

> Hermeneutical rapprochement has its dangers because Scripture is central to both Judaism and Christianity. The erosion of distinctly Jewish and Christian interpretations cannot help but weaken each community's identity and power, resulting in a tastelessly lukewarm Judeo-Christian tradition good for nothing except to be spewed out, as the Book of Revelation says of the Church at Laodicea.[15]

Lindbeck disapproves of the disappearance of the distinct features of each community. The survival of each community is fundamental to the vibrancy of Israel as a people of God, or a "nation among nations" comprised of Jews and gentiles.[16] Ephraim Radner also recognizes the diversity within the understanding of the church as a people of God. It is not a "monolithic

---

13. Radner, *Church*, 130. Radner agrees with this configuration of the church as Israel. He posits that it is a term that is difficult to explain. However, this concept of church rightly "involves a relationship of Jew (believing or non-Christian) and Christian believer (whether Gentile or Jewish) that is ordered together to an obedience of God that will finally give rise to a common praise, as the vision of Revelation 7 indicates."

14. Lindbeck, *Church in a Postliberal Age*, 110.

15. Lindbeck, *Church in a Postliberal Age*, 112.

16. Radner, *Church*, 81. The notion of the church as "a nation among nations" is used by Radner to describe the church as a nation that is tasked with a mission for the sake of nations.

cultural understanding of the Church."[17] The gentile church and the Jewish synagogue are diverse aspects of the "*Ekklesia* or Church of Israel itself."[18]

Kinzer similarly affirms a distinction between gentile and Jewish fragments of the church of Israel in his concept of the "bilateral ecclesiology." The unity does not erode the particularities of each people group. This differentiated unity exists in solidarity with Israel. The *ekklesia* is "bilateral—one reality subsisting in two forms."[19] However, Kinzer sets a boundary between the two which cannot be transgressed. Gentiles are gentiles, and Israel is Israel. Gentiles are not Israel, but "have been associated with Israel."[20] The church is a "transnational entity" which is composed of Jewish and gentile communities in solidarity with Israel.[21] While Lindbeck affirms the distinction between Jews and gentiles, he explicitly posits that the church is Israel. Kinzer does not completely accept this Israel-like concept of the church. He speaks of the incorporation of gentiles into the life of Israel in a different way. The Jewish fragment remains in "solidarity with the Jewish people as a whole, but the Gentile *ekklesia* is thereby brought into meaningful relationship with 'all Israel.'" The gentiles do not become Jewish, but they are "joined to an extended multinational commonwealth of Israel and can legitimately identify with Israel's history and destiny."[22]

JEWS AND GENTILES: DWELLING MUTUALLY AS ONE PEOPLE IN CHRIST

Though Kinzer sets a strict boundary between Israel and the church in *Postmissionary Messianic Judaism*, he affirms that both of them can mutually exist together. The coexistence between Jews and gentiles is defined as "mutual-indwelling."[23] It seems that the way this notion of mutual indwelling works is by securing and maintaining the diversity of groups or particularities of groups in their communion with each other. It is a collective of different groups (Jewish and gentiles) that are spiritually linked together. Kinzer's notion of a collective unity is pronounced in the way he conceives different groups (i.e., the Catholic Church, Jewish Catholics,

---

17. Radner, *Church*, 130–31.
18. Radner, *Church*, 130.
19. Kinzer, "Bilateral Ecclesiology," 152.
20. Kinzer, "Bilateral Ecclesiology," 156.
21. Kinzer, "Bilateral Ecclesiology," 152.
22. Kinzer, "Bilateral Ecclesiology," 152.
23. Kinzer, *Searching Her Own Mystery*, 174.

Messianic Jews, and the wider Jewish world) mutually enriching each other. The benefit of maintaining this notion of collectiveness is the protection of the particularities of groups and the opportunity available for these different communities to learn from each other. There are several questions that one may ask in order to understand Kinzer's notion of mutual indwelling: What is the nature of this mutual indwelling? Is Christ somehow related to this mutual indwelling? According to Kinzer, the relationship between the two groups is a mystery, but Christ is somehow related to and involved in the relationship between gentiles and Jews. He explains that "Jesus is as much the mystery hidden in the depths of the Jewish people and the Jewish way of life as he is the mystery of the ecclesia."[24] Kinzer draws this insight from Pope John Paul II's understanding of the messianic identity of Christ as the mystery in which Jews and gentiles are linked together.[25] Kinzer calls this understanding as "Israel-Christology" which affirmatively "entails a relationship of mutual-indwelling."[26] Commenting on how Christ is related to the notion of mutual indwelling, Kinzer records,

> The relationship of mutual-indwelling that Jesus has with both communities creates the "spiritual bond" that joins each to the other. Because he dwells in them both, they also dwell in one another. Through the unbreakable relationship that Jesus forges with his own flesh-and-blood, genealogical-Israel abides in the heart of the *ecclesia*. Through her baptismal union with Jesus, the *ecclesia* likewise abides in the heart of the Jewish people. Only through humble and persistent self-searching can either discern this mutual-indwelling, but once it is perceived, new vistas open to the eyes of faith.[27]

Kinzer affirms the dynamic and interpenetrative relationship that exists between the church and the Jewish people through Christ. Though he conceives of *ekklesia* as part of the extended "commonwealth of Israel," the distinction of the communities is stressed.[28] However, if Christ is a mystery hidden in both groups, does Kinzer think that Christ is also related to the strict boundary he sets between gentiles and Jews? The distinction between the two is not denied, but what is potentially worrisome in Kinzer's writings is the reluctance to frame the church as Israel. While the christological determination of the unity is significant, Kinzer's insistence on the separation

---

24. Kinzer, *Searching Her Own Mystery*, 174.
25. Kinzer, *Searching Her Own Mystery*, 173–74.
26. Kinzer, *Searching Her Own Mystery*, 174.
27. Kinzer, *Searching Her Own Mystery*, 174–75.
28. Kinzer, *Searching Her Own Mystery*, 178.

between Israel and church seems to provide a conceptual avenue through which the church could self-determine herself apart from Israel—a kind of self-determination which has historically been an "ecclesiological scar" and a result of sin. Kinzer still stresses two people groups and does not explicitly acknowledge both as one people (or church) of Israel.[29] Kinzer's concept of mutual indwelling appears to be undergirded by the notion of unity-in-diversity, and it appears as though, for Kinzer, the potential danger of regarding Israel and the church synonymously could lead to confusion over their meanings and the dissolution of identities.

However, the Israel-like concept of the church, which Lindbeck and Radner affirm, could satisfactorily bolster the notion of mutual indwelling of Jews and gentiles as one single people by precluding the option for the church to self-define herself apart from Israel. The linguistic framing of the church as Israel in Lindbeck's thought cherishes the Jew-gentile relation and respects both of their identities. Radner is also insightfully instructive in his understanding of how the identity of single peoplehood—characterized by the figure of Israel—is expressed in Christ. Israel and the church are perceived as one single adopted children of God. According to Radner, the church and Israel, through adoption in Christ, are "scripturally figured in Christ." It is this christological grounding that renders the task of dwelling together as a single people possible. Adoption is "only one way of expressing the gracious act of God's calling and animating his people." The church as "a people of adopted children is exactly what Israel is, not something other than Israel."[30] While Radner acknowledges Christ is central to the church and Israel as one people, he still stresses the notion of the church as Israel.[31] The decoupling of the church from Israel has led to many historical sins of the church directed against Israel. The reaffirmation of the church's "Israel-identity" challenges the church "to face itself responsibly, take account of

---

29. It would be interesting to know what principles would ensure the practical success of mutual indwelling. What sort of conceptual frameworks would undergird such coexistence? The conceptual understanding of Christ as the mystery hidden in both groups does (or could) bring people together to coexist, but there are more factors involved in ensuring the success of two groups to coexist. There are so many factors that would contribute to its success, such as people's attitudes, sensibilities, sense of toleration, values, openness, etc. Furthermore, Kinzer's "mutual indwelling" would have to address (and develop a practical way of combatting) conceptual self-understandings of Israel and the church respectively that could potentially compromise the integrity of their unity through mutual indwelling. The mindset of a single peoplehood through Kinzer's notion of "mutual indwelling" could potentially be compromised if the church is able to self-define herself apart from Israel.

30. Radner, *Church*, 145.

31. Radner, *Church*, 95–116.

its actions, repent, and be renewed."[32] The church—made up of Christians whose national origins are Jewish and gentile—is conceptualized by Radner as the "Christian part of Israel" and the Jews represent the Jewish part of Israel.[33] As Israel, both of them "adopted" into Christ, "as Children by flesh of the First Adam are made children by grace of the Second."[34] Such treatment of the church as Israel attempts to see the figural connection between Israel and the church. It sees the Christian church as something that is "given to us in the forms of Scripture's reference, logically prior to the Church's actual historical embodiment."[35] Israel as a scriptural referent describes the church's own life in the world. Thus, the church's life could never be understood apart from Israel's actual life.

The church is constituted as one people of Israel in Christ for a particular purpose and mission. The church as a whole does not exist for herself. In fact, the whole church—Israel and gentiles together as one people of Israel—is "a people called and animated by God in Spirit to gather all peoples in Christ together in praise of their Creator."[36] Radner notes that this ecclesiological definition is expressed in the "genealogical outworking and experience of Israel. From them the Christ is born, and he takes them to himself and sends them in his Spirit to the nations."[37] As a people, they have been adopted by God to be his people, and the calling of God on their lives is visibly witnessed to by their baptism. For Radner, baptism "marks the hearing of that call and its receipt and recognition all at once."[38] The church testifies that she will be committed to living her new life in Christ which is missional. It is not the case that only a small fraction of the people of God is truly called to be missionaries, and the remaining group is not. Acts 1:8 expresses that the calling of God for the whole church, which is empowered by and baptized with the Holy Spirit, is to go forth as a witnessing people "in Jerusalem, and in all Judea and Samaria, and to the ends of the earth" (NIV).

When the church engages the world, she cannot forget that she is constituted as one holy people by grace. However, her historical sins humble her before the eyes of the world. The world is historically aware of her horrific and unspeakable acts that have oppressed, repressed, and unfortunately resulted in the persecution and murder of Jewish people. Christian

32. Radner, *Church*, 100.
33. Radner, *Church*, 105.
34. Radner, *Church*, 145.
35. Radner, *Church*, 102.
36. Radner, *Church*, 144.
37. Radner, *Church*, 144–45.
38. Radner, *Church*, 146.

supersessionism and Christian persecution of Jews have darkened her witness in the world. While the theology of the single peoplehood of Jews and gentiles in Christ could be taught, it is important, however, for such unity to materialize in a tangible manner. In John 17:20–23, Jesus prays the following prayer for all of his disciples to be unified:

> My prayer is not for them alone. I pray also for those who will believe in me through their message, that all of them may be one, Father, just as you are in me and I am in you. May they also be in us so that the world may believe that you have sent me. I have given them the glory that you gave me, that they may be one as we are one—I in them and you in me—so that they may be brought to complete unity. Then the world will know that you sent me and have loved them even as you have loved me. (NIV)

As Jesus's prayer alludes, the unity which all of his disciples (i.e., Jewish and gentile) share together as one people will notify the world that Christ was sent by the Father for the life of the world. The unity of the Trinity must ground this oneness between believers. The believability of the gospel relates to our rootedness in the Trinity as one people.

A divided people of God cannot properly give witness to the triune God in an honorable way before the world. The gentile church has historically been proclaiming the good news to the world, but she must repent from sins of anti-Semitism and supersessionism that continue to sever the fellowship between gentiles and Jews in Christ. The proclamation of the gospel by a divided church does not faithfully honor Jesus's prayer in John 17. Christ did not commission a divided *ekklesia* to proclaim his gospel. Jesus's prayer challenges the whole *ekklesia* (Jewish and gentile fragments together) to consider the cruciality of ecclesial unity in relation to her mission in the world. The implication of this truth challenges the gentiles in the church to rethink ecumenism in a way that also engages the other Jewish fragment of the church. Moreover, it also dispels the notion of supersessionism because both fragments (gentile and Jewish) are one people of God in Christ. The division between the gentile and Jewish aspects of the *ekklesia* undermines the hallowing of God's name in the world. The church, which has been adopted and animated by God, can faithfully honor the mission she received from Christ by living in the world as one people.

CONCLUSION

Christianity was primarily a Jewish movement. This realization should certainly encourage modern gentile Christians to learn more about the Jewish roots of their Christian faith and repudiate supersessionist ideologies expressed in Christian gentile circles. One must comprehend that Jerusalem was the center of Christianity in the first century. This Jewish center existed in peace and harmony with gentile gatherings. The Jerusalem church provided leadership and guidance to gentile gatherings. Though there is a continuity between Israel and the church in Lindbeck's thought, there is a clear distinction between the Jewish and gentile *ekklesias*. Unlike Kinzer, Lindbeck and Radner affirm the Israelhood of the church. Gentiles and Jews dwell mutually in Christ as one church of Israel. This paper has attempted to show that Lindbeck's Israel-like concept of the church helps one understand better how the gentile and Jewish fragments of the church are fundamentally connected as an inseparable people without obliterating their particularities. Dividing these two fragments will have irreversible supersessionist consequences and will breed violence of some kind against the vulnerable fragment. It has historically been the Jews who have suffered atrociously at the hands of so-called Christians. If the church seriously wants to honor Christ in her missionary activity in the world, she should first make serious efforts to repair and reconcile broken relationships internally—and that fundamentally includes her familial relationship with the Jews.

BIBLIOGRAPHY

Batlajery, Agustinus M. L. "Ecumenical Activities of John Calvin." *Journal of Reformed Theology* 11 (2017) 223–48.

Betz, Hans Dieter. "Is the New Testament Canon the Basis for a Church in Fragments?" In *The Church in Fragments: Towards What Kind of Unity?*, edited by Miklós Tomka and Giuseppe Ruggieri, 35–45. Concilium 1997/3. Maryknoll, NY: Orbis, 1997.

Brown, Shaun C. *George Lindbeck and the Israel of God: Scripture, Ecclesiology, and Ecumenism*. Pathways for Ecumenical and Interreligious Dialogue. Cham, Switz.: Springer International, 2021.

Frymer-Kensky, Tikva, et al., eds. *Christianity in Jewish Terms*. Radical Traditions. Boulder, CO: Westview, 2000.

Kinzer, Mark S. "Bilateral Ecclesiology in Solidarity with Israel." In *Postmissionary Messianic Judaism: Redefining Christian Engagement with the Jewish People*, 151–79. Grand Rapids: Brazos, 2005.

———. "Healing the Schism." In *Postmissionary Messianic Judaism: Redefining Christian Engagement with the Jewish People*, 303–10. Grand Rapids: Brazos, 2005.

———. *Postmissionary Messianic Judaism: Redefining Christian Engagement with the Jewish People*. Grand Rapids: Brazos, 2005.

———. *Searching Her Own Mystery: "Nostra Aetate," the Jewish People, and the Identity of the Church*. Eugene, OR: Cascade, 2015.

Kortner, Ulrich H. J. "A Lost Fragment: Jewish Christianity." In *The Church in Fragments: Towards What Kind of Unity?*, edited by Giuseppe Ruggieri and Miklós Tomka, 47–54. Concilium 1997/3. Maryknoll, NY: Orbis, 1997.

Lindbeck, George A. "Church." In *The Church in a Postliberal Age*, edited by James J. Buckley, 145–65. Radical Traditions. Grand Rapids: Eerdmans, 2003.

———. *The Church in a Postliberal Age*. Edited by James J. Buckley. Radical Traditions. Grand Rapids: Eerdmans, 2003.

———. "Confession and Community: An Israel-like View of the Church." In *The Church in a Postliberal Age*, edited by James J. Buckley, 1–9. Radical Traditions. Grand Rapids: Eerdmans, 2003.

———. "Postmodern Hermeneutics and Jewish-Christian Dialogue: A Case Study." In *Christianity in Jewish Terms*, edited by Tikva Frymer-Kensky et al., 106–13. Radical Traditions. Boulder, CO: Westview, 2000.

———. "What of the Future? A Christian Response." In *Christianity in Jewish Terms*, edited by Tikva Frymer-Kensky et al., 378–87. Radical Traditions. Boulder, CO: Westview, 2000.

Louthan, Howard P., and Randall C. Zachman, eds. *Conciliation and Confession: The Struggle for Unity in the Age of Reform, 1415–1648*. Notre Dame, IN: University of Notre Dame Press, 2004.

Nicholas of Cusa. *The Catholic Concordance*. Edited and translated by Paul E. Sigmund. Cambridge Texts in the History of Political Thought. Cambridge: Cambridge University Press, 1991.

Radner, Ephraim. *Church*. Eugene, OR: Cascade, 2017.

———. "Division Is Murder." In *A Brutal Unity: The Spiritual Politics of the Christian Church*, 63–120. Waco: Baylor University Press, 2012.

———. "The Limits of Consensus." In *A Brutal Unity: The Spiritual Politics of the Christian Church*, 221–67. Waco: Baylor University Press, 2012.

———. "The Procedural Quest for Unity and Its Obstacle." In *A Brutal Unity: The Spiritual Politics of the Christian Church*, 269–310. Waco: Baylor University Press, 2012.

Chapter 12

Jewish-Christian Reconciliation Is Inseparable from Christian Leadership
1 Timothy 3:2 Interpreted in Light of Zizioulas

Calvin Pais

> Faithful is the WORD, whoever aspires to be an overseer desires a noble task. Now the overseer . . . is to be faithful to his wife . . . able to teach. (1 Tim 3:1)

THIS VERSE ABOVE MAY not at first glance seem to be about Jewish-Christian reconciliation, but the following essay seeks to offer such a proposal. To begin with, "WORD" in this verse should not be taken as simply meaning a 'trustworthy saying' as some translators suggest (NIV, etc.). God is *himself* the WORD in the New Testament.[1] And if God is being referenced, an amplified version of the text might be rendered, "Faithful is *God*."

The Greek behind "WORD" in the text is *logos*, is meaning a "cosmic" logic that "govern[s] the organization of the universe" that is "synonymous

---

1. Consider the following New Testament references beginning with John—"In the beginning was the Word, and the Word was with God, and the Word was God" (John 1:1 NIV)—but additionally Luke—"Many have undertaken to draw up an account of the things that have been fulfilled among us just as they were handed down to us by those who from the first were eyewitnesses and servants of the word" (Luke 1:1–2 NIV). See also Jeffrey: "In his reference to 'eyewitnesses, and ministers of the word' (Luke 1:2) he is certainly speaking of the person as well as the words" (*Dictionary of Biblical Tradition*, 460).

with . . . 'God.'"[2] Taken altogether, the verse suggests that God is the undergirding wisdom of all. Additionally, God is faithful. Together, Paul is developing how the logos of God, or more simply the logic of God, is faithfulness. Hence, faithfulness is the underlying logic behind all things in which they are invited to participate in, and if so, must bear upon the remainder of the verse.[3] Christian leaders are to be faithful as God is faithful.[4] Further, the faithfulness of Christian leaders in the area of marriage in the second portion of the verse ("faithful to his wife") is epexegetical of God.[5] The God of Christianity is none other than Jehovah who marries Israel at Sinai.[6] And insofar as Israel is a priest to the nations, Israel's marital relationship with Jehovah's is revelatory to all of him.[7] Therefore, Christians are those who worship the one who reveals his name to be "Jealous" which calls us to a faithfulness worthy of his own loyalty (Exod 34:14).

The linkage between God's marriage and his corporate people as a vehicle of self-revelation is not without difficulty. In Torah (the Christian Old Testament) Israel is considered to be the bride of Yahweh (Isa 54:5). However, in the New Testament, the church is considered to be the bride of Christ (Eph 5:25–32). Together, this creates an uneasy issue; namely, is Israel God's bride and the church illegitimate? Or vice versa, is Israel an adulterous bride divorced and replaced with the church? Or perhaps something else? As marital imagery is used in relation to both parties it bears an impact to how we understand God's relationship to each group as well as how they can relate to one another. But it also informs our marital and sexual ethics. For instance, if we say that God replaces neither and maintains both, it provides rationale for polygamy. Amid these difficulties, we propose that God

---

2. For a helpful primer on the Stoic understanding of logos, see Gregory Hays, "Introduction," in Marcus Aurelius, *Meditations*, xx.

3. When we say "the word [logos] becomes flesh" we are saying God's logic joins creation to himself. Meaning, creation is put on like a glove upon the logic and life of God. This is at least a preliminary image and definition of participation. See David Schindler's definition on participation referenced below.

4. A consequence of such a definition is to suggest that many Christian leaders are in a state of unfaithfulness. Not necessarily adultery, but apathy. Like Martin Luther's negative and positive peace, there is perhaps negative faithfulness (adultery), positive faithfulness (akin to steadfastness and love), and void, an apathy that is neither here nor there.

5. By epexegetical we mean the addition of words that clarify what's before.

6. Hersey, "Marriage at Mount Sinai."

7. Regarding Israel's priestly vocation, see Brueggemann, *Theology of Book of Jeremiah*, 10–14. He does not make the point that God's husbandry is in view, but if God is husband as per Oliver Hersey's work previously referenced, it is inextricable to the priestly vocation.

is eternally faithful to Israel by inviting gentiles into Christ, who is a person that is irrevocably Israelite. Christian leaders are those who participate in the logic of Christ's marital fidelity. Therefore, not only should overseers be faithful to their wives, but they are perhaps participants in the larger purposes of Christ's marriage with Israel.

THE CORE ISSUE: WHO IS THE NEW JERUSALEM?

The New Testament reveals a future state in which a "new Jerusalem" is called God's "bride" with varying problems for Jewish-Christian relations (Rev 21:2 ESV). If as previously mentioned God has two brides, one named the new Jerusalem and "previously" Israel, the explanation is either replacement or polygamy. The polygamous paradigm sees two brides of God—Israel and the new Jerusalem—that issue from a Christian dispensational[8] paradigm in which a separate pathway for salvation exists for ethnic Jews who reject Jesus as LORD.[9] We normalize polygamy in this option because two are maintained eternally. For the Christian, defined here as those who are in Christ and participating in the life of God, they are free to engage in God's polygamous example. There are certainly also notions of a singular bride, yet one that simultaneously suggests her continued Israelite identity is missing. It too leaves open the possibility for the new Jerusalem to be a replacement for the former wife. As the LORD and Israel "divorce" in the time of Jeremiah, it is logical to consider that God chooses a different wife hereafter that is not Israel (Jer 3:8). In such a case Jerusalem would be a name perhaps taken from the word's component parts suggesting a quality of "peace" in the people without continuity of the Israelite identity and ethnicity.

New Jersualem's scriptural location within John's Apocalypse creates other complications in interpretation foremost because of the apocalyptic character and related mixed metaphors as bride, palace and city.[10] The recently deceased John Zizioulas, who was a professor and bishop of the Metropolitan of Pergamon, is lauded as one of the most influential Eastern Orthodox thinkers and offers a contrarian approach and much wisdom

---

8. Dispensationalism is a popular Christian piety which is generally favorable towards non-Christian Jewish pieties. Dispensationalists often see there to be two ways of salvation, one for Jews and another for gentiles.

9. See, for instance, Fruchtenbaum, *Israelology*.

10. The apocalypse has complex images, e.g., seven-headed monsters (Rev 12), angels equally as frightful (Rev 7), and images of God being like an emerald (Rev 4:3). For a discussion of the apocalyptic genre, see Collins, *Apocalyptic Imagination*, ch. 1.

regarding how *not* to view the bride.[11] Specifically, the bride is *not* to be understood as being an autonomous hypostatic person apart from God.[12] Concretely he is arguing against a "middleman" hypostasis where biological persons (such as yourself) and God (a set of persons for Christians) are united with a middleman or -woman who is not God, say, for instance, Mary. Rather, God takes biological persons directly into himself. The church as bride is a group of people that are directly connected to God and receive their identity directly from God.[13] Zizioulas argues that the church and bride are to be christologically interpreted.

Zizioulas's Theological Ecclesiology as Rationale for Why the Bride Does Not Have a Hypostasis of Its Own

Zizioulas contends the church has no personal hypostasis in *The Mystery of the Church in Orthodox Tradition*, arguing that the church be situated in God. He believes "*ecclesiology must [first] be situated within the context of Trinitarian theology.* We must begin with a clear distinction of Persons in the Trinity as the Cappadocian Fathers insisted," which is to serve as a "basic theological presupposition."[14] God for Zizioulas reveals himself through the ecumenical councils to the church fathers, which he describes as the

---

11. Rowan Williams, for instance, who is the equivalent of Rome's pope, but to the Anglican communion, writes positively of Zizioulas (Williams, "Eastern Orthodox Theology"). For an overview of the alternative proposals to Zizioulas, see McPartlan, "Who Is the Church?"

12. *Hypostasis* is a Greek word whose component parts, "hypo" and "stasis," mean "under" stasis or under constancy. Its usage is varied in history but in the third century begins to be drawn into theological and philosophical discourse regarding how God consists of three persons or hypostases. In terms of a definition as per Zizioulas's corpus more broadly, Zizioulas would not say that hypostatic persons are simply constant, bearing an eternal dimension or under stasis. Persons are those also in *ek-stasis*, that is, out of constancy in a movement towards communion with God and all else. This is because God is definitional of persons as those who are true persons who as Father, Son, and Spirit have always existed and therefore are *constant*, aka under stasis, but simultaneously are not distant and separate from one another but constantly giving themselves to the other in love or communion. See Zizioulas, *Communion and Otherness*, 209. For a short history on how hypostases develop, see Zizioulas, *Lectures in Christian Dogmatics*, 50.

13. A good support for this are the root words of church. The Greek *ekklessia* comes from *ek* (out) and *klessia* (called). Church is at its core a vehicle of exiting all to live entirely *in* Christ. In its verb form, the New Testament states "out of [*ekalesa*] I have called my son," quoting Hosea as a reference to the exodus (Matt 2:15).

14. Zizioulas, *One and the Many*, loc. 3145 of 8191; emphasis in original.

"Cappadocian revolution."[15] To them, the Father is the *only* source and cause of the Trinity and therefore ascribes an initiating logical priority to the Father *and not the Son* or the Spirit.[16] "The Church exists first of all because *the Father*—as a distinct divine person—wills her to exist. It is the initiative and the good pleasure *of the Father* that brought her to existence. And not only that, but it is *to the Father*—as a person other than the Son—that she will finally be brought when Christ submits everything to Him."[17] Since creation flows from the Father who is the initiating source of all things, here alone does creation find the wisdom of its design.

As Trinity, God exists as three distinct persons who are in unending relationship. Their hypostases represent a constancy and eternal distinctiveness. This in turn issues several relationships amid them which creation is graciously brought into. Their distinctive relationships are the ground for Zizioulas's dialectic explanation. He proposes that there exists a church-Christ dialectic and a Christ-and-the-Father dialectic, as well as the created-uncreated dialectic. Regarding these he apologizes to his readers, exclaiming, "What a complexity of dialectics!"[18]

Zizioulas's Uncreated-Created Dialectic: Creation Is Not the Uncreated God

Zizioulas begins with a clarification of the term and doctrine *ex nihilo*. Alongside God, there is "absolute nothingness" which is void of "ontological content" with "no relationship whatever to being."[19] What he means by this is that there was a period in which even 'nothingness' did not exist. Thus when Genesis states "in the beginning God created," it should be understood that before the beginning, *only* God existed (Gen 1:1). In contrast to God, creation has a beginning that is insurmountable and definitive to what it means to be created. Creation has a starting point and can never not have one.

---

15. Zizioulas, *Lectures in Christian Dogmatics*, 50.

16. Zizioulas, *Lectures in Christian Dogmatics*, 78. For Zizioulas and other Eastern Orthodox theologians, this doctrine is termed the "monarch of the Father." See Chiapetti, "Zizioulas' Reading of the Fathers." This issue also treads on another aged issue, the *filioque* clause, a clause inserted into the Nicene Creed by the now-Western rite, which the East did not accept and which was a major contributor to the East-West schism.

17. Zizioulas, *One and the Many*, locs. 3143–44 of 8191; emphasis in original.

18. Zizioulas, *One and the Many*, loc. 3233 of 8191.

19. Zizioulas, *Communion and Otherness*, 254.

The created-uncreated dialectic framework results in not only a temporal distinction but a spatial one. Zizioulas notes that "the notion of beginning is tied up inseparably with that of distance . . . with the possibility of absence" again implying it was not present before the beginning.[20] Creation cannot *reach* into eternity past. It has a starting point, from which it is bracketed off and distanced. Creation is that which exists and is bound spatially inside of and in time.

Consequently, creation is bracketed from the uncreated in terms of time (eternal vs. temporal) but also a spatial distancing from uncreated life. This bracketing of creation means it bears a mortal frailty, an existence that can choose eternal life, but does not inherently possess it on its own. Zizioulas believes this is hallmark of the patristics, citing Athanasius who writes that creation coming from nothing is to be understood as being "incapable of independent perseverance" because creation "knows that it was not spontaneous."[21] Creation "naturally contains, at its heart, no power of survival" which for Zizioulas by way of Athanasius is the definition of mortality.[22] Creation's reliance on another to give it being betrays its finitude and inability to claim an inherent eternality.

Nevertheless, God declares these distinctions between himself and creation to be "good" (Gen 1) which includes the distinctiveness of the first created person: Adam, who was begotten in Eden. As eternal life is inherent to God, created persons are entirely reliant on God's own personal being to receive eternal life. This is again because in the beginning, *only* God existed. Only God was ever eternal. Eternality is *not a quality separable* from God, but *only a description* of his being. Therefore, since only God bears eternal constancy, which can never be extraneous to himself, access to eternality is in God, with him and inside him alone.

WHY THE CHRIST-CHURCH DIALECTIC IS SOTERIOLOGICALLY ESSENTIAL AND MAINTAINS THE CREATOR-CREATION DISTINCTION

Creation is enabled to metaphysically participate in the Creator's life without transgressing the insurmountable distinction with its Creator. "To speak of metaphysical participation is to say that one thing has what it is *with* and indeed *after* and *in pursuit of*, another: it has its reality, in other words,

---

20. Zizioulas, *Communion and Otherness*, 221n23.

21. Zizioulas, *Communion and Otherness*, 221, 269n6. Zizioulas references Athanasius, *Inc.* 3.

22. Zizioulas, *Communion and Otherness*, 269n6.

in something other than itself."²³ God presents his life to creation coterminously.²⁴ While our magnitude is lesser than God's we may be "caught up" in the entirety of the relationship between the Father and Son not merely as observers but with the same identity as the Son, albeit knowing that this is a foreign life gifted to humanity that is not itself inherent. To be concrete, those in the Son are not a second-class brother but rather granted the position to be included *into* the son himself with qualification.

For Zizioulas, eternal life is the intra-Trinitarian relationship of the Father and the Son and Spirit such that participation is essential to soteriology. God is our Father who by definition of the name Father is one always freely willing a relationship with his Son. This relationship with their Spirit of love are their eternal living. Eternal life is nothing short of this relationship between Father, Son, and Spirit. Humanity is thus required to enter into to access that life as the son informs us that he "is the way to true life and no other access to the Father exists" (John 14:6 ESV).

Zizioulas wants to guard against a "trialectic between the church, Christ and the Father" where Christ becomes a "go-between mediator, a third person, who listens first to the Church speaking to Him and then like a messenger transmits the prayer to the Father."²⁵ At stake is direct access to our Father.²⁶ A trialectic is for Zizioulas a "demonic" heresy akin to "monophysitism."²⁷ This heresy purported that Christ was only divine and did not *actually* take become human. What Zizioulas has in view is that the son taking on flesh is a type of case study or track record demonstrating that God is able to unite flesh into himself, including ours. If Christ can't or doesn't take on our flesh, he couldn't have taken on flesh to begin with. Our flesh too must be assumed.²⁸

This anti-trialectic thinking the underlying rationale of why the church is not itself hypostatic. Zizioulas concludes:

> The church is at the same time maximalized and minimalized. She is maximalized in that she will survive eternally when her true identity will be revealed in the Parousia. And she is

23. Schindler, "What's the Difference?," 1; emphasis in original.

24. Coterminous angles are a helpful concrete illustration. A 90-degree angle and 180-degree angle overlap, but one is far *greater* in the *degree* of movement.

25. Christ is "mediator" (1 Tim 2:5 NIV), but he mediates not trialectically but dialectically (Zizioulas, *One and the Many*, loc. 3198 of 8191).

26. Consider the following Scripture as well: "For *through* [Christ] we have access to the Father by one Spirit" (Eph 2:18 NIV; emphasis added).

27. Zizioulas, *One and the Many*, loc. 3245 of 8191, in the context of sec. 3197.

28. Scripturally, see the KJV's inclusion in Eph 5:30: "We are the flesh of him, the bones of him."

> minimalized in that she has no hypostasis of her own but draws her identity from Christ and the Kingdom to come. By existing in history "in persona Christis," she is guaranteed the glory and eternal life of her Head. But for the very same reason she is no autonomous entity vis-à-vis either Christ or the Kingdom. Her existence is iconic.[29]

In sum, for Zizioulas, God lives constantly by virtue of being uncreated without beginning or end in contrast to creation's inherent fragility. Creation however is reliant upon its Creator for it to sustain itself and is incapable of independence. This leads to Zizioulas definition of an icon.[30] The term iconic is to be "an image of something else that transcends her" but also "transparent" so that she is not the focus, but Christ is.[31]

Zizioulas's Catholic-Orthodox context roots icon in terms that Protestant and Jewish sensibilities *rightly* abhor. Paul's usage is simpler as he states that "we all having been unveiled in face, beholding as in a mirror the glory of the Lord are being transformed into the same icon" (2 Cor 3:18 BLB). We can "hold" God's image in us as mirrors do by reflection. The light photons are held within the mirror extraneously and only while focused on the other.[32] A mirror focused on the sun with adequate intensity can heat, bend, and disfigure/refigure/transform the mirror, of course, as well, all while maintaining its nature.

---

29. Zizioulas, *One and the Many*, loc. 3269 of 8191.

30. "Icon" comes from the Greek word *eikon*, meaning an image or picture, a copy of sorts, and not the same thing necessarily.

31. Zizioulas, *One and the Many*, loc. 3274 of 8191.

32. Consider further that Christians "are members of his body, of his flesh, and of his bones" (Eph 5:30 KJV). The church is certainly made up of us mortals but are to be seen as only component parts, "flesh and bones," of Christ. But note, "the flesh counts for nothing" (John 6:63 ESV). The point is that when it comes to the collected saints, we must have "called-out" eyes that do not look to the physical but look to how they cohere in Christ. Out of Christ one might see individual humans together, a social group, or a vision of God himself constituted by the many. So too, with biological people as you and I, we can be taken in lust with our beauty or reprehensibly with our disfigured body parts instead of as a cohesive person. The church's iconic life is one of transcendence where we see beyond the body parts and unique people and instead, in its spirit, the Spirit of Christ that is not only transcendent but immersive.

EXAMPLES OF TRIALECTIC CHURCH HYPOSTASES

Biological Hypostases

In distinction from the divine persons exist us created biological hypostases, which are frustrated by our spatio-temporal roots.[33] We are frustrated since we cannot be in multiple spaces and times. *Created persons* are contained *in* biological bodies that are subject to the time constraint of birth at a specific moment and an eventual death. So Zizioulas states we succumb to a "classic tragedy [that] enslaved its heroes—human and divine—in the destiny of natural or moral order and rationality," as if suggesting these are slavery by their fearsome incapacity to transcend death (Heb 2:15).[34] All *created persons* begin life in contained in specific times and spaces, e.g., Adam, begotten of dust *in Eden* and dying in an obscure yet specific place outside there. Adam is neither begotten nor dies in New York in the second millennia. Additionally, biological persons are also limited spatially in the degree of which they can grow. Adam's existence is confined to a physical body with standard height and weight limits always displacing matter along the way. Adam entering a bathtub displaces water; or for us moderns, entering a crowded bus leads to another exiting the bus. Returning to Adam's biological profile, it matters not whether Adam may have been seven foot two and four hundred pounds, but rather, we know that no *created person* has ever been able to grow to a height and mass that can expand across the earth and heavens. Not so with God, whose hypostases are *not created* and are unbound by both time and space and thus free.[35]

Adam's limited freedom enslaves all who overcommit to him. In the crudest sense, this looks like an obedience to Adam to go and be everywhere he is. And since he dies in a specific place, this is a desire to go to that place and live inside of that dead body is impossible due to decomposition. If it is another created person this is a problem as well. While two hands can hold, cells must be crushed and die for there to be entire unreserved spatial overlap. Nevertheless, *partial* entry into another biological person *is* possible. Intercourse, for example, permits entry into empty space. Similarly, childbearing is limited by a woman's biological clock with a predetermined

---

33. Zizioulas, *Communion and Otherness*, 221.

34. Zizioulas, *Communion and Otherness*, 103.

35. N.b. the incarnation is the addition of created *bodies and flesh* to an uncreated person. The eternal Son does not receive created personhood but created flesh and bodies.

cut-off whether octuplets or nonuplets; and still it is seasonal: an adult can never return to the womb. The point is that the biological is restrictive, and to enter a created hypostasis is to absurdly put on the entirety of their spatio-temporal limits in reductive and deleterious ways. Seeking to enter Jesus's mother, Mary, or ancestor Jacob/Israel in their biological and created being is too, if not necromantic. Against these possibilities, Jesus's eternal hypostasis is witnessed to take flesh and blood to new places, by appearing in flesh and body to nearly five hundred people all at the same time in different places. Even more than that today, millions of people are able to unite and enter him now expanding his indwelling presence to all (1 Cor 15).

The Incapacity of Non-Biological Created Corporate Personalities

Another category of "persons" exists, legal entities.[36] As many churches are constituted by these, they are worth discussion and also consideration for their rejection of the possibility of replacing Israel. Though created corporations offer gifts to biological persons that can include new rights and resources, they too do not transcend the final limitations of creation—the temporal bracketing from eternity. As such they are not only insufficient but additionally enslave a person by arbitrary limits. Even when scripturally informed, they are themselves not Scripture in their entirety, and so they are limited insofar that they do not provide the fullness of scriptural potential.

While the church are those that live inside of Christ in a particular way—that is, *in persona Christis*—when misinterpreted, even the Christ is insufficient.[37] Recall that a trialectic approach with Christ exists where a person or groups of people pray to Jesus with no direct access to the Father. Zizioulas calls this demonic and heretical.[38] So too, there are perhaps some that masquerade as being *in Christ* but are only "among us" (1 John 2:19 BLB).[39]

---

36. Davoudi et al., "Historical Role of the Corporation."
37. Zizioulas, *One and the Many*, loc. 3269 of 8191.
38. Zizioulas, *One and the Many*, loc. 3245 of 8191, in the context of sec. 3197.
39. There are various scriptural discussions of people who are amid the saints and yet are not *in Christ* but only present "among us." For instance, the parable of the weeds and the tares (Matt 13:24–30) suggests dandelions are masquerading among daffodils, to which Christ will eventually say, "I never knew you" (Matt 7:23 ESV; 25:12)

CHALCEDONIAN LOGIC: THE HYPOSTATIC LOGOS IS IRREVOCABLY ISRAELITE[40]

As the church does not quite receive an identity of its own but enters Christ's identity, we must understand that which informs us. The Chalcedonian Creed which dogmatically rules our conception of the Son affirms that the flesh he is born with he maintains fidelity to "without division, without separation."[41] The NT offers pictures of his fidelity to the flesh he received at birth extending *through* his crucifixion and death, and into his resurrection and ascension. After being resurrected from his death, Christ says to us, "Look at my hands and my feet. It is I myself! Touch me and see; a ghost does not have flesh and bones, as you see I have. . . . Put your finger here; see my hands. Reach out your hand and put it into my side. Stop doubting and believe" (Luke 24:39 ESV). Here we find that his resurrection body *continues* to have the *same wounded* "side" that allows Thomas to put his fingers "into" (John 20:27 BLB). While there is, of course, profound *change* to his body and flesh, it is still the "same body" and not a replacement, a switching of coats.[42] The nails have made a "mark," like a seal might, to suggest that *this* coat is the one that touched the nails of the cross before the resurrection and has passed through death (John 20:25). A replacing of coats, as it were, would not maintain the mark the nails make that are shown to Thomas. Further, to argue otherwise is an invitation for self-harm as if God pierces himself again. Christians confess that a person who *was* crucified shows those marks yet again and has ascended as the "lamb who *has been slain*" (Rev 5:6 ESV; emphasis added). This specific body has been united to a person and ascended to the throne which offers us "a new and living way opened for us through the curtain, that is, his flesh" (Heb 10:20 BLB). And we are told, according to my translation that more accurately follows the word position of the Greek, "put on the Lord Jesus Christ, namely the flesh, and make not provision for your desires" (Rom 13:14). The meaning being, his flesh is to wrap around ours.[43]

---

40. Chalcedon refers first to a Greek town, but the term is a metonym for an ecumenical council held there in AD 451, which decided that Christ had two natures, human and divine, and has particular dogmatic terminology laid out in what is termed the Chalcedonian Creed.

41. Bettenson, "Chalcedonian Formula."

42. Pålsson, "Angelic Humans, Glorious Flesh." Jerome emphasizes "sameness of the body" and profound change in the resurrection. For a history, see Widdicombe, "Wounds and Ascended Body."

43. Even in the direct flow of the Greek text, "but put on the Lord Jesus Christ, and of the flesh provision not make for desires," the idea remains that Christ's flesh is to be placed upon ours. We share *his* flesh now, so do not use it for perverse desires as those with the resurrection life.

Christians—those who live in Christ—are those united to this person's body. He is not ethnically ambiguous (e.g., one who becomes a new ethnicity—South American), nor does he cease to be Jewish as in some interpretations of Gal 3:28 and Col 3:11.[44] This son received flesh and body from a Mary, a Jew who descended from David. In graphic detail, the original manuscripts of the Scriptures describe the son descending from David *not in idea* but from the *spermatos* (σπέρματος) "of David" (Rom 1:3). He further has a maternal genealogy tracing back to Jacob and Abraham (Luke 3).[45] Moreover, insofar as Chalcedon is a dogmatic that governs Christianity's interpretation of Scripture, its reference to the son's human "nature" being inseparable applies epexegetically to Rom 11 when it too discusses human "nature."[46] The key term is that human nature in the context of Israelite ethnicity is said to be "a gift and calling of God that is irrevocable" (Rom 11:29 ESV). Israelite human nature bestowed through the maternal line from Jacob through Judah until today does not cease at the level of nature. Rom 11:24 and 29 is of course true for the son's incarnation as well. Since Christ keeps his human nature "without division, without separation" it is *impossible* to accept the person of Jesus and reject these characteristics.[47] Christianity, therefore, confesses not simply that Jesus is of Israel and is Israelite, but continues to be so indefinitely.

God's call applies entirely to the Son's hypostasis as well. "It is not so much a matter of *communicatio idiomatum* between divine and human *natures* as it is a matter of *hypostatic union* in which the *hypostasis* or person freely assumes and refers creation to God."[48] Between the lines here is the error of ascribing the irrevocable Israelite call of Christ's body and flesh *only* to his body and flesh—we again fall back into a Monophysite demonic isolation. To suggest only his flesh and body are Israelite is to believe that only the flesh and body is received in Mary's womb without his person passing through as well. All that is of the flesh and body is true of his hypostasis. This is also because natures should not be construed as bearing its own existence but as descriptors *of* hypostases.[49] A person takes on a body of flesh which is what, in part, is definitive of being human. Human nature alone

---

44. My point here is not so much to interpret either verse but to suggest how they cannot be interpreted in light of the broader swatch of Scripture and church history.

45. Bockmuehl, "Son of David."

46. "Nature" is *physis* in the Greek used in both Rom 11:24 and in the Chalcedon formula and *must* inform one another lest we reject Chalcedon.

47. See Irenaeus, *Haer.* 5.7; Justin Martyr, *On the Resurrection* 2.

48. Zizioulas, *One and the Many*, loc. 3293 of 8191; emphasis in original.

49. Zizioulas states, "There is no bare essence, no nature-as-such" (*Lectures in Dogmatics*, 52).

does not exist. Persons exist and are described to be human (Jesus, Adam, etc.) or not (our Father, the Spirit, the Son *before* his incarnation).

ISRAEL AS GENITIVAL OF GOD, GOD AS GENITIVAL OF ISRAEL, AND THE BRIDE AS GENITIVAL OF ISRAEL

Israel becomes *God's* name that is gifted to the church genitivally.[50] Since Jesus our God takes on an Israelite character, God himself is Israelite. And therefore, it may be that those who enter him can claim an Israelite identity.

The genitival nature of the church is implied specifically concerning Israel in Zizioulas. "The Church is not a sort of Platonic 'image' of the Trinity; she is communion in the sense of being the people of God, Israel, and the 'body of Christ,' i.e., in the sense of serving and realizing in herself God's purpose in history for the sake of the entire creation."[51] The Platonic way is to render the church bearing an image that is "empty of reality."[52] In that sense, a Platonic Israelite church would be a title incoherent with who Israel is: that is, a church that is without genealogical birth but also apart from the rest of the people of Israel in the past and the future.

Since the church is participative, it is Israelite only to the extent that it partakes of Jesus's own Israelite person. Christians confess that the LORD has taken on Israel's nature and "calling" (Rom 11:29), which is to believe that God is Israelite and is now *called* Israel. 'Calling' and 'name' are of course different words, yet they are granted meaning by God, and not by grammar. While there is a long history of falsely naming others as Israelite, Jesus is an Israelite par excellence considering his birth and lineage. He is constituted and made up of David and Abraham's seed, and shares in all of Israel's life and destiny, giving meaning to the name Israel.[53]

On this basis we take the Israelite constitution of Christ applying to the bride also:

> "Come, I will show you the bride, the wife of the Lamb." 10 And he carried me away in the Spirit to a mountain great and high, and showed me the Holy City, Jerusalem, coming down out of heaven from God. 11 It shone with the glory of God, and its

---

50. Zizioulas, *One and the Many*, loc. 3156 of 8191.
51. Zizioulas, *One and the Many*, loc. 1429 of 8191.
52. Zizioulas, *One and the Many*, loc. 1433, expounded in loc. 3269 of 8191.
53. Since Rom 11 affirms ethnicity as being irrevocable, this applies not only to ethnic Israel but also to the nations. The nations do not cease to bear their ethnicity. They join a new nation and can never forget it. Participating in God's Israelite life is *always* as a foreigner.

brilliance was like that of a very precious jewel, like a jasper, clear as crystal. 12 It had a great, high wall with twelve gates, and with twelve angels, and names having been inscribed, which are of the twelve tribes of the sons of Israel [Ἰσραήλ]. (Rev 21:9–12 NIV)

Though several names are described, they are secondary names of the bride. This essay assumes Israel was the *first* bride of the Lord on the basis that Jer 3 and the Sinaitic covenant are a marriage ceremony between the Lord and Israel.[54] The covenant clarifies the gift and promises to her where Israel is explicitly called the wife of the Lord (Isa 54:5–8). This privilege is the irrevocable gift and calling *to Israel* (Rom 9:3–4; 1:29). Note, these gifts and callings are not specified to the other sons however in these passages. Therefore, because Israel was the first bride, and this calling cannot be removed, and the final bride bears inscriptions that are constituted with Israel we understand that the bride is eternally Israelite.

The bride receives Israelite identity because Christ is constituted with Israelite life. Her being is not her own but *in* the Israelite personhood of Christ. This person is also a "Word" who takes on Israelite identity (John 1:1). All that we've said about the person is true of the word such that the word of Christ is Israelite as well. Hence, those who join themselves with theological Israel receive an Israelite Word, resulting in a new identity. This word, however, does differentiate and prevent replacement. Gentiles receive this identity *contrary to nature* (*para physin* [Rom 11:24]) in a way that is foreign and "wild" (*agrielaois* [11:24]) to their nature. Ethnic Israel instead are offered a double portion and a reaffirmation according to nature (*kata physin* [11:24]) from the "roots" (11:19). Such an analysis is finally an expansion of Israel that hopes to realize the promises of Israel that is a metanarrative of Israel. It believes that Israel was a name bestowed upon Jacob unchangingly but then taken up also by God in a creative new way that was otherwise unimaginable.

A CANONICAL INTERPRETATION FOR LEADERSHIP

Faithful is the Word, whoever aspires to be an overseer desires a noble task. Now the overseer . . . is to be faithful to his wife . . . able to teach. (1 Tim 3:1)

Jesus is the eternally faithful word and logic. Christ's own faithfulness must inform the overseer's marital life, especially considering the genitival

---

54. Hersey, "Marriage at Mount Sinai."

notions previously discussed. We are to be "partakers [of God's] divine nature" (2 Pet 1:4 ESV) instead of Platonic imitators replacing his way of life in displacement of him, which produces a counterfeit oversight.

Lexically, the term "overseer" is a translation of the Greek word *episcopos*, which in its pre-Christian usage referred to a military inspector who oversaw others from a higher rank.[55] This reflects the word's component parts, *epi-* (on) and *skopos* (the mark). Those who seek to be episcopal must literally work "toward the mark" (*skopos*) of God in Christ Jesus (Phil 3:14). Christ is our target "model" and *skopos*, which we are to align ourselves with and be upon (Phil 3:14, 17). This mark is marital fidelity, which is a mimicry of God.

Episcopal mimesis of God involves consideration of several challenging scriptural contours of his marriage. God himself is caught in moments of polygamy (e.g., Jer 3). Against normalization, consider that the creation of the kingdom of Judah as a separate entity from Israel, where they are both first called brides explicitly, is a consequence of *her and Israel's divisive actions* that is finally accidental and not of God's initiation. This is not God's intended plan. Instead, polygamy should be seen as a concessional permission in the Torah. In support of the idea that polygamy and divorce are not God's intention is Jesus's statement that "it was because you were so hard-hearted that Moses allowed you to divorce your wives, but it was not like this from the beginning" (Matt 19:8 NRSV). God's promises to them both are not his sinfulness and affirmation of polygamy, but his continued care and commitment to Israel with the foreknowledge that Judah will not continue as bride but finally be "joined" in Israel's final destiny (Jer 3:18). This applies to the other supplementary brides as well, e.g., Oholah of Ezek 23 and all the others. They, like Judah, are children of Israel who by the genealogical sin of division continue in a cursed heritage of divisiveness yet are nevertheless returned to be building blocks of Israel.

In any case, reconciling with Israel, whatever her status, cannot be avoided. This is brought to bear especially considering that the *episcopon*—those *on the mark*—are to be a "husband of one wife" and "able to teach" or "live" in accord (1 Tim 3:2 ESV; Jas 3:13). Thus, Christ's own faithfulness to Israel is the content of any Christian episcopacy's teaching life such that it is to reconfigure the direction and structures of our ecclesial vision. It applies to individual marital ethics of congregants, but also to the broader marital state of Israel and the church. Episcopacies are to be devoted to reconciliation. This is the faith and faithfulness of Christ.

---

55. Ernst Fuchs, "σκοπος," *TDNT* 7:948.

CONCLUSION

There are multiple ways to deal with Israel being God's bride and the church being Christ's bride. Per Zizioulas, the church cannot have its own hypostasis. Rather, the church can only take Christ's hypostasis. According to Chalcedonian logic, Christ's hypostasis must be "of Israel." Indeed, Israel is a genitive of God, a name of God. Therefore, Jews and gentiles are one (also seen in Eph 3). This vision is interpretive to the broader swath of Scripture insofar as Christ's life is the logos or logic of all. Hence the leaders who are to replicate him must also be like him. But further, they are to reorient pastoral care accordingly. This is at once so that Christ might be constitutive of the individual family units, but also that their faithfulness might bring forth a movement of Christians in Christ's own lamentable marriage with Israel.

BIBLIOGRAPHY

Bettenson, Henry, trans. "The Chalcedonian Formula." Anglicans Online, last updated May 23, 2017. From *Documents of the Christian Church* (Oxford: Oxford University Press, 1947), 73. https://anglicansonline.org/basics/chalcedon.html.

Bockmuehl, Markus. "The Son of David and His Mother." *JTS* 62 (2011) 476–93.

Brueggemann, Walter. *The Theology of the Book of Jeremiah*. Old Testament Theology. New York: Cambridge University Press, 2007.

Chiapetti, Dario. "Part 1: Zizioulas' Reading of the Fathers: The Notion of Person and the Doctrine of the Monarchy of the Father." In *The Father's Eternal Freedom: The Personalist Trinitarian Ontology of John Zizioulas*, 9–84. Bristol: Clarke, 2022.

Collins, John J. *The Apocalyptic Imagination: An Introduction to Jewish Apocalyptic Literature*. Biblical Resource. Grand Rapids: Eerdmans, 1998.

Davoudi, Leonardo, et al. "The Historical Role of the Corporation in Society." *Journal of the British Academy* 6 (2018) 17–47. https://doi.org/10.5871/jba/006s1.017.

Fruchtenbaum, Arnold G. *Israelology: The Missing Link in Systematic Theology*. Tustin, CA: Ariel, 1989.

Hays, Gregory. "Introduction." In *Meditations: A New Translation*, by Marcus Aurelius, vii–lvii. Modern Library. New York: Modern Library, 2003.

Hersey, Oliver. "The Marriage at Mount Sinai: Reading Exodus in the Context of Ancient Near Eastern Diplomatic Marriage." PhD diss., Trinity International University, 2019.

Jeffrey, David Lyle, ed. *A Dictionary of Biblical Tradition in English Literature*. Grand Rapids: Eerdmans, 1992.

King, Martin Luther, Jr. "Letter from a Birmingham Jail [King, Jr.]." African Studies Center, Apr. 16, 1963. https://www.africa.upenn.edu/Articles_Gen/Letter_Birmingham.html.

Marcus Aurelius. *Meditations: A New Translation*. Translated by Gregory Hays. Modern Library. New York: Modern Library, 2003.

McPartlan, Paul. "Who Is the Church? Zizioulas and von Balthasar on the Church's Identity." *Ecclesiology* 4 (2008) 271–88.

Pålsson, Katrina. "Angelic Humans, Glorious Flesh: Jerome's Reception of Origen's Teachings on the Resurrection Body." *ZAC* 23 (2019) 53–81.

Schindler, David. "What's the Difference? On the Metaphysics of Participation in a Christian Context." *Saint Anselm Journal* 3 (2005) 1–27.

Widdicombe, Peter. "The Wounds and the Ascended Body: The Marks of Crucifixion in the Glorified Christ from Justin Martyr to John Calvin." *Laval Théologique et Philosophique* 59 (2003) 137–54.

Williams, Rowan. "Eastern Orthodox Theology." In *The Modern Theologians: An Introduction To Christian Theology Since 1918*, edited by David F. Ford and Rachel Muers, 572–88. 3rd ed. Oxford: Wiley Blackwell, 2005.

Zizioulas, John D. *Communion and Otherness: Further Studies in Personhood and the Church*. Edited by Paul McPartland. London: T&T Clark, 2006.

———. *Lectures in Christian Dogmatics*. Edited by Douglas H. Knight. Translated by Katerina Nikolopulu. London: Zed, 2021.

———. *The One and the Many: Studies on God, Man, the Church, and the World Today*. Edited by Gregory Edwards. Alhambra, CA: Sebastian, 2010. Kindle.

Epilogue
The Unprecedented Unique Bond Between Christians and Jews

Charles McVety

IT WAS A PRIVILEGE to host the symposium that gave rise to this volume at Canada Christian College, and in light of that I felt to conclude these essays with my personal thoughts. It is critically important that Christians live their lives in alignment with the truth, and this is why it was my honor and privilege to host the first symposium of the Eckstein Institute for Jewish-Christian Relations, the platform which hosted many of the papers in this volume. Christians worship the God of truth—the God of Abraham, Isaac, and Jacob. But somehow, somewhere, encrusted in the annals of history, many Christians have lost their way. These Christians came out of alignment with scriptural realities due to the confluence of Roman paganism and Christianity advanced by Constantine beginning in AD 325. Christians, since then, exhibited an inordinate hatred toward Jews—an outlook entirely antithetical to the Bible which was bequeathed to Christians by the Jewish people. This anti-Jewish mentality is completely antithetical to what Scripture teaches, yet it is a factual reality, perhaps one that is hard to accept. Many Christians have forgotten that the Jews are God's chosen people. They have turned away from the divinely ordained teachings of history; yet as the common saying suggests, history is the greatest teacher. People should look to history as their guide—the good, the bad, and the ugly—and turn away from biased fallacies to be reintroduced to the truth of matters. It is hard to accept that, for two thousand years, Christians, with few exceptions, persecuted Jews. Millions of Christians, however, since the mid-nineteenth century have been reawakened to the truth of Scripture, and as a result, have been the recipients of an unprecedented outpouring of God's blessing.

About two thousand years ago, there were an approximately equal number of Jewish and Chinese individuals—around 12 million each. Unfortunately, due to persecution of the Jewish people by Christians and many others, the population of Jews today remains roughly similar—around 16 million total—while the Chinese population has grown remarkably to around 1.5 billion. A significant, yet simple question, must be asked: Why would Christians persecute the Jewish people? The answer, I suggest, is bad theology based upon a distortion of the events of Scripture. Thankfully, however, around two hundred years ago, the progressive revelation of God rooted first in the Reformation led our Christian forefathers to wholly believe in the entirety of the Bible—they began to respect, honor, and love the Jews, and significantly, began to treasure the state of Israel.

Today, Jews and Christians are bonded together in an unprecedented way. Christians and Jews, like no other faith groups in the world, have a unique and peculiar bond. Today, many are working together to fight against anti-Semitism–they are fighting alongside each other for peace and security, to stamp out insidious hatred, and to live peaceably with one another. Christians are now proudly standing shoulder to shoulder with their Jewish brothers and sisters, with the outcome of this bond being the rebirth of the state of Israel after nearly two millennia. This miracle did not occur by Jewish effort alone, but through the joint efforts of Bible-believing Christians and Zionist Jews who love Israel. The rebirth of the state of Israel is demonstrative of what can happen when Christians and Jews come together, united by God, to work alongside one another to further the kingdom of God.

As a result of Christians and Jews working together, the state of Israel is alive and well, reconstituted after its initial establishment over three thousand years ago. Bible-believing Christians who love Israel and the Jewish people are, whether knowingly or unknowingly, are experiencing the favor of God, the outcome of Christian's blessing Israel. When God's people work together in tandem, they experientially live out the mission of Scripture. As a result, God pours out his blessings upon his people—both Christians and Jews.

It is beyond unreasonable, and to be sure, entirely antithetical to Scripture for any so-called Christian to hate Israel. How can someone pray for blessings from the God of Israel and then curse Israel? This, of course, is nonsensical. Cursing Israel does not bring blessings; instead, it brings peril to the ones with curses with their mouths or in their hearts. Perhaps more importantly, it is disingenuous for a Christian to worship Jesus Christ and not love Jewish people. People, and some percentage of Christians specifically, seem to forget that Jesus himself was Jewish and considered himself to be familially related to his Jewish brethren. He practiced Judaism, worshiped in a synagogue, called the Jewish temple his "Father's house," was called rabbi by many of his followers, and often wore a Jewish prayer shawl. Jesus of Nazareth was a direct descendant of Abraham, Isaac, and Jacob; he was in the kingly succession of the line of King David. To hate the Jewish people is also, in an indirect but nevertheless significant sense, to hate Jesus—or at the very least, to hate the ethnic background that the triune God willingly chose for him to be incarnated into.

How is it possible for Christians to worship a Jew named Jesus in order to secure their eternal salvation, and then simultaneously, hate the Jewish people? In fact, it is ridiculous for Christians to do so, and it is equally absurd for them to hate Israel while simultaneously preaching about the prophets, priests, and kings of Israel. It is ludicrous to preach on the Pentateuch—Moses's writings—let along the rest of the Old Testament, all written by Jews, and to denounce or defame the Jewish people. In that same vein, the entire New Testament was written by Jews. Mary, Joseph, Matthew, Mark, John, Peter, Jude, James, Paul, and the twelve apostles were all Jews. So how can someone possibly say they are a Christian—a follower of the Jewish Messiah Jesus—but simultaneously be anti-Semitic and not support Jewish neighbors living across the street? How can someone possibly say that they love the God of Israel but hate Israel? The answer, once more, is bad theology.

On my reading of history, I am thankful that the Reformation freed the Bible from those who kept it locked up in Latin, which, was incomprehensible to the vast majority of the populace save the Medieval priesthood. Understanding of Scripture has progressed, and Bible-believing Christians are now able to decide their theological outlooks for themselves. In the nineteenth and twentieth centuries, it became clear to many Christians that they must pray for Israel and love the Jewish people. They internally realized the truth espoused by Rom 15:27: "For if the Gentiles have been partakers of their spiritual things, their duty is also to minister to them in material things" (NKJV). Here, God tells Christians that believers have been spiritually blessed by the Jews; therefore, Christians are indebted, practically materially, to them. Thankfully, tens of millions—indeed, perhaps even hundreds of millions—of Christians around the world are now obeying Scripture by passionately supporting Israel and the Jewish people.

The direct result of blessing Israel is blessing and prosperity. Psalm 122:6 says, "Pray for the peace of Jerusalem: May they prosper who love you" (NKJV). This is a divinely scientific equation—pray for the Jewish people and prosper. Thankfully, today, large numbers of Christians support

Israel, love the Jewish people, fight against anti-Semitism, and, in turn, are blessed by the God of Israel.

In 2004, there was a historic gathering of Christians and Jews at Canada Christian College for a fundraising benefit related to Israel war bonds; approximately 650 prominent Christian leaders gathered together, shoulder to shoulder with their Jewish brethren, to deposit their financial "treasures" into solidarity with Israel. Matthew 6:21 says that "for where your treasure is, there your heart will be also" (NKJV). At the event, the prime minister of Israel, Benjamin Netanyahu, spoke via video and made a remarkable statement about the fact that Christian Zionism antedated formal political Jewish Zionism. Indeed, he aptly acknowledged that seven years before the First Zionist Congress, Christian leaders had already fostered a political movement aimed at the rebirth of Israel.

The first major Christian Zionist initiative was led by a preacher named William Blackstone, who, significantly, was associated with Dwight L. Moody's church in Chicago. Blackstone was a successful businessman who later shifted his life toward sharing the gospel on an exclusive basis. He authored a book called *Jesus Is Coming* that sold several million copies and attained a tremendous following within nineteenth-century Evangelicalism. Blackstone believed that the Jewish people were the "apple of God's eye" and that the rebirth of Israel was the historical focus of God. He was appalled by the reports of Russia's violent discrimination against the Jewish people during their various pogroms. And thus, in November 1890, he called for a gathering of Christian and Jewish leaders to discuss the reconstitution of the state of Israel.

On November 25, 1890, pastors, rabbis, politicians, and leaders gathered together to speak about the reestablishment of Israel to as a nation-state. Israel's original establishment, of course, dated back over three thousand years prior, though due to persecution of both the Roman Empire and subsequent spread of Islam, Jews were kept from retaining their God-given nation. At this pivotal conference, Blackstone argued:

> Why shall not the powers which under the treaty of Berlin, in 1878, gave Bulgaria to the Bulgarians and Serbia to the Serbians now give Palestine back to the Jews? . . . These provinces, as well as Romania, Montenegro, and Greece, were wrested from the Turks and given to their natural owners. Does not Israel rightfully belong to the Jews?

The result of this historic meeting was the 1891 Blackstone Memorial—a significant political document signed by over four hundred leaders and supported by four United States presidents. This document, though unknown by the majority of Americans today, became the cornerstone of US foreign policy.

As news of this meeting spread throughout the Western world, leaders such as Theodore Herzl began to organize movements in support of the indigenous people of the region to have a homeland—i.e., Israel. In 1897, Herzl organized the famous First Zionist Congress in Basel, Switzerland. He went on to develop his vision and, today, is honored as the forefather of the state of Israel. Herzl was supported in his efforts by many Christian leaders, including William Heckler, whom Herschel referred to as the first Christian Zionist. The bond between Christians and Jews in Chicago, Switzerland, London, and Washington, DC—as well as around the world—has grown over the past 130 years; its fruits have proven to be a formidable force in the international community.

The focus of the Blackstone Memorial was Gen 12:3: God blesses those who bless Israel. Blackstone incorporated this document due to having been deeply affected by the Niagara Bible Conference of 1878. At that conference thirteen years prior, the major tenets of Christian Evangelicalism were codified. In fact, fourteen tenets were penned, with the final tenet referencing the restoration of Israel: "Hence that the Lord Jesus will come in person to introduce the Millennial age, when Israel shall be restored to their own land."[1]

One of Blackstone's protégés was a Canadian pastor, A. B. Simpson, who pastored a now-historic Presbyterian congregation in New York City. Simpson was so struck with Blackstone's passionate support for Israel that he traveled to Jerusalem. There, he began to publicly speak in hopes of fostering a deep commitment to Israel and love for the Jewish people. In respect to these commitments, he placed a stained glass menorah in the main window of his church building. Simpson went on to be the father of the Pentecostal movement, as he was convinced of God's supernatural activities due to his prayer resulting in the miraculous healing of his own heart disease. Thereafter, he began preaching about the contents of Mark 16, which include mentions of signs, wonders, healing, prophecy, and tongues. His followers went on to establish other significant Christian movements, such as the Assemblies of God, Foursquare Church, and the alike. Today, over 600 million people adhere, knowingly or unknowingly, to Simpson's

---

1. S. V. Robinson, stenographer, *Report of the Believers' Meeting for Bible Study, Held at Niagara-on-the-Lake, Ontario July 18-25, 1888* (Toronto: Toronto Willard Tract Depository), 16. https://upload.wikimedia.org/wikipedia/commons/f/fa/Report_on_the_Believers%27_Meeting_for_Bible_Study_%28microform%29_-_held_at_Niagara-on-the-Lake%2C_Ontario%2C_July_18-25%2C_1888_%28IA_cihm_05879%29.pdf.

theology. From a Christian perspective, this modern Pentecostal revival is an important example of how the God of Abraham, Isaac, and Jacob pours out his blessings upon those who love and support Israel and the Jewish people.

Due to Blackstone's profound influence upon twentieth-century Western political thought, former British Prime Minister and Christian Zionist Lord Arthur Balfour authored the now-famous Balfour Declaration. Britain won the war with the Ottoman Empire and liberated Israel in 1917. With the Balfour Declaration in hand, General Edmund Allenby proudly marched into the city of Jerusalem, liberating it from 1,800 years of oppression, with the goal of restoring Jerusalem as the eternal capital of the Jewish people. The United States and the British Empire marched toward the path of blessing Israel, and in fact, both nations were truly blessed by God. Indeed, there was a time that it was common to say that the sun never set on the British Empire—approximately one third of the world was under its governance. However, as students of the Bible well know, there is another half to this great equation of blessing Israel, and that is the reality that those who curse Israel will be cursed. Numerous insidious forces within the British Empire in the ensuing three decades persuaded the British government to turn its back on promises made in the Balfour Declaration; from a spiritual standpoint, this abandonment of God's people resulted in Britain losing much of God's blessing. Today, Britain is reduced to a fraction of what it once was. This great empire, this great nation, once the flagship of Christianity, has now been reduced to just 3 percent of its population identifying as "churchgoing," causing its grand churches and cathedrals to be reduced to mere monuments. God's blessing has faded from Britain.

In the years where this divine blessing was gradually lost, over six million Jews were killed in the Holocaust by the most detestable genocidal regime in human history—Adolf Hitler's Third Reich. Though a portion of Christians protected their Jewish brethren, not enough was done. As a result, many leaders began to recognize the horrors of anti-Semitism and that the Jews must have their land returned. The push was on to reestablish the state of Israel and the Jewish homeland, and on May 14, 1948, this aspiration became a reality. The culmination of great Zionist efforts, both Christian and Jewish, gave rise to the state of Israel as a modern nation-state.

Unfortunately, Israel's rebirth as a nation did not end anti-Semitism or the persecution of the Jewish people. Bad theology persists among Christians, even until today. However, some Bible-believing Christians reflected upon the horrors of the Second World War and were enlightened through their reexamination of Scripture. Additionally, a great leader, John Hagee, rose to prominence. Beginning in 1982, Hagee began to host an annual

Night to Honor Israel, and in 2006, he invited over four hundred prominent Christians to formally establish an outstanding organization known as Christians United for Israel (CUFI). Today, CUFI is the largest pro-Israel group in the world with over ten million active members who understand both the necessity of supporting Israel and the Christian imperative to love the Jewish people. Another major Christian initiative related to Israel also began in the early eighties—the International Christian Embassy of Jerusalem, which established offices in over sixty countries and inspired Christians to fulfill their biblical mandate to support God's chosen people. On the Jewish side, Rabbi Eckstein established the International Fellowship of Christians and Jews; today, this organization raises over $100 million every year to support Jewish charities and fund aliyah for desirous Jews. In more recent years, the Knesset aligned with the notion of building bridges with Christian Zionists, and in 2004 MK Yuri Shtern founded the Knesset Christian Allies Caucus, which presently has pro-Israel caucuses in fifty-two parliaments around the world.

All that being said, a lesser-known source of present-day attempts at relationship building between Jews and Christians can be traced is the teaching of the Rabbi Meir Lau. On October 27, 2002, Rabbi Lau visited Toronto and spoke at the Shaarei Shomayim Synagogue. His topic was, as the title of this essay states, that an unprecedented unique bond exists between Christians and Jews. Rabbi Lau recalled his remarkable story on stage, detailing how he was one of the youngest survivors of the Holocaust. Lau was just eight years old when he was taken to the Buchenwald death prison. Eventually, in 1945, this prison was liberated, and he rose through the ranks to become the chief rabbi of Israel a deep interest in the bond between Christians and Jews. This was because Lau had grown up in the same city where Pope John Paul II formerly had served as a priest. Meir Lau's father was a rabbi alongside Pope John Paul II, and the two of them developed a strong friendship—the future pope was even known to play on the Jewish soccer team.

In addition to recalling his life stories, Rabbi Lau discussed prophecies found in Isa 11. In these texts, the prophet mentions that the anticipated Messiah will bring peace upon the earth. He stated that many of his rabbinic counterparts are skeptical that this could ever happen, and instead, view the passage as an important allegory related to our striving for peace; however, Lau believed that it will happen. He contended that the truth of Scripture will take place, as is spoken of in Isa 11:

> The wolf also shall dwell with the lamb,
> The leopard shall lie down with the young goat,

> The calf and the young lion and the fatling together;
> And a little child shall lead them. The cow and the bear shall graze;
> Their young ones shall lie down together;
> And the lion shall eat straw like the ox.
> The nursing child shall play by the cobra's hole,
> And the weaned child shall put his hand in the viper's den.
> They shall not hurt nor destroy in all My holy mountain,
> For the earth shall be full of the knowledge of the Lord
> As the waters cover the sea.

Speaking on this passage, Rabbi Lau proclaimed that this will take place because it has already occurred once in history. There was a 150-day period of peace on Noah's ark in which numerous animals, big and small, alongside a group of human beings, lived harmoniously together. Rabbi Lau went on to say that that peace was not just related to the glory of God but was also necessary in the face of a common enemy. He explained that, today, Christians and Jews face common enemies of all kinds: diseases, cancer, starvation, mental illness, ignorance, hate crimes, weapons of mass destruction, terrorism, and so on. Christians and Jews are in the same boat together, he suggested, and the only way forward is to do as the people and animals aboard Noah's ark did—respect one another, and live peaceably.

The rabbi's appeal was especially piercing: he said, "Surely we know as much as the mice of Noah's ark." Rabbi Lau gave the same speech in numerous nations across the world in the ensuing years, and it greatly impacted Christian and Jewish communities alike. Christian and Jewish leaders began to take up his talking points and discern how to best build a bond between them—an unprecedented unique bond. They discussed how they could stop focusing on the differences between their faiths, and instead, work toward the common good for their respective communities. Many leaders, Christian and Jew alike, agreed to put their hand to the same plough, to till the field of support of Israel, to fight against anti-Semitism, and to engage in many other humanitarian tasks. When people put their hands to the plough, they stop looking at their differences and focus on the task at hand. And indeed, what arose from such discussions include over twenty years of Christian and Jewish initiatives. For example, in 2003, a historic journey of twenty prominent Canadian and American Christians, including myself, traveled to Israel to sit down with Knesset Cabinet leaders to foster the growth of this unique bond. One notable statement was made by the speaker of the house at the time, former President Reuven Rivlin, who proclaimed that Christians and Jews look to the same Messiah to come and bring peace on earth.

To be sure, Christian support for Israel was not just led by religious leaders; it was also facilitated by popular politicians such as the evangelical Stephen Harper—a member of the Christian and Missionary Alliance, which was a denomination founded by A. B. Simpson. During his tenure as the prime minister of Canada from 2006 to 2015, Harper was widely known as a staunch supporter of Israel, including his push to reverse Canada's horrific 50-year record of voting against Israel at the United Nations. Harper also condemned the election of Hamas in Gaza and designated them as a terrorist group. He also was steadfast at the Francophone summit, single-handedly leading them to affirm a more balanced position on the Gaza War. Recently, Harper even stated that Israel is the most remarkable country in the world and even participated in a tremendous PragerU video in support of Israel that, at the time of this writing, has amassed over four million views.

In 2018, with the support of Christian faith advisors, President Donald Trump stood against the tide of the international community and moved US embassy to Jerusalem. In doing so, he addressed a shameful reality—countries inherently practice anti-Semitic postures by refusing to locate their embassies in the true and eternal capital of Israel. While much about his personality and tenure as president can be debated, President Trump pioneered a position based upon Christian beliefs that Israel must be treated with respect and dignity—the same way that any other democracy is treated by Western countries. Simply stated, it was the right thing to do, and it brought about blessing upon blessing as peace ensued with the United Arab Emirates, Bahrain, and many other countries in the ensuing Abraham Accords. Many rabbis have publicly commented upon this wave of peace as a "second miracle." They suggest that first miracle was the rebirth of the state of Israel; the second being the acceptance and support of Israel by millions of Christians and Jews alike.

With a flurry of advances in the relationship between Jews and Christians, their unique bond has flourished. CUFI, under the leadership of John Hagee, has now organized hundreds of Nights to Honor Israel across the world, including its flagship Washington Summit that gathers six thousand supporters every year. Held in the US capital every July, throngs of Christians and Jews develop relationships with one another, celebrate the nation-state of Israel, and formally appeal to the American government in support of Israel and against anti-Semitism. These appeals have resulted in tremendous victories over opponents of the state of Israel, such as those aligned with the "boycott, divest, and sanctions" movement.

Given the flurry of positive developments between Christians and Jews, one might think that anti-Semitism and the hatred of Israel are in steep decline; yet, nothing could be further from the truth. Alongside the strengthening bond between Christians and Jews, anti-Semitism is spreading worldwide like wildfire. Due to the spread of social media and other technologies, the teachings of radical Islamic terrorist organizations ranging from Al-Qaeda to Boko Haram to ISIS are spreading unabated. Persecution is so prevalent in Western cities like New York, Toronto, Paris, and London that visible Jews find it difficult to be in public areas without being accosted or even attacked.

Of course, we cannot forget the most severe event against Jews in recent memory: on October 7, 2023, the fiftieth anniversary of the Yom Kippur War, thousands of vicious Hamas butchers poured over the Gazan border to invade Israel. They slaughtered over 1,200 innocent men, women, and children. They took over 200 hostages, and war ensued. And in the shadow of this tragedy, Israel actually *lost international support*. It is beyond sickening that, right now, our streets are filled with Hamas supporters and our universities are actively spreading anti-Jew hatred at a rate not seen since Hitler's Third Reich.

This hatred is not just directed against the Jewish people; it is equally against Bible-believing Christians. Globally, Christians are the most persecuted group on the planet. Terrorist organizations and Iranian proxies are attempting to wipe Christians out from their historical homelands in the Middle East. Of course, proponents of Christianity's destruction are not just radical Islamists; many are aligned with leftist political entities in the West. It is remarkable how radical Islam and "woke" leftism have found common ground, since logically speaking, their ideologies are opposed to one another. A few years ago, the vice prime minister of Israel, Moshe Ya'alon, described this relationship as the "red-green alliance"—radical Islam with radical leftist ideology.[2] They work together not because they enjoy each other's company, but because they affirm the common saying that "the enemy of your enemy is your friend." Radical Islam wants to eradicate the entirety of the Judeo-Christian ethos, and radical leftists are staunchly opposed to Judeo-Christian morality. Now, more than ever, Christians and Jews need to solidify their unique bond with one another.

On January 27, 2006, the United Nations—sixty years too late—finally voted to formally observe International Holocaust Remembrance Day. Every speaker testified that the Holocaust did not begin with Auschwitz, but rather began with the marginalization of the Jewish people. Today, the marginalization of both Jews and Christians is rampant, traveling at hyperspeed through social media and the internet. The fruit of this poisoned tree

---

2. In personal conversation with author.

is giving rise to authoritarianism in traditionally democratic countries and causing swathes of society to truly hate freedom, peace, toward security. Hence, Christians and Jews must make a choice: to stand united or to fall divided.

If hundreds of millions of Christians alongside millions of Jews make the choice to uphold their unique bond with one another, the result will be peace, security, and freedom. Together, Christians and Jews can fight and emerge victorious against the evils of the day. Together, Christians and Jews, standing shoulder to shoulder, shall stand, and God will do exceedingly and abundantly above all that Christians and Jews ask or think.

Ancient Sources Index

OLD TESTAMENT

Genesis

1	90, 111, 125, 191
1–2	89, 113, 126
1:1	190
1:26	88, 91
1:27	145
1:31	145
2:18	145
2:18a	146
2:20	145
2:23	146
3	126
8:12	113n17
11	28, 112n14
11:1–9	112
12:3	207
18	89, 90
18:2	89n28
18:8	89n28
28:12	90
31:13	66
32:30	113
40:8	113–114n18

Exodus

3:6	117n24
5	111
5:2	111
15	113
19	9
20:2	117
29:18	113n17
33:11	113
34:14	187

Leviticus

16:8	113–114n18
18:22	146
19–20	101
19:1–4	117
19:18	101
19:27	101
20	95

Numbers

12:8	113
14:14	113
17:12	26

Deuteronomy

5:4	113
6:4–9	58–59, 95
6:5–6	58–60
28	5
29:22	5
30	5, 11
30:5	5
30:18	26
31:17–18	130
31:20	113–14n18
32:7–8	28
32:9	28

Deuteronomy (continued)

33	113
34:10	113

Judges

13:8	113n18
18:5	113n18

1 Samuel

13:9–13	114
15:22–23	111
28	113–14n18

2 Samuel

19:12	5
23:1	5

1 Kings

6:12–13	113
8:27	113
13:1–10	23
22:7	113n18

2 Kings

19:14–34	113n18
20:8–11	113–14n18
21:1–9	113–14n18
23:16–18	23

2 Chronicles

2:6	111

Nehemiah

8:18	5

Job

	109n7, 118, 122, 123
4:7–8	127
7:9	117n24
8:3–7	127
11:13–20	127
19:25–27	117
21:14–15	113–14n18
36–41	113

Psalms

	67, 113, 122
2	70–71
6:5	117n24
8:4	67
9:10	111
19:1–4	141
19:8	105
24:1–2	111
27:2	41
30:9	117n24
34:9	108n6
44	130
44:8	130
44:9	131
44:13	131
44:17	130
44:19	131
44:22	131
44:23–24	131
45	169n79
49:15	117n24
50:1	83
50:12	113
50:13–15	113
51:16–17	114
82	83, 87, 87–88, 91
82:1	83
82:6	82, 83
82:7	87
88:8–12	117n24
94:11	118
97:5	73
97:9	113
107:8–9	141
111:15	111
115:8	91
121	113
122:6	205

Proverbs

3:11–12	122
19:3	124

Ecclesiastes

	107–19
1:1	107n2
1:2	115
1:11	107, 108
1:13	109n7, 116
1:14	109, 115
1:16	114n19
1:17	109n7, 117
2:1	115
2:1–10	114n19
2:11	109n7, 115
2:13	118
2:15	115
2:15–17	118
2:17	115
2:19	115, 117
2:21	115
2:23	115
2:24	108
2:24–26	108, 109n7
2:26	109n7, 115, 117
3:11	109n7, 116, 118
3:11–15	116
3:12–13	108, 109n7
3:13	108, 109n7
3:14	108, 109n7, 117, 118, 119
3:14–15	109n7
3:17	109n7
3:19	115
3:21	117
3:21–22	117n24
3:22	108, 109n7, 116
4:4	115
4:7–8	115
4:16	115
5:1	117
5:1–6	108, 118
5:1–7	109n7, 114
5:2	110
5:6	119
5:7	109n7, 115, 117
5:10	115
5:18–20	108, 109n7
5:20	109n7
6:2	115
6:4	115
6:9	115
6:11	115
6:12	113, 116, 117
7:1–13	118
7:6	115
7:13	117, 118
7:13–14	118
7:14	109n7, 116
7:18	117
7:23–24	116, 116n23
7:23–29	115, 116
7:24	116
7:25–28	116, 116n23
7:26	116n23
7:28	116n23
7:29	116n23, 124
8:1	117
8:7	116, 117
8:10	108n6, 115
8:10–13	117
8:12–13	108, 109n7, 117, 118, 119
8:13	109n7
8:14	115
8:15	108, 109n7
8:17	117, 118
9:1	117, 117n25
9:5	117
9:5–6	107
9:7	109n7
9:7–10	108
9:9	108
9:11	117
9:11—10:20	118
9:12	116, 117
10:2	118
10:8–11	116
10:14	116, 117
10:15	117
11:2	116, 117
11:5	116, 117, 118
11:6	117
11:7—12:1	108, 109n7
11:8	115
11:9	109n7, 117

Ecclesiastes (continued)

11:10	115
12:7	117n24
12:8	115
12:13	108, 109n7, 117, 118, 119
12:14	109n7

Isaiah

	9
1:2–3	113–14n18
7:11	113–14n18
11	209–210
26:19–21	117n24
38:18	117n24
42:1	90
44:6	5
53:3	29
53:11	69, 70
54:5	187
54:5–8	199
55:8	4
55:8–9	111
66:20	73

Jeremiah

	122
3	199, 200
3:8	188
3:18	200
32:2–3	113–114n18

Ezekiel

	67
5:14–15	24
23	200

Daniel

	70, 73
7:9–14	67–68, 69, 71, 72
7:13	67
7:14	69
12:2–3	117n24

Hosea

14:2	103

Joel

2:28	113–14n18

Jonah

1:9	111

Micah

6:8	111

Habakkuk

	122
3:17–19	114

Zephaniah

3:9	12

Zechariah

	9–10, 10
8	10

Malachi

3:16	36, 39

ANCIENT NEAR EASTERN TEXTS

Babylonian

A Dialogue About Human Misery	109n7
A Pessimistic Dialogue Between Master and Servant	109n7

Egyptian

A Dispute Between a Man and his Ba	109n7

Mesopotamian

Atra-Ḥasis   112

The Epic of Gilgamesh

    109n7
Gilgamesh III:1–13   109n7

DEUTEROCANONICAL BOOKS

4 Ezra

65, 67, 68, 71, 72, 73–75, 91, 158, 158n23
13   71, 72–73, 73
13:1–4   71
13:1–13   71
13:4   73
13:5–13   71–72
13:10   73
13:13   73
13:14–20   72
13:21–58   72
13:25–26   72
13:32   72, 73
13:32–38   72
13:37   72
13:51–52   72

4 Maccabees

    91

OLD TESTAMENT PSEUDEPIGRAPHA

1 Enoch

65, 91, 158
6–11   70n23
37–71   67, 68, 68n18, 70–71, 72–74
38:2   68–69
45:3–4   69
46:1   69
46:2   69
46:3–4   69
47   69–70
47:1   70
47:4   70
48:2–3   70
48:5–6   70
51:3   69
55:4   69
61:8   69
62:2–5   69

Jubilees

    158

Testament of Moses

    91

Testament of Naphtali

3:2–5   149

DEAD SEA SCROLLS

67, 74, 89
4Q427   87
4Q491c   87

ANCIENT JEWISH WRITERS

Josephus

Against Apion (Contra Apionem)
2.24   149, 149n28

Jewish Antiquities
13   147n20

Philo

On Abraham
35   149, 149n29

De somniis
5:417–19   66–67, 66n11

Letter of Aristeas

152	149
162	149

Pseudo-Phocylides

line 188	149n30
line 191	149n30
line 192	149, 149n30

RABBINIC WORKS

Talmud

b. Shabbat

127b	101–2, 102n12
b. Sotah 11a.	42, 42n30

Deuteronomy Rabbah

	91

Genesis Rabbah

	88, 89
8:10	88, 90
15:4	41
68:12	90

Sifre to Deuteronomy

	87–88

Midrash Tehilim

	41–42

MEDIEVAL JEWISH WRITERS

Ibn Ezra

Leviticus/Va' Yikra

148	147, 147n22

Maimonides (Moses ben Maimon)

Commentary on Mishnah Aboda Zara

1:3	6, 6n2

"Eight Chapters"

§4	104–5, 105n19

The Guide for/to the Perplexed

	123
3.10, 266	123, 123n10
3.12	124, 124n12
3.22, 297	123, 123n7
3.23, 303	123, 123n8
510–11	102–3, 103n14
599–600	104n18
638	103, 103n15

Mishneh Torah, Kings and Wars

11.1	7–8, 8n4, 10

Responsa of Maimonides

no. 149	6–7, 7n3, 10, 10n5

Saadiah Gaon

Book of Theodicy

	122
124	122, 122n2
125–26	122, 122n3–5

NEW TESTAMENT

Matthew

	162
2:15	189n13
5–7	162–164
5:44	163, 163n50
6	26
6:6	26

6:21	206	2:18	157
7:1–2	162	2:19–21	157n17
7:23	195n39	3:2	154
8:25	26	3:15	26
13:24–30	195n39	3:19–20	155
13:29–30	162	3:25	155
18:11	26	4:7	154n6
19:8	200	4:9	157
20:16	30	4:22	155n7, 157, 164n58
22:32	117n24	4:31	154
23	43, 162, 163	4:39	154n6
25:12	195n39	4:46	154n6
27:24–25	70, 70n23	5:1	155, 157
27:25	162, 163	5:10	155
		5:10–11	154
		6:4	155, 157
		6:25	154

Mark

10:42–45	30

		6:52	157
		6:63	193n32

Luke

		7:1	155
		7:2	155
1:1	186n1	7:41	157
1:1–2	186n1	8:12	166n67
1:52	25	8:17	154
3	197	8:21–24	154
6:39	26	8:31	155n7
15:24	26	8:44	155, 164, 164n58, 165, 166, 166n67
16:15	22		
18	26	8:47	155
24:39	196	8:59	155
		9:2	154

John

		9:22	155
		10:34	154
	84, 153–69, 169	10:34–35	83
1:1	186n1, 199	11:8	154, 155
1:1–18	164–65n61, 164–67, 164n60, 166n67	11:29	154
		11:31	155n7, 157
1:4–5	165	11:33	155n7
1:6	165	11:36	155n7
1:8	165, 165n62	11:45	155n7, 157
1:9	165	11:54	155
1:12–13	166	11:55	155, 157
1:14	63	12:11	155n7, 157
1:19	155	12:20	154n6
1:38	154	12:42	155
1:49	154	13:13–14	154
2:6	155, 157n17	13:33	154
2:13	155, 157	14:6	192

John (continued)

16:2	155
17:20–23	183
18:28	154n6
19:1	154n6
19:20	157
19:38	155
19:40	155, 157n17
19:42	155
20:16	154
20:19	155
20:25	196
20:27	196

Acts

1:8	182
5:34–39	84
11:18	176
14:17	141
17	29
17:24–25	113
17:26	29

Romans

	169
1	140
1:3	197
1:18–25	142
1:18–32	140
1:20	141
1:20–25	142
1:21	141
1:22	111n10
1:25	144
1:25–26	144n15
1:26–27	140n5, 142, 148
1:29	199
2	31
3:10	28, 31
3:23	29
5:19	30
6:3–8	85
6:5	85
8:2–11	85
8:10	85
8:11	85
8:15	83
8:17	85
8:22–23	85
8:29	85
9:3–4	199
11	93, 197, 198n53
11:2–21	21–32
11:19	199
11:20–21	23, 25, 26
11:24	197, 197n46, 199
11:29	197, 198
11:32	29
11:32–36	29
11:33	30
12:2	86
12:5	85, 86
13:14	196
15:27	205

1 Corinthians

1:30	87
2:6—3:4	99
2:16	86
3:18–20	118
6:17	85, 86
10:11	22
12:12	86
12:12–13	85
12:13	86
13:5	85
15:39	145–46, 195

2 Corinthians

3:18	85, 86, 193
4:4	85
4:8–12	85
4:10–11	85
4:17	85
5:17	85
5:21	30, 80, 80n6, 86
8:9	30, 80, 80n6
12:1–10	85

Galatians

	169

2:20	85
3:28	85, 197
4:19	85
5:9	27
6:15	85

Ephesians

	169
2:5	85
2:6	85
2:13	29
2:14	29
2:15	29
2:16	29
2:18	192n26
3	201
5:25–32	187
5:30	192n28, 193n32

Philippians

1:21	85
1:29	85
2	27, 68
2:5–8	86
2:6–8	30
2:6–11	63
3:1–10	86
3:10	85
3:14	200
3:17	200
3:21	85
4:7	29

Colossians

1:15	85
3:1	85
3:4	85
3:11	197

1 Thessalonians

5:18	141

1 Timothy

2:5	192n25
3:1	186–87
3:1–2	186–201
3:2	142, 200
3:16	63
6:16	143
6:17	22

Hebrews

2:15	194
10:20	196
10:39	32

James

	169
3:13	200

1 Peter

	169

2 Peter

1:4	30, 84, 200

1 John

2:19	195
3:1–3	30
3:2	84–85

Revelation

2:8	30
3:16	178
4:3	188n10
5:6	196
7	28, 178n13, 188n10
12	188n10
21:2	188
21:3–4	129
21:9–12	198–99

EARLY CHRISTIAN WRITINGS

Athanasius

On the Incarnation of the Word of God

54	80n3

Augustine

On Christian Doctrine (De doctrina Christiana)

3.24	169, 169n80

The City of God (De civitate Dei contra paganos)

17.16	169, 169n79

The Confessions

7.12.18	125, 125n14, 125n16
On the Free Choice of the Will	125
Homily on Psalm 81	81, 81n10

Clement of Alexandria

Protrepticus

7.122.4–7.123.1	83, 83n16

Irenaeus

Against Heresies (Adversus Haereses)

	54
1.1–5	53, 53n25
1.3.2	53, 53n24
1.3.6	54n27
1.4.4	53, 53n26
2.27.1	54, 54n29
3.6.1	83, 83n15
4.6.7	54, 54n28
5, preface	80n3
5.7	197, 197n47
8.1	53, 53n26
9.2–4	53, 53n26
9.28	53, 53n26

Justin Martyr

Dialogue with Trypho

124	83, 83n14

On the Resurrection

2	197, 197n47

Origen

On First Principles

2:4.2.9	168–69, 169, 169n76, 169n77
2:4.3.1	169, 169n77

Thomas Aquinas

Summa Theologiae

1.2.69	104

CHRISTIAN PSEUDEPIGRAPHA

Pseudo-Dionysius

Ecclesiastical History

1.3	80

GRECO-ROMAN LITERATURE

Lucian

Dialogues of the Dead

9	147n20

Pseudo-Aristotle

Οἰκονομικά

1.1343a	56n33

Περι Κοσμος/*De mundo*
    5   56–57, 57n34

QUR'AN
Surah Al-Anbya
  (21) 22   57, 57n35

Subject and Name Index

Aaron, 111
abad, 26
Abel, 29
Abelard, Peter, 47n2
abomination, 147
abortion, 40
Abraham, 1, 9, 89–90, 89n28, 157n17, 197–98, 205
Abraham Accords, 211
ἀχάριστος, 142
Adam, 88, 90, 97, 145–46, 182, 191, 194
Adams, Marilyn McCord, 128–29
adoption, 81, 83, 181–83
adultery, 33, 139, 187, 187n4. *See also* faithfulness
aeons/eternities (Gnostic), 53, 53n23
Africa, 11
After Auschwitz (Rubenstein), 129–30
afterlife, 117n24, 123
Against Heresies (Irenaeus), 52, 54
Agamben, Giorgio, 55
agency, 56, 98, 100, 105
agnosticism, 127–28
Ahab, King, 23
Alexander (Syrian king), 147n20
aliyah, 209
ἀλλήλους, 143
Allenby, Edmund, General, 208
Al-Qaeda, 212
ambition, 23, 108, 108n6, 109n7
Ammonius, 147n20
ancient Near East, 109–14, 109n7, 111n10, 112n12, 112n14, 116–18, 147. *See also* Middle East

Ancient of Days, 67–68. *See also* Antecedent of Days
angels, 28, 88–92, 97, 124, 188n10
anger, 127–28, 130
Anglican church, 25n4, 63
animals, 113–14, 128, 145–46, 149n30, 210
Anselm, 129
Antecedent of Days, 69–70. *See also* Ancient of Days
anti-Judaism, 153–69, 153n2, 154n3, 159n25, 164n56, 164n59
anti-Semitism. *See also under* Judaism/Jews
  vs. anti-Judaism, 154n3
  Christians and, 7, 10, 22, 27, 153n2, 159n25, 183, 204–5
  global, 1, 211–12
  the Third Reich and, 208
apathy, 187n4
apocalyptic texts, 67, 75, 188–89, 188n10
apollumi, 26
apologetics, 154, 159, 159n25
apotheosis, 91. *See also* deification of humans
Aquinas, Thomas, 27, 37, 102–5
Aristotle, 34, 80–81n7, 102–3
ark, Noah's, 210
ἄρσενες ἐν ἄρσεσιν, 143
ἄρσην, 143, 145
Articles of Religion (Anglican Church), 63
asceticism, 82, 92
ἀσχημοσύνη, 143

asherisms (ašrê), 104
Assemblies of God, 207
assimilation, hermeneutic, 178
Assmann, Jan, 47, 59
Athanasius, 30, 80n3, 81n9, 191
atheism, 127–30
atonement, 29
attīq yōmīn, 67
Augustine
   on deification of humans, 81, 81n9
   on Jews, 24
   on potentiality, 34
   on the problem of evil, 125–26, 131
   on Scripture, 169
   on theology, 3
   theology of, 27
Auschwitz, 128–29, 212
authoritarianism, 212–13
authority, 7, 48, 50–52, 51n18, 54, 58, 135–40. See also under Scripture/the Bible

Babel, tower of, 112–13, 112n14
Babylonian Job, 117
Balfour, Arthur, Lord, 208
Balfour Declaration, 208
baptism, 98, 180, 182
bar enash, 67–68. See also Son of Man
Barbour, Ian G., 96n1
Barrett, C. Kingsley, 164n58
Barth, Karl, 27, 30, 160
βδέλυγμα, 147
the Beatitudes, 104
Beck, Norman A., 164n58
behavior/conduct, 34, 38–39, 41–43, 69. See also ethics, Judeo-Christian; morality
belief in Jesus Christ, 166–67, 166n67, 167n71
Bello, Rafael, xiii, 95–106
benevolence, 122, 126, 169
Berkovits, Eliezer, Rabbi, 131–32
Berlin, Treaty of, 206
Beth-El, 66
Betz, Hans Dieter, 175n2
Beutler, Johannes, 164n59
the Bible. See Scripture/the Bible
Bible and Sword (Tuchman), 5

binary, male-female, 137, 143–45
Blackstone, William, 206–8
Blackstone Memorial, 206–7
blessings, 97–99, 111, 122–23, 204–5, 207–8
blood, innocent, 70n23
blood libel, 10
blood-curse, 162–63
bloodshed/murder, 11–12, 37, 40, 124, 182
The Bodies of God and the World of Ancient Israel (Sommer), 64
body, physical, 52, 135–40, 140n4, 143–46, 150
body of Christ, 86, 193n32, 198
Boko Haram, 212
Book of Theodicy (Saadiah), 122
boundaries on humans, 109n7, 116–18
Boyarin, Daniel, 64–65, 68, 70, 72–75
Braiterman, Zachary, 126
bride, 187–89, 198–201
Britain, 208
Brown, Raymond, 158
Bruce, F. F., 47
Brueggemann, Walter, 187n7
Buchenwald, 209
Bultmann, Rudolf, 160–61
Bunta, Silviu Nicolae, 79, 86–87
Burnett, David, 79

Cain, 29, 169
Calvin, John, 27, 51–52, 51n18, 60
Canaan, 109n7, 111
Canada, 211
Canada Christian College, 2, 203, 206
canon, 48–52, 48n7, 51n18, 54–55, 57, 59–60
canon criticism, 161
canon within a canon, 161
canonical approach, 49–52
Cappadocian fathers, 189–90
carnal Christians, 99
Carson, D. A., 126–27
Cary, Phillip, 125
Chafer, Lewis Sperry, 97, 99
Chalcedonian Creed, 196–98, 196n40, 197n46, 201

Subject and Name Index

character, stability of, 98–99, 103–5
Charles, R. H., 71
Charlesworth, James H., 68n18
childbearing, 147n20, 194–95
Childs, Brevard, 49, 52
the Chosen One, 69–70
Christian and Missionary Alliance, 211
Christianity/Christians. *See also* the church
  adoption by God, 181–83
  anti-Judaism in, 7, 10, 22, 27, 153n2, 159n25, 183, 204–5 (*See also* "the Jews" in the Gospel of John)
  carnal, 99
  deification in, 82–86, 83n13
  gentiles and Jews in, 174–80, 178n13, 181n29, 183–84
  as grafted in branches, 22, 26
  Jewish views of, 2–3, 6, 10–12
  Messianic Jews and, 23, 25, 80
  persecution and, 11–12, 212
  Second Temple Judaism and, 64–65, 73–75, 84, 84n17
Christians United for Israel (CUFI), 209, 211
Christology, 64–75, 156, 167n72
Chrysostom, John, 159
the church. *See also* canon; Christianity/Christians
  as the body of Christ, 86, 193n32, 198
  as bride, 187, 189, 198–99, 201
  early, 174–76
  as *ekklesia*, 176–77, 179–80, 183–84, 189n13
  as icon, 192–93, 193n32
  as Israel, 22, 27n6, 175–84, 178n13, 181n29, 198–99 (*See also* supersessionism)
  mission of, 182
  sin of, 31, 175, 181–83
  unity of gentiles and Jews in, 174–84, 181n29
church fathers, 30, 81–83, 189–90
circumcision, 155, 175, 175n2
city *(polis)*, 56–57

Clement of Alexandria, 82–83
clouds, riding on, 68, 71, 73
Coakley, Sarah, 27
Cohen, Hermann, 58–59
Collins, Adela Yarbro, 68, 70
Collins, John, 71–74
colonialism, 31
commandments of God, 8, 36–40, 59, 147–48, 162–64, 163n50, 169
communities
  canon and, 50–52, 55, 60
  Johannine, 156, 158
  morality and, 38–39, 43
  Qumran, 74, 87, 89, 158
  textual, 47–48, 50, 60
concentration/death camps, 128–29, 131, 209, 212
conduct/behavior, 34, 38–39, 41–43, 69. *See also* ethics, Judeo-Christian; morality
Cone, James, 27
confession/repentance, 41, 102–3, 127, 154, 176, 182–83
Constantine, 203
contemplation, 90–92, 103, 105
content criticism. *See Sachkritik* (content criticism)
control, 107, 110, 112, 114, 118, 147n20
conversion, 7, 10, 98
coronavirus pandemic, 27, 126
corporations, 195
cosmology, 52–60. *See also* the world
covenant
  with Israel, 27n6, 58, 104, 130, 177–78, 199
  love in, 60
  new, 21
COVID-19, 27, 126
Craig, William Lane, 128n25
creation
  evil and, 123–25
  ex nihilo, 122, 190–91
  finitude of, 190–91, 193
  as good, 125
  of humans, 36–38, 88–89, 122, 131–32, 145–46
  in Mesopotamian myth, 112

creation *(continued)*
  in relationship to God, 187n3, 190–93
  revelation and, 38, 141
Crisp, Oliver, 96
criticism, canon, 161
criticism, content. *See Sachkritik* (content criticism)
Crossan, John Dominic, 153n2
the crucifixion, 29, 162, 196
the Crusades, 2, 7, 10–11
CUFI (Christians United for Israel), 209, 211
Culpepper, R. Alan, 157n16, 164–65n61
curses, 5, 114, 126, 163, 204, 208
Cynics, 80–81n7
Cyril, 81n9

Daniel, 7, 91
David, King, 23, 41, 197–98, 205
De Jonge, Henk Jan, 156
De mundo (Pseudo-Aristotle), 56–57, 60
De Ruyter, B. W. J., 156
Dead Sea Scrolls, 67, 74, 87, 89
death of God theology, 129–30
death/concentration camps, 128–29, 131, 209, 212
death/mortality, 88, 116n23, 117, 117n24, 123, 137, 191, 194
deception/lies, 137–39, 144–47, 144n15
deificare, 87, 92. *See also* deification of humans
deification of humans, 79–92, 80n3, 81n9, 83n13
deificatus, 92. *See also* deification of humans
delusions, 107–8, 109n6, 110, 114, 118–19
demons, 55, 113, 126
desires. *See* emotions/feelings
determinism, 167
Deuteros Theos (Second God) (Philo), 66
the devil/Satan, 126, 155, 164–66, 169

The Dialogue of a Philosopher with a Jew and a Christian (Abelard), 47n2
the diaspora, 157, 157n17
discipline/instruction of God, 122–23
disease/illness, 124, 210
dispensationalism, 188, 188n8
divination, 112–14, 114n18, 116
divinity, functional vs ontological, 68, 70, 72
divorce, 187, 188, 200
Dizon, J. Luis, xiii, 63–77
The Doctrine of Deification in the Greek Patristic Tradition (Norman Russell), 81–82
doctrines, 96–97
Dodson, Joseph, 105n20
Draper, Paul, 128
dualism, 131, 167, 167n72
Duodecad (Gnostic), 53
duplex gratia, 96, 100

"The Earliest Patristic Interpretations of Psalm 82, Jewish Antecedents, and the Origin of Christian Deification" (Mosser), 83n13
Ecclesiastes. *See* Qohelet
ecclesiology, 179, 181–82, 189. *See also* the church
Eckstein, Rabbi, 209
Eckstein Institute for Jewish-Christian Relations, 1, 2, 203
ecumenism, 174n1, 176, 183, 189, 196n40
Egypt, 109n7, 111
ekklesia, 176–77, 179–80, 183–84, 189n13
El-Shaddai, 130
emotions/feelings, 117, 136–39, 140n5, 141–44
Encyclopedia of Christian Civilization, 84
end times, 68, 177. *See also* eschatology
enemies
  common of Jews and Christians, 210, 212
  of David, 41

of Jesus, 155, 162
love for, 163–64
of the Messiah, 71
of the Son of Man, 72–73
energies of God, 82
Enlil, 112n12, 114
Enoch, Parables of, 68, 73, 74
Enoch, Similitudes of, 67–72
Epicurus/Epicureans, 80–81n7, 126
episcopos, 200
Esau, 29
eschatology, 10, 80, 83, 85, 97, 159n27
essence of God, 82
eternal life, 114, 143, 191–93. *See also* immortality
eternities/aeons (Gnostic), 53, 53n23
ethics, Judeo-Christian. *See also* morality; virtue
 as common ground, 33, 38–39, 78
 holiness and, 101–3
 sexuality and, 135–50, 135n1
ethnicity, 23, 177, 188, 197, 198n53, 199, 205
εὐχαριστέω, 141–42
Evangelicalism, 25, 97–99, 105, 127, 207
evangelization of Jews, 24–25, 31
Eve, 83, 126, 146
evil, the problem of, 4, 116–17, 121–33
Evodius, 125
ex nihilo, 122, 190–91
exegesis, 54n27, 97, 160–61. *See also* Sachkritik (content criticism)
expropriation of Israel's identity, 177–78
extispicy, 113
Ezekiel, 67

Fackenheim, Emil, 124
Faith After the Holocaust (Berkovits), 131
faith in God
 all humanity and, 10–11
 canon and, 48–51, 55, 60
 evil/suffering and, 127, 130–31
 Jewish *vs.* Christian, 41–42
 justification and sanctification and, 99
 theology and, 3–4
 uncertainty/anxiety and, 111, 114
faithfulness
 of God, 186–88, 199
 to God, 25, 42, 88, 177
 to spouse, 186–88, 187n4, 199
the fall of humanity, 83, 126
falsehood. *See* lies/deception
Al-Faruqi, Ismail, 58, 58n37
fate, 112–13
fathers, church, 30, 81–83, 189–90
fear of God, 108, 108n6, 109n7, 110, 110n9, 115, 117–18
feelings/emotions, 117, 136–39, 140n5, 141–44
Fehige, Yiftach, 34–35
female-male binary, 137, 143–45
First Things, 33–34
First Zionist Congress, 206, 207
Foursquare Church, 207
free will, 97–98, 125, 131–32
Frey, Jörg, 166n67
fringes of garments, 43
functional divinity, 68, 72
the future, 112–14, 113n18, 116–17. *See also* divination

Gabriel (angel), 89–90
Gagnon, Robert A. J., 146n19
Galilee, 157
Gamaliel, 84
Gamel, Brian K., xiii, 153–73
Gaza, 211, 212
gentiles, 35, 154n6, 174–75, 175n2, 188n8, 199. *See also* the church
Gideon, 114
Gilgamesh, 109n7
Gnosticism, 53–54, 53n23, 54n27
God. *See also* image of God *(imago Dei)*; revelation, divine; theodicy; the Trinity; the Word of God
 essence *vs.* energies of, 82
 as eternal, 191
 evidence of, 141
 faithfulness of, 186–88, 199

God *(continued)*
  grace of, 81, 83, 97–100, 103–4, 122, 132, 182
  hiding his face, 130–31
  love for, 59–60
  nature of, 63–65, 80, 82, 101, 113–19, 143
  omnipotence of, 126, 128–30, 132
  rejection of, 141–42
  sovereignty of, 109n7, 110, 115–16
  unknowability of, 4
God, Freedom, and Evil (Plantinga), 129, 131
gods/pantheons in polytheism, 55–56, 59, 109n7, 110–14, 111n10, 112n12, 112n14, 117–18
good, greater, 122, 128
Goodman, Lenn, 123
Gospel of John, "the Jews" in, 153–69, 154n5, 155n7
the Gospel/Good News, 21, 30, 161, 161n38, 166n67, 183. *See also* kerygma
grace of God, 81, 83, 97–100, 103–4, 122, 132, 182
gratitude, 118, 141–42, 144–45
Greeks, 154n6
Gregory Palamas, 82
Grentzbegriff, 33
The Guide for the Perplexed (Maimonides), 123
γυναικεῖος, 147

hador ha'acharon, 5
Hagee, John, 208–9, 211
Hakola, Raimo, 155, 167n73, 168
Halakhah in a Theological Dimension (Novak), 37
Hamas, 1, 211, 212
happiness, 103, 108–9n6, 125
Harnack, Adolf, 83n13
Harper, Stephen, 211
Hartley, John, 147
hebel, 115, 115n20, 118
Heckler, William, 207
Heim, Knut Martin, 108–9n6
Hellenism, 110

hermeneutics, 161n40, 178. *See also Sachkritik* (content criticism)
Herod the Great, 68n18
Hersey, Oliver, 187
Herzl, Theodore, 207
Heschel, Abraham Joshua, 36, 126–27
hester panim, 130–31
heterosexuality, 142–46
higher life movement, 98
high-mindedness. *See* pride
historical-critical approach, 49
history, human, 4–6, 21, 31–32, 72, 131, 198, 203
Hitler, Adolph, 60, 208. *See also* concentration/death camps; Nazis
holiness, 95–111, 96n1, 108n6, 110n9, 113, 118–19
holiness code, 101. *See also under* law
the Holocaust/Shoah, 31, 126–31, 156, 159, 208–9, 212
the Holy Spirit, 64, 85, 98–99, 182, 189n12, 190, 192. *See also* the Trinity
ὅμοιος αὐτῷ, 145
ὁμοίως, 136–44
homosexuality, 136–49, 140n5, 144n12, 146n19, 149n30
Hoshaya, Rabbi, 88
house *(oikos)*, 56–57
humankind. *See also* history, human; image of God *(imago Dei)*
  as biological hypostases, 194–95
  bodies of, 136–38, 140
  boundaries on, 109n7, 116–18
  as contingent beings, 125
  creation of, 36–38, 88–89, 122, 131–32, 145–46
  deification of, 79–92, 80n3, 81n9, 83n13
  the fall of, 83, 126
  responsibility of, 109n7, 126, 131–32
  weakness of, 107–8
  will of, 97–98, 125, 131–32
Hume, David, 126
humility, 11, 26–27, 43, 180, 182. *See also* pride
ὑπόθεσις, 53–54

Hurtado, Larry W., 74
hypostasis, 67, 189–90, 189n12, 192–95, 197, 201
hypothesis (Gnostic), 53–54

Ibn Ezra, 147
icons, 6, 10, 192–93, 193n30, 193n32
identity
    in ancient Near East, 112
    Christian, 156, 158, 168, 177, 181–82, 189, 192–93, 199
    human, 47, 89, 91, 136–39, 144, 146
    Jewish, 155, 157n17, 158, 166n67, 177, 199
idolatry, 6, 10, 41, 81, 91
'inyan rā ', 116
illness/disease, 124, 210
image of God *(imago Dei)*
    as basis of natural law, 34, 36, 38
    in both Judaism and Christianity, 2, 92
    deification of humans and, 80, 83, 88
    denial of God and, 142
    human search for God and, 36
    human sexuality and, 136, 145
    humans as icons and, 193
image of humans in heaven, 90
The Image of the Non-Jew in Judaism (Novak), 35
immortality, 89, 109n7, 112, 143. *See also* eternal life
impulses. *See* emotions/feelings
incantations, 113
the incarnation
    definition of, 194n35
    human deification and, 80, 82
    Islam on, 58
    Judaism on, 63–65
    permanence of, 196–97
    unity between Jews and gentiles through, 29
inscriptions, 114, 114n19, 199
Institutes of the Christian Religion (Calvin), 51
instruction/discipline of God, 122–23

International Christian Embassy of Jerusalem, 209
International Fellowship of Christians and Jews, 209
International Holocaust Remembrance Day, 212
οἱ Ἰουδαῖοι *(hoi Ioudaioi)*, 153–69, 154n5, 157nn16–17
Irenaeus of Lyons, 30, 52–55, 60, 80n3, 82–83
Isaac, 205
ISIS, 212
Islam/Muslims, 6, 12, 47, 57–58, 58n37, 206, 212
Israel, kingdom of (Northern), 200
Israel, land of, 4–5, 11, 101
Israel, modern nation-state of, 10–12, 204–8, 211–12
Israel, people of
    behavior of, 41–42
    the church as part of, 22, 27n6, 175–84, 178n13, 181n29, 198
    ethnicity of, 197, 198n53, 199
    exile of, 5
    as kingdom of priests, 187, 187n7
    as married to God, 187–88, 199
    mission of, 9–10
    Mosaic law and (*See under* law)
    other nations and, 28–29

Jacob, 29, 90, 195, 197, 199, 205
Jaspers, Karl, 55
jealousy of God, 187
Jehovah. *See* God
Jeroboam, King, 23
Jerome, 81n9
Jerusalem, city of, 9–11, 175–76, 184, 208, 211
Jerusalem, new, 188–89
Jerusalem Council, 175n2
Jesus Christ. *See also* the incarnation; the Trinity
    belief in, 166–67, 166n67, 167n71
    crucifixion of, 29, 162, 196
    divinity of, 63, 71
    gentiles and Jews and, 29, 179–80, 181n29
    human nature of, 197

Jesus Christ *(continued)*
  Jewish identity of, 154–56, 197–99, 205
  as mediator, 192, 192n25
  as model, 200
  resurrection and, 117n24, 195–96
  as the Word of God, 80n3, 155, 165–66, 186–87, 186n1, 187n3, 199
Jesus Is Coming (Blackstone), 206
Jesus the Jewish Theologian (Young), 84n17
Jewish Christianity. *See* Messianic Judaism
Jewish-Christian Dialogue (Novak), 33, 34, 38–39
"the Jews" in the Gospel of John, 153–69, 154n5, 157nn16–17
Job, 109–10, 109n7, 118, 122, 126–27
Job, Babylonian, 117
John Chrysostom, 159
John Paul II, Pope, 180, 209
John the Baptist, 165
Jonas, Hans, 130
Jones, Jordan W., xiv, 107–20
Josephus, 147n20, 149
Josiah, King, 23
Journal of the Evangelical Theological Society, 49–50
joy, 108, 108n5, 109n7, 110n9, 118–19
Judah, kingdom of, 200
Judaism/Jews
  in the Gospel of John, 153–69, 154n5, 157nn16–17
  on Messiah, 63–75
  Messianic, 23, 25, 180
  mission of, 9–10
  monotheism of, 58–59
  as natural branches, 22
  persecution of, 6–7, 11–12, 163, 182–84, 203–4, 206, 208–9, 212
  rabbinic, 65, 73–75
  Second Temple, 64–75, 83n13, 84, 149, 155, 158, 162
Judea, 157, 157nn16–17
judgment/judging
  by God, 83, 114, 117, 130
  human, 51

  of Israel, 41, 163
  by Messiah, 74
  of others, 101–2, 162
  by Son of Man, 68–69, 72
Juel, Donald H., 74–75
justice, 4, 9, 18, 112n14, 123–24, 127
justification, 99–100, 105
Justin Martyr, 82–83

Kant, Immanuel, 33
Kasemann, Ernst, 161
Katz, Steven, 131
Kavka, Martin, 37
Kazadi, Axel, xiv, 174–85
Keefer, Arthur, 115
Keller, Tim, 132
kerygma, 161, 161n40, 168. *See also* the Gospel/Good News
Keswick convention center, 98
kingdom of God, 34, 68, 101, 179, 193, 204
kingdom of priests, 187, 187n7
Kinzer, Mark, 25, 175–76, 177, 179–81, 181n29, 184
Kissell, Ian, xiv, 47–62
the Knesset, 209, 210
Knesset Christian Allies Caucus, 209
knowledge, human, 53–54, 113–18, 113n18, 123–24

ladder of Jacob, 90
Laodicea, church in, 178
Lau, Meir, Rabbi, 209–10
law
  Islamic, 58, 58n37
  Mosaic, 25, 39–40, 96, 100–105, 147–49, 175
  natural, 33–38, 40–41, 43
  Noahide, 33, 35, 38, 40
  rabbinic, 6–7, 33, 40
Law and Theology of Judaism (Novak), 37
leaders, Christian, 187–88, 187n3, 199–200
leftist politics, 212
legalism, 102, 104
Leo the Great, Pope, 30
Levenson, Jon D., 161–62n44

Levi, Primo, 132
Levi, Rabbi, 91
Lewis, C. S., 55–56
LGBTQ ethic, 135–39
libel, blood, 10
lies/deception, 137–39, 144–47, 144n15
life
   after death, 117n24, 123
   eternal, 114, 143, 191–93 (*See also* immortality)
   human, 37, 107–8, 110, 114, 118, 141
   new, 85, 182
Lindbeck, George, 26–27, 175–79, 181, 184
Lisbon earthquake, 126
literacy, 47–48, 47n2, 60
Litwa, M. David, 79
logic, 186–87, 187n3, 201
logos, 55, 66–67, 186–87, 187n3, 201
lost/perishing, 26
love
   disordered, 125–26
   for enemies, 163–64
   for God, 59–60
   God's, 60, 163, 168
   for Israel, 204–6
Lucian, 147n20
Luther, Martin, 2–3, 27, 161, 164, 169, 187n4
Luz, Ulrich, 162–63, 162n46

macarisms, 105
Mackie, J. L., 129, 130, 132
magic, 113
Maimonides, Moses, 6–11, 63, 96, 102–4, 123–24
male-female binary, 137, 143–45
Manichean dualism, 131
manipulation of God/gods, 110, 112, 114, 118
Marcus, Joel, 159n25, 159n27
marginalization, 212
marriage, 186–88, 187n4, 199–200
Marshall, John, 158n23
Martyn, J. Louis, 158
Marx, Karl, 60, 60n45

Mary, 189, 195, 197
μάταιοι, 118
McDermott, Gerald, xiv, 84n17
McVety, Charles, xiv, 203–13
Meachem, Jon, 153n2
Meir, Rabbi, 131
memory, 48
menorah, 207
Menorah Review, 34
Mesopotamia, 109n7, 111–12
the Messiah, 7–9, 29, 63–75, 84, 209–10. *See also* Son of Man
Messianic Judaism, 23, 25, 180
μεταλλάσσω, 144n15
metaphysics, 102–3, 105
Michael (angel), 89–90
Middle East, 11, 212
Milevsky, Jonathan, xiv, 33–44
Milgrom, Jacob, 147
mirror, 193
Mishneh Torah, Kings and Wars (Maimonides), 7, 10
missionaries, 175n2, 182, 184
Mittleman, Alan, 101–3
moderation, 96, 105
Molinist view, 128
Monad (Gnostic), 53n23
monarch of the Father, 190n16
monophysitism, 192, 197
monotheism, 47–48, 55–59, 64, 74, 86–87
monuments, human, 108, 111–12, 114, 208
Moody, Dwight L., 206
morality, 9, 33, 35–40, 43, 103–4, 126, 148. *See also* ethics, Judeo-Christian; virtue
Mormonism, 80
mortality/death, 88, 116n23, 117, 117n24, 123, 137, 191, 194
Moses, 91, 111, 155, 200
Mosser, Carl, 79, 82–83, 83n13
mṣ', 116, 116n23, 118
murder/bloodshed, 11–12, 37, 40, 124, 182
Muslims/Islam, 6, 12, 47, 57–58, 58n37, 206, 212
myths, 55, 112

Naselli, Andy, 97–99
nations, 8–11, 28–30, 41–42, 68–69, 71–73, 187, 198n53
"Natural Law, Halakhah, and the Covenant" (Novak), 38
Natural Law in Judaism (Novak), 38
natural theology, 105
nature, human, 82, 143–45, 197–98
Nazareth, 7–8, 65, 157n17
Nazis, 60, 121–22, 124, 127, 208. *See also* concentration/death camps
neo-Platonism, 80–81n7
Netanyahu, Benjamin, 206
the new Jerusalem, 188–89
new life, 85, 182
the New Testament, 75, 78, 84, 84n17, 153–69, 205
Niagara Bible Conference, 207
Nicene Creed, 190n16
Nickelsburg, George, 69
Nietzsche, Friedrich, 126, 127, 129, 130
Nigeria, 12
Night (Wiesel), 127
Night to Honor Israel, 209, 211
Nineveh, 41
Nissinen, Martti, 149
Noahide law, 33, 35, 38, 40
Noah's ark, 210
Novak, David, 21–22, 27, 30, 33–41, 43
nuclear war, 37

obedience, 38–39, 87–88, 113, 118–19, 132
oikos (house), 56–57
Olson, Daniel C., 68n19, 69
omnipotence of God, 126, 128–30, 132
On the Free Choice of the Will (Augustine), 125
ontological divinity, 68, 70
ὄρεξις, 143
Origen, 159, 168–69
OrthodoxWiki, 84
Ottoman Empire, 208
overseer. *See* leaders, Christian
Ozymandias, 108

paganism, 6, 81, 109–10, 119, 130, 203
Pais, Calvin, xiv, 186–202
pandemic, 27, 126
pantheons/gods in polytheism, 55–56, 59, 109n7, 110–14, 111n10, 112n12, 112n14
"Parable of the Madman" (Nietzsche), 129
Parables of Enoch, 68, 73, 74
parallelism, 35–36
παρέλαβον (*parelabon*, welcome, accept), 166
passions. *See* emotions/feelings
Paul, 84, 100n8, 174, 205
Paul the Jewish Theologian (Young), 84n17
peace, 29, 209–10, 211
Pennington, Jonathan, 104
Pentecostalism, 98–99, 207–8
perfectionism, Christian, 97–98
perichoretic union, 85
persecution, 6–7, 11–12, 163, 182–84, 203–4, 206, 208–9, 212
personification, 105n20
Pew Research, 144n12
Pharaoh, 111
Pharisees, 43, 156, 162, 162n47
Philo of Alexandria, 66, 149
philosophy, 80, 83n13
phylacteries, 43
φυσικός, 142, 142n8
φύσις (*physis*), 142–44, 149, 149n30
piety, 36, 43, 54
Pilate, Pontius, 154n6
Piper, John, 49–52
Plantinga, Alvin, 129, 131, 132
Plato, 80–81n7, 198, 200
Plotinus, 80–81n7
pogroms, 206
polemics, 159n25, 162, 162n46, 167–68
polis (city), 56–57
polydoxy, 161–62n44
polygamy, 187–88, 200
polytheism, 55–57, 59, 109n7, 110–14, 111n10, 112n12, 112n14

Postmissionary Messianic Judaism (Kinzer), 179
potentiality (Augustine), 34
poverty, 124
power. *See also* authority
  to become children of God, 165–66
  the church and, 27
  of evil, 112
  of God, 111, 131–32, 141, 176
  harmonization through, 60
  Judeo-Christian tradition and, 59
  of the Messiah, 63–64
  polytheism and, 56, 59
  of the Son of Man, 67
powers, two, theology of, 65–67
prejudice. *See* anti-Judaism; anti-Semitism
presuppositions, 37, 51, 60, 161, 189
pride, 22–24
priest, French, 11
priests, Israelite, 114, 156
priests, kingdom of, 187, 187n7
problem of evil, 4, 116–17, 121–33
process theology, 130
prodigal son, 26
progressive revelation, 204
prophecy, biblical, 4–5, 22–23, 84, 113–14n18, 209–10
Protestantism, 129, 161
Pseudo-Aristotle, 56–57, 60
Pseudo-Dionysius, 79–80
Pseudo-Phocylides, 149
punishment, 122–23, 127, 129, 131
Puritans, 5

qādōš (holy), 107–10, 108n6
qahal, 176
q'dushá (holiness), 95
qitrug, 34, 41–43
Qohelet, 107–19, 107n2, 108–9nn4–7, 109n7, 110n9, 116n23, 117n24
Qumran community, 67, 74, 87, 89, 158
the Qur'an, 58

Radner, Ephraim, xiv–xv, 21–32, 25n4, 176n9, 178–79, 181–82, 184

Rapoport, Chaim, Rabbi, 147–48
Rashkover, Randi, 37, 39
rationality, 35, 55, 194
Rawls, John, 33
Al-Razi, 124
"Reading the New Testament as Second Temple Literature" *JSNT*, 84n17
Reardon, Michael M. C., xiv, 1–18, 78–94
"Reason with Baggage" (Milevsky), 36
reception theory, 49
recompense/restitution, 123
reconciliation, 29–30, 59, 200
redemption, 7, 9, 30, 70, 72–73
the Reformation, 10, 168, 204, 205. *See also* Calvin, John; Luther, Martin
Reformed model of holiness, 95–100
Reichstheologie, 60. *See also* Third Reich
Reinhartz, Adele, 157n17, 159, 159n30, 167–68
rejection, 29–30, 131–32, 141–42, 167, 188
Rendtorff, Rolf, 49
repentance/confession, 41, 102–3, 127, 154, 176, 182–83
Responsa of Maimonides (Maimonides), 6–7
response of humans to God, 36–37, 141, 167
responsibility, human, 109n7, 126, 131–32
restitution/recompense, 123
the resurrection, 117n24, 195–96
retribution, 109–10
revelation, divine. *See also* canon; Scripture/the Bible
  in both Judaism and Christianity, 34, 38–39
  canonical approach and, 49–52
  as distinct from text, 160–61
  of God's character, 118
  human body as, 140
  in nature, 141
  progressive, 204
  relationship with Israel as, 187

rewards, 4, 42, 103, 122–23
the rich, 22, 30
the Righteous One, 68–70
righteousness
   of Abraham, 90
   absence of, 29, 116n23
   believers become, 30, 80n6, 86
   of God, 118
   human deification and, 92
   of the law, 101
   of Son of Man, 69
   suffering and, 123, 126
rituals, 101, 110, 112–14, 118. *See also* sacrifices
Rivlin, Reuven, 210
Roman Empire, 154n6, 175, 206
Rowe, William, 128
rûaḥ (wind), 109n7
Rubenstein, Richard, 129–30
rule of truth. *See* canon
Russell, Bertrand, 127
Russell, Norman, 81–82, 84
Russia, 206

Saadiah Gaon, 122–24
Sachexegese, 160
Sachkritik (content criticism), 154, 160–69, 161n38, 161n40, 167n73
Sacks, Jonathan, Rabbi Lord, 149
sacraments, 82, 92
sacrifices, 112–14, 113n17
Sadducees, 117n24, 156
Saldarini, Anthony J., 164n56
salvation/soteriology, 21–22, 79, 82, 97–98, 155n7, 165n65, 188, 191–93
Samaritans, 154n6, 157
same-sex practices, 136–49, 140n5, 144n12, 146n19, 149n30
sanctification, 95–100, 104–6. *See also* holiness
Sargon of Akade, 114n19
saru (wind), 109n7
Satan/the devil, 126, 155, 164–66, 169
scribes, 162
Scripture/the Bible. *See also* literacy
   authority of, 7, 50–52, 51n18

   canon of, 48–52, 48n7, 51n18, 54–55, 57, 59–60
   as community-forming, 50–52, 55, 60
   cosmology and, 54
   critical approaches to, 49–52, 154, 160–69, 161n38, 161n40, 167n73
   Gnosticism and, 53–54, 54n27
   interpretation of, 48–50, 52–55, 54n27, 168–69
   spreading knowledge of, 9–10
second blessing, 97–98
Second Temple Judaism, 64–75, 83n13, 84, 84n17, 149, 155, 158, 162
Segal, Alan, 65–66
the self, 60, 110n9, 137–38, 140
Seow, C. L., 115
sephirot, 64
the Sermon on the Mount, 104, 162–64, 162n49
sex, biological, 145, 194
sexual ethics, 135–50, 135n1, 148
sexual identity, 136–38
Shaarei Shomayim Synagogue, 209
the *Shahādah*, 57–58
Shapira, Rabbi, 132
shekhinah, 64
Shelley, Percy, 108
the Shema, 58–60, 95
Sheol, 117n24
the Shoah/Holocaust, 31, 126–31, 156, 159, 208–9, 212
Shtern, Yuri, 209
Simai, Rabbi, 87–88
Similitudes of Enoch, 67–72
Simpson, A. B., 207–8, 211
sin. *See also* ethics, Judeo-Christian; morality; virtue
   of the church, 31, 175, 181–83
   free will and, 132
   hiddenness of God and, 130–31
   intention and, 97
   of Israel, 131, 177
   Jesus Christ and, 30, 80n6
   repentance of, 41, 102–3, 127, 154, 176, 182–83
   sexual, 148

Subject and Name Index

suffering and, 126–27
Sinai, Mount, 40, 187
Sinaitic covenant, 199
social media, 212
Sommer, Benjamin, 64, 75
Son of Man, 65, 67–74. *See also* the Messiah
sonship, 83, 85–86
soteriology/salvation, 21–22, 79, 82, 97–98, 155n7, 165n65, 188, 191–93
source theory, 49
sovereignty of God, 109n7, 110, 115–16
speaking in tongues, 98
Spirit, Holy, 64, 85, 98–99, 182, 189n12, 190, 192. *See also* the Trinity
standard for behavior. *See qitrug*
stasis, 189n12
Steinberg, Jonah, Rabbi, 88, 90–91
Stock, Brian, 47
Stoicism, 80–81n7
Stump, Eleanore, 132
submission to God, 60
suffering, 69–70, 122–33. *See also* problem of evil
the Suffering Servant, 69
summum bonum, 103–4
supersessionism, 21–22, 27n6, 29–30, 177–78, 183, 184
Symeon the New Theologian, 81n9
synagogues, 51, 155, 158, 179, 205

ta'amei hamitzvot, 38, 40
Talking with Christians (Novak), 33, 36
al tawḥīd, 57–58
the Temple, 9, 21, 113, 175–76
terrorists, 210–12
teshuvah, 102–3
testing, 122
thankfulness. *See* gratitude
The Mystery of the Church in Orthodox Tradition (Zizioulas), 189
θῆλυς, 142, 145, 145n17
θηλύτερος, 145n17
theodicy, 4, 116–17, 121–33

theology, 3–4, 26–27, 41, 65–67, 105. *See also* Second Temple Judaism
theopoiesis, 91. *See also* deification of humans
theos, 67
theosis, 84, 87, 91. *See also* deification of humans
"Theosis Through Works of the Law: Deification of the Earthly Righteous" (Steinberg), 88
third blessings, 98–99
Third Reich, 60, 121–22, 124, 127, 208. *See also* concentration/death camps
Thomas, 196
Thomas Aquinas, 27, 37, 102–5
thrones, 67–68, 196
Time magazine, 129
Tiresias, 147n20
תּוֹעֵבָה, 147
tongues, speaking in, 98
the Torah, 6–8, 10, 42, 87–88, 92. *See also* Scripture/the Bible
tourism of modern state of Israel, 11
tower of Babel, 112–13, 112n14
traditions, adherence to, 3, 5–6
transgenderism, 137–38
Treaty of Berlin, 206
trialectic approach, 192, 192n25, 195
trials, suffering as, 122
the Trinity
 description of, 190
 the church and, 198
 eternal life and, 192
 Judaism and, 6, 10, 63–64, 74
 unity of believers like, 183
Trump, Donald, President, 211
truth
 canon and, 48, 54
 God's, 22, 142, 144, 144n15
 the material world and, 138–39
 modern thought on, 55
 religion and, 34
 rule of. *See* canon
 supersessionism and, 22
Tuchman, Barbara, 5
Two Powers in Heaven (Segal), 65–66
two powers theology, 65–67

tzaddīq, 69
tzelem elohim. *See* image of God (*imago Dei*)
tzitzit, 43

unbelief, 22, 25–26, 29. *See also* belief in Jesus Christ
Understanding the Jewish Roots of Christianity (McDermott), 84n17
underworld, 112
United Arab Emirates, 211
United Nations, 211, 212
United States of America, 208
universities, 212
Urim and Thummin, 114
Uruk, 109n7

Van der Horst, P. W., 149n30
vanities, 108nn5–6, 115n20, 118
the Vatican, 11
virtue, 96, 98–99, 102–5. *See also* ethics, Judeo-Christian; morality
Von Rad, Gerhard, 49

war, 37, 71, 124, 127n20, 208, 211–12
warrior, heavenly, 71–73
the weak, 30
Wesley, John, 97–98
Whybray, R. Norman, 108n5, 116n23
Wiesel, Elie, 127
will, human, 97–98, 125, 131–32
Williams, Rowan, 189n11
wind, 71, 109n7, 118
Wirkungsgeschichte, 154
wisdom, 39, 43, 107, 118, 123–24, 187

woes, 162
Wolicki, Pesach, xv, 1–18
women, 12, 116n23, 136, 144, 147, 147n20
the Word of God
 in the canon, 50–51, 60
 governance of the world by, 54
 Jesus Christ as, 80n3, 155, 165–66, 186–87, 186n1, 187n3, 199
the world, 8–11, 34, 53, 55, 182–83. *See also* creation; evil, the problem of; history, human; nations
World War II, 208
Wyschogrod, Michael, 25

Ya'alon, Moshe, 212
Yahweh/YHWH, 66, 73, 108n6, 110–11, 113, 117–18. *See also* God
Yaneff, Jeff, xv, 135–50
yd', 116–17
Yeshua. *See also* Jesus Christ; Messianic Judaism
Yeshua movement, 175
Yoder, Timothy S., xv, 121–34
Yom Kippur War, 50th anniversary, 212
Young, Brad, 84n17
yr' (to fear), 108n4

Zeus, 147n20
ziggurats, 112
Zion, Mt., 72
Zionism, 204, 206–13
Zizioulas, John, Bishop, 188–96, 189nn11–12, 198, 201

www.ingramcontent.com/pod-product-compliance
Lightning Source LLC
Chambersburg PA
CBHW072022240426
43667CB00044B/2210